50 Hikes in Northern Virginia

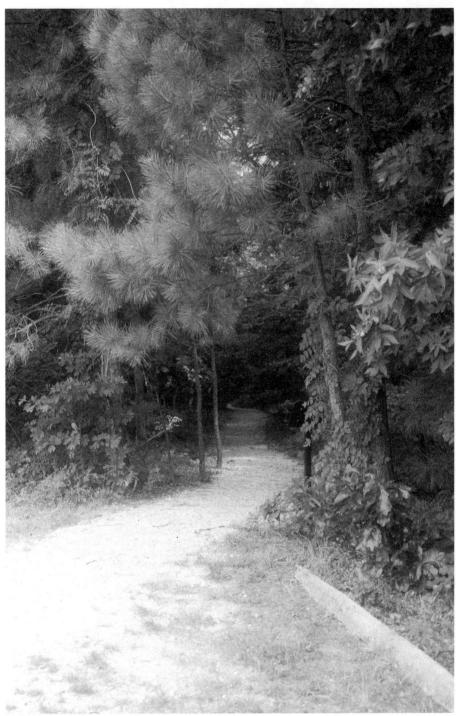

Cold Harbor Trail entering the woods

50 *Hikes*

In Northern Virginia

Walks, Hikes, and Backpacks from the Allegheny Mountains to the Chesapeake Bay

LEONARD M. ADKINS

Second Edition

Backcountry Guides

Woodstock, Vermont

An Invitation to the Reader

Over time trails can be rerouted and signs and landmarks altered. If you find that changes have occurred on the routes described in this book, please let us know so that corrections may be made in furure editions. The author and publisher also welcome other comments and suggestions. Address all correspondence to:

Editor
Fifty Hikes™ Series
Backcountry Guides
P.O. Box 748
Woodstock, VT 05091

Note:

Many water sources are identified for hiker convenience, but this is not an endorsement of their purity. All sources should be treated before consuming.

**Library of Congress
Cataloging-in-Publication Data**

Adkins, Leonard M.
50 hikes in Northern Virginia : walks, hikes, and backpacks from the Allegheny Mountains to the Chesapeake Bay / Leonard Adkins ; [interior photographs by the author].–2nd ed.
  p. cm.– (Fifty hikes series)
Includes bibliographical references and index.
ISBN 0-88150-444-0 (alk. paper)
1. Hiking–Virginia–Guidebooks. 2. Virginia–Guidebooks. I. Title: Fifty hikes in Northern Virginia. II. Title. III. Series.
GV199.42.V82 A35 2000
917.55'20443–dc21   99–058150

Series and cover design by Glenn Suokko
Interior photography by Leonard M. Adkins
Cover photograph of White Canyon Falls in Shenadoah National Park © William B. Folsom
Original trail maps by Richard Widhu;
New maps by Mapping Specialists Ltd., Madison, WI, © 2000 The Countryman Press

Published by Backcountry Guides
A Division of The Countryman Press
P.O. Box 748
Woodstock, VT 05091

Distributed by W.W. Norton & Company, Inc.
500 Fifth Avenue
New York, NY 10110

Printed in the United States of America
10 9 8 7 6 5

Every part of this soil is sacred.
Every hillside, every valley, every plain and grove
has been hallowed by some sad or happy event
in days long vanished.
Chief Seattle

**In memory of Leonard Wilson Adkins,
who understandingly said to me,
"I know you need to go hiking, son, so go."**

I think I know now the secret of making the best person.
It is to live in the open air and sleep with the earth.
Walt Whitman

OTHER BOOKS BY LEONARD M. ADKINS

A Walking Guide to the Caribbean:
From the Virgin Islands to Martinique

Seashore State Park: A Walking Guide

Walking the Blue Ridge:
A Guide to the Trails of the Blue Ridge Parkway

The Appalachian Trail: A Visitor's Companion

Adventure Guide to Virginia

Wildflowers of the Appalachian Trail

Acknowledgments

My name may be on the front cover of this book, but I owe a debt of gratitude to all of the people who willingly devoted time, energy, and expertise in seeing that the information presented is as complete and accurate as possible:

Bob Tennyson, Bud Risner, James Hunt, Dave Benavitch, Ronald Swann, David Rhodes, Cynthia Snow, and John Coleman with the U.S. Forest Service; Emond Raus, Michael Andrus, Donald Pfanz, Deanne Adams, Janet Stombock, James Burgess, Arthur C. Webster III, and Donald W. Campbell with the National Park Service; Karen Michaud and the staff of Shenandoah National Park; Tim Vest, Scott Shanklin, Paul Billings, Shawn Spencer, John A. Reffit, Charli Conn, Jeff Foster, Kathy Budnie, and Forrest Gladden III with the Virginia Division of State Parks; Vance Coffey with the Virginia Department of Forestry; Kristi Barber and Becky Holliday with the Newport News Park; Calvin Pearson with the City of Hampton; Darrell Winslow with the Northern Virginia Regional Park Authority; Glen Rowe with the Lancaster Public Works; Dede Smith, Elizabeth Murray, and R. J. Bartholomew with the Ivy Creek Foundation; Vaughn Stanely with Stratford Hall Plantation; J. E. Raynor with the Old Dominion Appalachian Trail Club; Henry Bashore of Kilmarnock, Virginia; and good trail friends Bob Ellenwood, Pat Love, Bill Foot, Steve Gomez, and Ann Messick.

Carl Taylor, Robin Dutcher, and Gretchen Gordon—thank you for helping make my foot travels become this book. Kathleen, John, Timmy, and Jay Yelenic—thanks for opening your home and family to me. Nancy Adkins—thanks for life, Mom. Laurie—thanks for sharing life with me.

A thunderous round of applause to the builders and maintainers of all trails.

50 Hikes at a Glance

HIKE	REGION
1. Grandview Natural Preserve	Chesapeake Bay
2. Newport News Park	Chesapeake Bay
3. Belle Isle	Chesapeake Bay
4. Hughlett Point	Chesapeake Bay
5. Hickory Hollow	Chesapeake Bay
6. The Northern Neck	Chesapeake Bay
7. Spotsylvania	Central Virginia
8. Prince William Forest Park	Central Virginia
9. Mason Neck State Park	Central Virginia
10. Bull Run/Occoquan River	Central Virginia
11. Manassas National Battlefield Park	Central Virginia
12. Sky Meadows State Park	Central Virginia
13. Lake Anna State Park	Central Virginia
14. Cold Harbor	Central Virginia
15. Willis River Trail	Central Virginia
16. Split Rocks/Jefferson's Rock	Central Virginia
17. Little Sluice Mountain and Cedar Creek	Blue Ridge and Massanutten
18. Big Schloss	Blue Ridge and Massanutten
19. Marys Rock	Blue Ridge and Massanutten
20. Stony Man	Blue Ridge and Massanutten
21. Old Rag	Blue Ridge and Massanutten
22. Cedar Run/Whiteoak Canyon	Blue Ridge and Massanutten
23. Hawksbill	Blue Ridge and Massanutten
24. Rapidan Camp	Blue Ridge and Massanutten
25. Brown Mountain/Rockytop	Blue Ridge and Massanutten

DISTANCE (in miles)	BACKCOUNTRY CAMPING	GOOD FOR KIDS	WATERFALLS	VIEWS	NOTES
3.6		★		★	Chesapeake Bay shoreline
5.6		★			Easy terrain; Civil War site
5.0		★		★	Hike beside cultivated farmlands
1.8		★		★	Optional miles–long beach walk
2.5		★			Swamp exploration; wildflowers
4.0		★		★	Horsehead Cliffs fossils; Washington's birthplace
5.3					Site of major Civil War battle
13.5					Streams & isolation close to D.C.
3.0		★			Turtles, eagles, muskrats, and ducks
11.0					Hike is along streams most of the way
5.2					Site of two major Civil War battles
5.4	★	★		★	Best view of the Piedmont
9.0					In the rolling woodlands of the Piedmont
1.0		★			Civil War trenches
15.3	★				Most rugged hike in Piedmont; for the experienced
6.9				★	"A view worth a voyage across the Atlantic."
11.7	★			★	Mountains along Virginia/West Virginia border
4.4				★	Excellent views and interesting rock outcrops
3.6		★		★	Opportunity for 360-degree view
3.5		★		★	Spruce & fir forest; Shenandoah Valley view
7.7				★	Arduous, with rock scrambles, but very popular
8.0 or 9.3	★		★		Almost continuous waterfalls
2.8		★		★	High point of Shenandoah National Park
7.4	★				President Hoover's mountain retreat; small streams
20.0	★			★	Two-day hike into isolated valley

50 Hikes at a Glance

HIKE	REGION
26. Riprap Hollow	Blue Ridge and Massanutten
27. Signal Knob	Blue Ridge and Massanutten
28. Woodstock Observation Tower	Blue Ridge and Massanutten
29. Duncan Knob	Blue Ridge and Massanutten
30. Ivy Creek Natural Area	Blue Ridge and Massanutten
31. White Rock Falls and Slacks Overlook Trails	Blue Ridge and Massanutten
32. Sherando Lake	Blue Ridge and Massanutten
33. Saint Mary's Wilderness	Blue Ridge and Massanutten
34. Crabtree Falls	Blue Ridge and Massanutten
35. Appalachian Trail	Blue Ridge and Massanutten
36. Mount Pleasant	Blue Ridge and Massanutten
37. Cold Mountain	Blue Ridge and Massanutten
38. North River Gorge	Western Virginia
39. Todd Lake Recreation Area	Western Virginia
40. Wild Oak National Recreation Trail	Western Virginia
41. Ramsey's Draft	Western Virginia
42. Shenandoah Mountain	Western Virginia
43. Elliot Knob/Falls Hollow	Western Virginia
44. Laurel Fork	Western Virginia
45. Hidden Valley	Western Virginia
46. Lake Moomaw	Western Virginia
47. Rich Hole Wilderness	Western Virginia
48. Beards Mountain	Western Virginia
49. Tuscarora Overlook	Western Virginia
50. Dry Run	Western Virginia

DISTANCE (in miles)	BACKCOUNTRY CAMPING	GOOD FOR KIDS	WATERFALLS	VIEWS	NOTES
9.6	★		★		Waterfall & swimming hole
10.4	★			★	Has become popular with mountain bikers
0.3	★	★		★	Very easy walk; great views
8.75	★			★	Off-trail scramble to view
5.0			★		A short drive from downtown Charlottesville
5.0	★	★	★		Along the Blue Ridge Parkway
1.6		★		★	Nice break from noisy campground
17.5	★		★		Two-day hike with remote campsite
5.8	★	★	★		Strenuous, but 1.5 miles of waterfalls
26.1	★		★	★	Has everything that makes hiking worthwhile
5.5	★			★	A protected Special Management Area
5.75	★			★	High mountain meadow
4.5	★				Nine river fords
3.8	★				Circuit hike of Trimble Mountain
26.1	★			★	Three hilly days with long, easy ridge walks
8.3	★				Popular Wilderness Area
10.6	★	★			Easiest long hike in Va. mountains; snowshoeing
9.0	★		★	★	Great sunrise and sunset spot
14.0	★		★		More like New England than Virginia
5.6	★				Wild trout fishing on side streams
6.6	★				Lakeshore camping
5.8	★			★	Accessible; lightly traveled; signs of black bears
7.1				★	Douthat State Park
9.6			★	★	Two waterfalls and a grand overlook
9.7	★				Secluded hemlock-lined stream with campsites

CONTENTS

IV. WESTERN VIRGINIA

Introduction

Only a person traveling by foot can truly appreciate the natural beauty to be found in Virginia. The two flower scars evident on a tiny red partridgeberry or the rich aroma and cool temperatures of an evergreen forest will be overlooked by those passing through in an automobile. Virginia's most impressive waterfalls are accessible only to someone who is willing to put forth a bit of effort to reach them, and the majestic serenity of a golden sunset shining on distant mountains is made all the more inspiring when you know you have reached the viewpoint under your own power. Only by walking on a quiet beach will you be permitted to study etchings in the sand that mark the movements of a ghost crab or have the time to watch the swooping silhouette of an osprey outlined by a silvery glow reflecting off salt water.

The topography of the northern portion of Virginia, stretching from the craggy summits of the Allegheny Mountains to the soft shores of the Chesapeake Bay, provides some of the widest variety of hiking terrain and sights to be found in any of the Middle Atlantic states. In the eastern part of the commonwealth—the coastal plain where land meets salt water—you will often find yourself hiking up and down minor changes in elevation and walking past herons and egrets as they fish in small swamps, brackish ponds, and slow-moving streams. The Piedmont in central Virginia is characterized by gently rolling land that will lead you into grassy meadows for open views almost as often as you will be treading in mixed hardwood forests. Influenced by narrow mountains and their spreading spur ridges, trails in the Blue Ridge and Massanutten Mountains either follow the rises and falls of fluctuating mountain crests or descend past quickly flowing streams and waterfalls into small valleys and coves. The mountains of western Virginia are the least populated, and it is here that you will find the most rugged yet isolated and quiet hiking and have the best chance of viewing the state's abundant wildlife.

This book was originally envisioned as a guide to 50 hikes throughout the entire state. It soon became apparent, however, that by trying to incorporate so much area, I would actually be limiting myself, and you, by having to reject and ignore far too many places deserving of your hiking time and attentions. By concentrating on only about half of the state, it is possible to include many of the most enjoyable and rewarding hikes in the northern part of Virginia. With descriptions of more than 360 miles of pathways, this book offers hikes for every degree of physical stamina and time constraint. Best of all, no matter where you happen be at any given moment (north of US 60), you are never going to be more than a 30- to 45-minute drive away from one of the hikes.

Like most guidebooks, this one will tell you where the hikes are and how to follow the pathways, and it will point out the plants, animals, and birds you may see along the way. It differs from many guides, however, in that it also contains interpretive information; by using it you will not be hiking "blind." Not only will you be told when to turn left, right, and so forth, but you will also receive background information on the plants, animals, and natural and human history or issues facing a certain area. You will come to understand why the pink lady's slipper grows in such an exotic shape, what animal likes what types of foods, and how to tell what an animal has recently eaten. You'll learn to look for signs that show if a bear or a turkey inhabits an area. You will also be able to determine why human history has left its mark on the land and what caused certain events to occur. There is, of course, much more to be learned than can be presented in this book. To help you gain an even greater awareness, enjoyment, and understanding of your surroundings, I urge you to read (and possibly carry) some additional books and field guides. (See "Suggested Readings and Field Guides" near the end of this introduction.)

Birds singing early in the morning, flowers opening wide to soak in the noontime sun, and owls hooting in the evening make it worthwhile to walk the same trail at different times of the day. Also, a trail walked in late spring is certainly going to be a different experience when you return to hike it in the fall. Therefore, be willing to visit an area more than once and don't limit your outdoor activities to just one or two seasons; hiking in Virginia can be a year-round activity. Of course, you must be prepared for sudden changes in the weather, but even on the highest mountains in Virginia there are numerous days when winter temperatures reach into the fifties and sixties.

To paraphrase a famous American humorist, I've never met a trail I didn't like. My wish is that this guidebook conveys to you the sense of excitement, joy, wonder, peace, and contentment that can only be found in the freedom of traveling the natural world by foot. Virginia awaits—go do some exploring!

How to Use This Book

This book includes a wide variety of hikes—ranging from pleasant strolls on nearly level ground to challenging, several-day backpacking trips over rugged terrain—so that everyone, no matter what their level of hiking experience or physical stamina, can choose an excursion that best fits their schedule, lifestyle, or expectations. The headings at the beginning of each hike were designed to give you—at a quick glance—an overview of what to expect.

I arrived at the total distance for each hike by walking with a surveyor's measuring wheel. If you compare some of my distances with those of other guidebooks or information from the Forest Service, state parks, or other sources, you may notice some discrepancies. Most often these sources give distances from a beginning trailhead, not taking into account how far you must walk to reach that trailhead. In order to give you as true a picture as possible of how far you are actually going to walk, I measured the hike from the point you leave your automobile to where you are able to return to it.

A one-way hike is just that—you walk in one direction, ending the hike at a different point from where you started. A one-way hike necessitates a car shuttle. On a round trip, you go to your destination and then return by way of the same route. On a circuit hike, which represents the vast majority of the hikes presented in this book, you will take a circular route to return to your starting point, rewalking very little, if any, of the same trail or trails.

So that you can quickly determine which distances relate directly to the hike you are taking, I express distances in two different ways. A distance written as a figure (e.g., 3.6 miles) is referring either to a distance in the driving directions or to the cumulative distance you have walked since beginning a hike. Distances to places you do not actually reach on your hike (via side trails, roads, and so on) are spelled out (e.g., two and three-tenths miles).

The hiking time is the minimum amount of time that it would take a person of average ability to do a trip at a leisurely pace. Some of you may go faster, a few of you slower. Begin with some of the shorter hikes and compare your time with those stated. This way you can approximate how long it should take you to do the more extended excursions. Do keep in mind that the stated time does not figure in any rest breaks, meals, resupplying for water, or time out for sight-seeing and nature study, and that in hiking, it is not how fast you go, but how much you enjoy the trip. Robert Louis Stevenson may have said it best: "To travel hopefully is a better thing than to arrive."

The vertical rise is probably the most accurate factor for determining how strenuous a hike will be. It represents the sum total of all the uphill hiking you will do and is not, as most other guides provide, just the difference in elevation between the lowest and highest point of a hike. This rise was determined using information from United States Geological Survey (USGS) maps.

The map heading at the beginning of each hike includes the specific USGS maps that cover that particular hike. Because the actual hike route—traced out from USGS maps—is reproduced for you in this book, you will probably not need to purchase them. However, they are nice to have along to help you identify various features, such as nearby peaks or waterways, and they can help you become proficient in orienteering. They may be obtained by writing the United States Geological Survey, Box 25286, Federal Center, Denver, CO 80225. Be aware that, as the headings point out, you may need several maps to

Natural staircase on Old Rag

complete just one hike, and the price of each is now in the multiple dollars range.

The other maps I identify can be obtained (often free of charge) at the appropriate contact stations, visitors centers, or Forest Service district offices.

If you are going to be hiking any of the Forest Service trails, I suggest you purchase the inexpensive map of the entire George Washington National Forest. (See page 24 for the Forest Service address.) Although they are usually easy to follow, trails in the national forest are generally not as well maintained or marked as those in the national, state, or regional parks. Not only will the map give you a broad overview of the areas in which you will be hiking, but because it shows all of the national forest's trails, it can also open up a whole new world of hiking options for you. The map marks the trails with official Forest Service inventory numbers and to help you orient yourself, I have included them in brackets (e.g., {FS 621}) in the hike descriptions. Like the Forest Service, I've used FDR (Forest Development Road) to refer to Forest Service roads (which are usually unpaved).

Please do not dismiss a hike or an area as being beyond your capabilities because you are intimidated by its length, time, or vertical rise. Because I enjoy walking so much, I have often described one of the longest and most meandering hikes to be taken in a particular area. Yet many places have numerous side trails or alternate routes you could take in order to shorten a hike. A good example is the Tuscarora Overlook hike in Douthat State Park. I describe a trip of more than 9 miles with a vertical rise of more than 2,000 feet, but there are so many interconnecting trails in the park that you could take a very rewarding circuit hike of about 3 miles with only a minimal change in elevation. Study maps and my descriptions and you will find that this is the case in many places.

Safety Tips for You and the Environment

All too often, people are given advice on how to prepare for and be safe while pursuing outdoor activities, and then, as an afterthought—or perhaps as something that is somehow unrelated to what they're doing—they are given tips on how to protect the environment. In reality, the two are inseparable, as you will see from the following discussions. Remember, what you do in the outdoors is going to have a direct impact on you, the people who come after you, and the natural areas you visit. So, to reduce your impact on the environment, please practice "no-trace" hiking and camping techniques.

There are just as many opinions on what constitutes proper clothing and equipment for hiking and backpacking as there are hikers. There are still a few people left who are "dyed-in-the-wool" and could never be persuaded to use any synthetic clothing materials; most others wouldn't dream of trusting their health and safety to anything but synthetics. The debate over the merits of external-frame versus internal-frame backpacks rages on. Technology is advancing the state of outdoor equipment every year, so these discussions will continue to grow and change. While there is disagreement as to specific brands or fabrics you should use, common sense and the experience of others can provide a general list of the things to take along while hiking.

As with any outdoor pursuit, you must be ready for abrupt fluctuations in the weather. Especially in the mountains, but even in the Piedmont and on the coastal plain, warm and sunny summer days may quickly become cold and rainy, and even on a spring or fall day that precipitation is just as likely be sleet or snow. Because people are caught off guard on days such as this, when the temperature dips into the low sixties and fifties, hypothermia may strike. A condition in which the body loses heat faster than it can produce it, hypothermia is one of the leading causes of hiker and camper deaths. Be prepared by carrying raingear and an insulating layer of clothing, such as a wool sweater or synthetic jacket, in your daypack. Because layering is a more effective means of keeping warm than wearing just one thick layer, carry several items of warm clothing for winter travel.

When you are going to be hiking more than an hour or so you should carry drinking water with you. Most everyone understands that Virginia's summertime heat and humidity will cause you to work up quite a dry mouth, but what many people don't realize is that in the cool temperatures of winter your body needs even

A copperhead (left) and two rattlesnakes (right)

greater amounts of water to keep from becoming dehydrated. Unfortunately, the days of being able to slake your thirst by dipping into a clear mountain stream or taking a sip of cold spring water are gone, most likely forever. The rise in the number of people visiting the natural areas of Virginia has brought about a corresponding increase in the appearance of giardia, a water-borne parasite. Water can also become tainted by viruses, bacteria, and man-made pollutants.

If your outing is going to last only a few hours, you should be able to carry all the water you need with you. On overnight trips, though, you are going to have to depend on a stream or spring. These sources could probably be made potable by boiling; however, only by using a water filter can you be somewhat assured of removing most man-made chemical pollutants. Consult trusted friends or your local outfitter to help you decide which filter or purifier is best for you.

Please note! For your convenience, I have pointed out water sources in many of the hike descriptions, but this is not an endorsement of their purity. All of these sources should be treated before drinking!

Your choice of a no-trace campsite can help assure that you are not the cause of any further water pollution. Select a site a minimum of 200 feet away from any source of water, including not just springs or streams but also lakes, ponds, and even wet meadows. Ditching or building trenches around your tent not only creates lasting scars but will also cause the topsoil to wash away, silting nearby water supplies. Carry water to some other point so that you can do all of your washing, including dishes, clothes, and yourself, well away from the source. Dig a hole and bury human waste under a minimum of 6 inches of soil and at least 400 feet away from any water.

While in camp, you can practice no-trace methods by cooking on a stove and not building a fire. A fire not only leaves charred spots but also destroys nutrients in the topsoil. Some places are so fragile that it could be years before any new growth will appear where there was once a campfire. So many otherwise beautiful places have been marred by literally dozens of fire rings and charred and barren spots on the earth that I recommend, and even request, that you refrain from building a fire on any of your camping trips. Modern backpacking stoves will add little weight to your pack and will cook your meal in a fraction of the time it will take to properly prepare a site, build the fire, and cook over it. If you want to enjoy the romance of a campfire, head to a developed campground with officially designated fire grates.

It is not necessary to subject your feet to the tortures of heavy-duty mountaineering-type boots in order to enjoy hiking in Virginia. Except for people who may have foot or ankle problems, comfortable tennis, walking, or running shoes would probably suffice for most of the hikes—especially the shorter ones—in eastern and central Virginia. Lightweight hiking boots or shoes should be sufficient for hikes in the mountains and on overnight backpacking trips.

Almost everyone agrees that in order to reduce friction and rubbing on your feet you should wear a thick sock over a thinner one. Yet for such a small item, there is a wide range of opinion on what proper hiking socks are. When I first started hiking, I found that, contrary to the advice I read in every book, cotton inner socks served me best. Now I prefer a wool-polypropylene blend. For outer socks, I find I am just as happy with the newer, thick synthetic socks that are now on the market as I am with my old ragg-wool socks. Experiment with different combinations to decide what is best for you. I have found that just changing the combination of socks I'm wearing can turn uncomfortable boots into ones that I wouldn't trade for anything.

To ensure a proper fit, wear the sock combination you have decided upon when shopping for new boots. In order to avoid discomfort, don't attempt an extended hike without breaking in your new boots or shoes. Apply moleskin (available at most pharmacies and outdoors outfitters) immediately to any "hot spots" on your feet to discourage blisters from developing.

Trails are built to let you and your boots travel from one place to another with different degrees of difficulty. They are also designed to drain off water with a minimum amount of erosion. Unfortunately, one of the most effective means of controlling this problem, the switchback, is one of the most abused by hikers. By cutting switchbacks to save a bit of energy and a few moments of time, you not only create scars on the earth but increase the amount of topsoil that is washed off the mountainside.

Mountain biking has become exceptionally popular in Virginia, especially in the national forest where a very large percentage of trails are open to bikes. Although most devotees of the activity I have met have been courteous, you should be prepared to quickly step aside at any moment as an unannounced bike goes zipping by you at a high rate of speed.

Staying on the main pathway is also a way to decrease the possibility of snake encounters. Virginia is home to a wide variety of snakes, but only three are poisonous. (Medical attention should be sought for any bite from a snake—poisonous or not—as it may transmit harmful bacteria.) You should definitely learn how to identify copperheads and rattlesnakes. Found only in the extreme eastern part of the state, the cottonmouth, or water moccasin, is less common; nevertheless you should know what it looks like, too. In addition to keeping to the main trail, you can do a number of other things to avoid risky contact with snakes. Step on a log first instead of stepping over it, and don't put your hands in places you can't see. Hike with a group, or use your walking stick so that its sound and the vibrations it sends through the ground will let the snake know you are coming.

Snakes are just as apprehensive about meeting you as you are of them, and given enough time and warning a snake will often leave an area before you arrive. Remember, you are walking through the snake's natural home and it has as much right, if not more, than you do to be where it is. If you do run across a snake, please refrain from killing it. Just walk around it, giving it a wide berth, and continue on your way.

In Shenandoah National Park, and on some of the other, more remote hikes, you have a very real chance of seeing black bears. It is exceedingly rare for a black bear to attack a human, but you must remember that they are wild animals and do not like to be approached at close range. Be especially careful not to get between a mother bear and her cubs. In any case, the wisest thing to do is to turn and walk (not run) away as quickly as possible. In the numerous meetings I've had with bears, they seemed just as relieved to walk away from me as I was from them. In fact, you should observe this rule for an encounter with any wild animal—give it plenty of room and leave it alone.

Due to the abundance of wildlife, hunting is extremely popular in Virginia, even in the more populated counties like Fairfax and Prince William. The usual season can run from October through January, and then there's a season again in the spring for turkey hunting. Because dates do vary, you should check with local authorities. During the hunting season, it may be best to hike in a group. In any case, don't venture forth without wearing some kind of blaze orange clothing. If you are hunting (or fishing), be sure to obtain the proper licenses and check about local regulations.

New England may be famous for its hordes of black flies, but Virginia certainly has its fair share of mosquitoes, gnats, no-see-ums, deerflies, ticks, and other insects. Bring repellent. (And remember that one of the pleasures of hiking during the colder months of the year is the absence of insects.)

Recent years have seen a rise in reported cases of Lyme disease, a bacterial infection transmitted by the bite of a deer tick. Preliminary research indicates that commercially prepared insect repellents may not work well against ticks, so as a precaution some people tuck pants legs into socks or boots and wear a long-sleeved shirt and a cap. Check yourself for ticks after each outing, remembering that the thing you are looking for could be as small as the period at the end of this sentence.

Poison ivy is found throughout Virginia; learn how to identify it. Most often you will see it as a woody shrub growing 2 to 3 feet high and lining or overtaking your route. You must also be wary of it when, as a hairy root-covered vine, it clings to the trunks of trees, reaching far up into the branches. Its white berries, which appear in the fall, are especially toxic, but all parts of the plant contain the poison—even in winter when it may look dead.

Stinging nettle grows so quickly that it can often overtake the best of maintained trails. One bout with this irritating plant will teach you to watch for it in the future.

Scientists continue to issue warnings about the sun's harmful effects; use a high-strength sunblock whenever you will be outdoors for an extended period.

Besides the sunblock, stash a first-aid kit, space blanket, small knife (I have never really found the need to carry a multitool, Swiss Army–type knife), flashlight, compass, toilet paper, and some waterproofed matches in your pack. Overnight hikes, of course, require additional items: full-sized backpacks, sleeping bags and pads, a tent, cooking utensils, and more. Again, there are many opinions as to what kind or brand you should use. Obviously it is not the intent of this guidebook to be a hiking or backpacking equipment "primer," so I'm going to suggest you solicit the advice of backpacking acquaintances, trail-club members, and outdoors outfitters. I am a firm believer, especially if you're a novice hiker, in supporting your neighborhood backpack shop instead of mail-order companies. Not only will the local folks help fit and adjust your equipment and be there to help you if you have any questions, but many shops also rent hiking and camping equipment—enabling you to try something before you decide to buy it.

A number of books are available if you feel the need for further information. Currently, two of the most complete books on the subject of outdoor travel are *Trailside Guide: Hiking and Backpacking* by Karen Berger and *A Hiker's Companion: 12,000 Miles of Trail-Tested Wisdom* by Cindy Ross and Todd Gladfelter. Although now becoming a bit outdated, *The Complete Walker III* by Colin Fletcher is not only informative but also makes for some entertaining reading. *Backwoods Ethics* by Laura and Guy Waterman is an excellent resource. It provides not only the "how" of no-trace camping but also the "why." If you don't have the time or inclination to read an entire book, at least obtain and study a copy of the Appalachian Trail Conference's (address below) no-trace ethic pamphlet—it is usually available free of charge.

Suggested Readings and Field Guides

Abercrombie, Jay. *Walks and Rambles on the Delmarva Peninsula: A Guide for Hikers and Naturalists.* Woodstock, Vt.: Backcountry Publications, 1985.

Adkins, Leonard M. *Adventure Guide to Virginia.* Edison Hill, N.J.: Hunter Publishing, 1998.

———. *The Appalachian Trail: A Visitor's Companion.* Birmingham, Al.: Menasha Ridge Press, 1998.

———. *Seashore State Park: A Walking Guide.* Centreville, Md.: Tidewater Publishers, 1990.

———. *Walking the Blue Ridge: A Guide to the Trails of the Blue Ridge Parkway.* Chapel Hill, N.C.: University of North Carolina Press, 1996.

———. *Wildflowers of the Appalachian Trail.* Birmingham, Al.: Menasha Ridge Press, 1999.

Breland, Osmond P. *Animal Life and Lore.* Rev. ed. New York: Harper and Row, 1972.

Brooks, Maurice. *The Appalachians.* Morgantown, W.Va.: Seneca Books, 1995.

Bull, John, and John Farrand Jr. *The Audubon Society Field Guide to North American Birds: Eastern Region.* New York: Alfred A. Knopf, 1977.

Byrd, Nathan, ed. *A Forester's Guide to Observing Animal Use of Forest Habitat in the South.* Atlanta, Ga.: U.S. Department of Agriculture, Forest Service, 1981.

Constantz, George. *Hollows, Peepers, and Highlanders: An Appalachian Mountain Ecology.* Missoula, Mont.: Mountain Press Publishing, 1994.

Dietrich, Richard V. *Geology and Virginia.* Charlottesville, Va.: University Press of Virginia, 1970.

Fletcher, Colin. *The Complete Walker III: The Joys and Techniques of Hiking and Backpacking.* 3rd ed., rev., enlarged, and updated. New York: Alfred A. Knopf, 1984, 1992.

Gupton, Oscar W., and Fred C. Swope. *Trees and Shrubs of Virginia.* Charlottesville, Va.: University of Virginia Press, 1989.

———. *Wildflowers of the Shenandoah Valley and Blue Ridge Mountains.* Charlottesville, Va.: University of Virginia Press, 1982.

Kephart, Horace. *Our Southern Highlanders.* Knoxville, Tenn.: University of Tennessee Press, 1984.

Little, Elbert L. *The Audubon Society Field Guide to North American Trees: Eastern Region.* New York: Alfred A. Knopf, 1994.

Martof, Bernard, et al. *Amphibians and Reptiles of the Carolinas and Virginia.* Chapel Hill, N.C.: University of North Carolina Press, 1989.

Peterson, Roger T. *A Field Guide to Eastern Birds: A Field Guide to Birds East of the Rockies.* Boston: Houghton Mifflin, 1984.

Peterson, Roger T., and Margaret McKenny. *A Field Guide to Wildflowers of Northeastern and North-Central North America.* Boston: Houghton Mifflin, 1975.

Petrides, George A. *A Field Guide to Trees and Shrubs.* Boston: Houghton Mifflin, 1988.

Simpson, Marcus B., Jr. *Birds of the Blue Ridge Mountains: A Guide for the Blue Ridge Parkway, Great Smoky Mountains, Shenandoah National Park, and Neighboring Areas.* Chapel Hill, N.C.: University of North Carolina Press, 1992.

Slone, Harry. *Trout Streams of Virginia: An Angler's Guide to the Blue Ridge Watershed.* Third edition. Woodstock, Vt.: Backcountry Guides, 1999.

Stokes, Donald W. *The Natural History of Wild Shrubs and Vines.* New York: Harper and Row, 1989.

Waterman, Laura, and Guy Waterman. *Backwoods Ethics: Environmental Issues for Hikers and Campers.* Woodstock, Vt.: The Countryman Press, 1993.

———. *Wilderness Ethics: Preserving the Spirit of Wildness.* Woodstock, Vt.: The Countryman Press, 1993.

Webster, William D., et al. *Mammals of the Carolinas, Virginia and Maryland.* Chapel Hill, N.C.: University of North Carolina Press, 1985.

White, Christopher P. *Appalachian Trail Guide to Central Virginia.* Harpers Ferry, W.Va.: Appalachian Trail Conference, 1994.

———. *Chesapeake Bay: Nature of the Estuary, A Field Guide.* Centreville, Md.: Tidewater Publishers, 1990.

Addresses

Hike 1:
Hampton Parks & Recreation
22 Lincoln St.
Hampton, VA 23669

Hike 2:
Newport News Park
13560 Jefferson Ave.
Newport News, VA 23603-1104

Hike 5:
Virginia Natural Heritage Program
217 Governor Street
Richmond, VA 23219

Hikes 3, 4, 6, 9, 12, 13, 48, & 49:
Department of Conservation and
    Recreation
203 Governor St., Suite 302
Richmond, VA 23219

Hike 7:
Fredericksburg & Spotsylvania
    National Military Park
120 Chatham Lane
Fredericksburg, VA 22405

Hike 8:
Prince William Forest Park
18100 Park Headquarters Rd.
Triangle, VA 22172

Hike 10:
NVRPA
5400 Ox Rd.
Fairfax Station, VA 22039

Hike 11:
Manassas National Battlefield Park
6511 Sudley Rd.
Manassas, VA 22110

Hike 14:
Richmond National Battlefield Park
3215 East Broad St.
Richmond, VA 23223

Hike 15:
Cumberland State Forest
929 Oak Hill Road
Cumberland, VA 23040

Hikes 16 & 35:
Appalachian Trail Conference
P.O. Box 807
Harpers Ferry, WV 25425

Hikes 17, 18, 27–29, 32–34, 36–47, & 50:
George Washington & Jefferson National
    Forests
5162 Valleypointe Parkway
Roanoke, VA 24019

Hikes 19–26:
Shenandoah National Park
3655 U.S. Highway 211 East
Luray, VA 22835-9036

Hike 30:
Ivy Creek Foundation
P.O. Box 956
Charlottesville, VA 22902

Hike 31:
Blue Ridge Parkway
199 Hemphill Knob Road
Asheville, NC 28801

Map Symbols	
– –	main trail
•••	side trail
Ⓟ	parking
⇇	view
⋏	Appalachian Trail
⋔	shelter

I

Chesapeake Bay and Eastern Virginia

Grand View Preserve

Ⓟ Parking

0 ————————————— 0.5 mile

0 ————————————— 0.5 kilometer

N

Light

Light

Northend Point

Light

Light

Light

Rip

Floods Hole

Spoil A

Dandy Pt

Grunland Point

Grunland Creek

Wallace RD

DANDY POINT RD

CANAL

LANE

Lighthouse (Aban'd)

Ⓟ

Hawkins Pond

State Park Road

WT

Grunland Creek

Fox Hill

BEACH RD

Grand View

Long Creek

RD

Light

Asbury Sch

Clark Cem

1

Grandview Natural Preserve

Total distance (round trip): 3.6 miles

Hiking time: 2 hours

Vertical rise: None

Map: USGS 7½′ Hampton

The Chesapeake Bay, America's largest bay, is the catch basin for a far-reaching drainage system that covers 64,000 square miles. Snow melt that begins its downstream journey near Cooperstown, New York, meets and mingles in the bay with rainwater that fell on the higher elevations of the Allegheny Mountains on the central West Virginia–Virginia border. The bay is considered an estuary, a body of water where tidal movements bring salt water upstream, where it comes in contact with the fresh water being carried toward the ocean by river currents.

There are many other estuaries throughout the world, such as Puget Sound in Washington, Cook Inlet in Alaska, and the fjords of Norway, but none of them are nearly as productive as the Chesapeake Bay. More than 200 million pounds of seafood are harvested from the bay each year, including 50 percent of America's supply of blue crabs and more than 20 percent of its oysters. A number of conditions combine to make the bay this productive. Probably the two most important factors are the large amounts of fresh water coming into the bay and the vast acreage of marshlands surrounding the bay, which provides an abundance of detritus and other nutrients. These wetlands are home to numerous shorebirds and are also major stopping over and resting areas on the Great Atlantic Flyway for migratory waterfowl, including a wide array of ducks, swans, and Canada geese.

Although the Chesapeake Bay has about 4,000 miles of shoreline—more than the entire U.S. Pacific coast (excluding Alaska)—a large percentage of it is privately owned, heavily developed, or both. It is our good fortune that the city of Hampton has set aside a 2- to 3-mile stretch of that shoreline as the Grandview Natural Preserve, where you and I can walk on a secluded beach, far removed from hordes of sunbathing vacationers, carnival-atmosphere boardwalks, high-rise condominiums, or busy shipping yards. Here, in a place of relative quiet, we can study the bay's waters, shoreline, and marshes at our leisure or just sit peacefully on the sand.

To reach the preserve, exit I-64 and follow Mercury Boulevard (US 258) east to make a left turn onto Fox Hill Road (VA 169). Fox Hill Road bears left onto, and becomes, Beach Road in less than 3 miles. Continue on Beach Road for 2.7 miles to make a left onto State Park Road. Park your automobile at the end of the street, being sure to obey the posted regulations. Be aware that there are no restroom facilities in the preserve and no potable water. Note too, especially if you're hiking in the cooler months, that the winds around the bay can teach your body the meaning of a windchill factor. There is no shade in the preserve, so be ready for the glare of sun hitting from above and reflecting off the water beside you and the sand underneath your feet. Regulations prohibit visitors from being in the preserve after sunset.

Walk through the gate, and immediately to the right you may see several turtles basking in the sun on and around Hawkins Pond. At dawn or dusk, you might see a raccoon searching for a meal at the pond, and despite all the houses and other developments in the area, deer have been spotted roaming about on the preserve. Arrive at the beach in 0.4 mile, and turn to your left (to the right is private property in a few yards), enjoying, as the name of this place suggests, a grand view of the Chesapeake Bay. Huge cargo ships often go slowly by, for the Norfolk-Hampton area is one of the busiest ports in the world. Off in the distance you may be able to make out the Chesapeake Bay Bridge-Tunnel, built in 1965 at a cost of $200 million. The bridge-tunnel spans the mouth of the bay—a distance of 18 miles—joining southeast Virginia with the Delmarva Peninsula. A trip across the bridge-tunnel to the peninsula is worthwhile; Jay Abercrombie thoroughly covers some good hikes in this area, which most people tend to overlook, in his book, *Walks and Rambles on the Delmarva Peninsula.*

Continue walking and doing a bit of beachcombing. You will find the shells of the jackknife clam, known locally as a razor clam because of its resemblance to the old-fashioned shaving razor. You might happen to see a few live ones wash up on the beach, but they are such quick burrowers that they will quickly disappear, making them next to impossible to dig up. The clams use a strong foot to anchor themselves in the sand as they send up siphons to feed on plankton and detritus floating about in the water.

Various body parts of the blue crab may be spread over the sand. In addition to being a favorite food of the shorebirds, blue crabs are one of the most important seafood species of the bay. Commercial watermen catch millions of pounds annually, with the same amount also estimated to be caught by weekend crabbers. The crabs bury themselves in the mud and become dormant in the winter, emerging as soon as the water temperature rises a few degrees. You will find large numbers of females here in late summer, as they move into this area from the north so that their young will be released into the more saline water found near the mouth of the bay. The interesting lives of blue crabs are described in superbly entertaining and nontechnical detail in William Warner's *Beautiful Swimmers: Watermen, Crabs, and the Chesapeake Bay* ("beautiful swimmers" is the English translation of the blue crab's Latin name, *Callinectes sapidus*).

The dune on your left was formed when sand, blown about by winds off the bay, became trapped in bits of beach debris. As the winds continued to blow more sand onto and over the dune, wind- and salt-resistant vegetation established itself and helped stabilize the dune. You may notice some discarded Christmas trees on top of the dune; they were placed there by the city of Hampton to aid in the stabilization of the dune.

Rounding a corner of the beach at 0.7 mile, look for brown pelicans resting on rocks in the water. Pelicans were once on the decline around the bay, but they have made a remarkable comeback since the banning of the pesticide DDT. It is now common to be able to watch one use its 90-inch wingspan to build up speed for a spectacular dive into the water. The cartoons you watched in your childhood may have convinced you that a pelican uses its pouch to carry fish, but in reality the pouch is primarily employed as a device to scoop the fish out of the water.

Looking back onto the beach, you'll see that the sand is dotted by small holes with scratch marks in front of them. These are the homes of small ghost crabs. If you wait and watch long enough, one of them will make a mad dash for the water, because they have to wet their gills on a periodic basis. Sadly for them, this is when they often become a meal for a circling gull or tern. In addition to the crab

Blue crab

holes, that string of tan capsules you find on the beach is whelk eggs. Many times the capsules did not hatch and, if you break them open, you'll find tiny whelk shells inside, identical to those of an adult.

Rounding another curve in the beach, you will notice the dune has become large enough to develop sand "cliffs," but by the time you have walked 1.7 miles, the dune will have disappeared and you can look out across the inland marsh where herons and egrets wade in search of food. At about this spot, the waves become larger and louder because the land no longer slopes gently into the water but rather drops steeply into the bay. The strip of land you are walking upon abruptly comes to an end in a few hundred feet. At one time you could have kept on walking a bit farther, but a violent storm that blew in from the northeast in the late 1990s breached the land and created the small channel in front of you. The newly formed island to the north of you is now a protected wildlife refuge zone, a sanctuary from human intrusion for least terns, black skimmers, and piping plovers, all of them struggling to find a place in our increasingly overdeveloped world.

This is the farthest you can walk in this direction. Turn around and stroll back to your car, delighting in the sunshine, the salty breeze, the antics of passing sea gulls, and the discovery of other sights, sounds, and small treasures you may have missed on the way out.

While in this area you should consider driving over to the City of Hampton's Sandy Bottom Nature Park (accessible from I-61 Exit 261A). A stroll along the several miles of pathways there will take you through lake edge, marsh, streamside, and forest habitats.

2

Newport News Park

Total distance (circuit): 5.6 miles

Hiking time: 3 hours

Vertical rise: 130 feet

Maps: USGS 7½' Yorktown; Newport News Park map

Golden Gate Park in San Francisco and Central Park in New York may be more famous than the Newport News Park, but these and other municipal parks often contain amusement rides, zoos, bandstands, and other highly developed areas spread out and connected by networks of paved roadways. With more than 8,000 mostly wooded acres, Newport News Park is one of the country's largest city-owned parks to provide hikers with multiple miles of walking routes through dense forests, well removed from automobiles and the resulting din of traffic noise—all the more amazing when you realize the park sits within the confines of one of Virginia's most heavily populated areas.

In order to meet the diverse recreational needs of so many people, the park provides bicycle and boat rentals, an archery range, a 36-hole golf course and driving range, picnic shelters, an arboretum, an interpretive center, an excellent seasonal schedule of naturalist-conducted programs, playgrounds, concessions, and a campground with close to 200 sites. Yet all of these facilities are concentrated on just a few hundred acres, and approximately 40 miles of pathways and fire roads can lead visitors away from intensely used areas around Lee Hall Reservoir and through dark stands of loblolly pine, by overgrown reminders of wars past, and into lushly green and quiet swamplands. The official state transportation map of Virginia may show this as metropolitan property, but you are in for a most decidedly un-urban walk. Park personnel and volunteers have inventoried 76 spring flowers; more than 100 summer and fall blossoms; 60 tree types; various shrubs, vines, and other plants; and so much wildlife that it takes an eight-page pamphlet just to list all of the native species. Take a look at the total vertical rise you're going to experience while on this hike of more than 5 miles and you will know you're in for an easy stroll over gentle terrain.

Exit I-64 in Newport News onto VA 105 East for less than 0.2 mile to make a left onto VA 143. In 0.5 mile, turn right into the park and continue about 1 mile to the Discovery Center, where you can obtain maps and other information about the park, which is open year-round.

You can leave your car either at the center or in the parking area across the road from it. Begin by crossing the bridge over Lee Hall Reservoir, which is open for the fishing of catfish, largemouth bass, northern pike, crappie, chain pickerel, bluegill, and white and yellow perch. At the far end of the bridge, bear left to follow the left branch of the Twin Forts Trail, where you'll see the first of many mounds and trenches that made up the Confederate lines of defense during the Civil War's battle of Dam Number One. The dam, now covered by the waters of the reservoir, is still visible below the footbridge you just crossed.

At the beginning of 1862, the Federal strategy of the peninsula campaign was for Major General George B. McClellan's Army of the Potomac to swiftly defeat the Confederate forces on the peninsula and move on to capture Richmond before it could be fortified. Remember that at this time the war was still in its early stages and the Union felt the fall of Richmond would depress Southern resolve and bring about a speedy conclusion to the rebellion. Preparing for the impending attack, the Confederates constructed, with the help of slaves from nearby plantations, a

series of fortifications (known as breastworks because soldiers could fire from the trenches but still be protected to the breast by the high mounds) stretching across the peninsula. Following a failed attempt to make it past the Warwick River on April 5, the Army of the Potomac was again repulsed on April 11 by soldiers entrenched behind the breastworks close to Dam Number One.

Some of the old breastworks found at other sites in Virginia have deteriorated to the point of being barely distinguishable, but the ones you'll see throughout your hike in the park are remarkably well preserved, many coming close to retaining their original shape and size. After the two skirmishes, McClellan halted frontal assaults in favor of large artillery bombardments. After suffering several weeks under the Union barrage, the Confederates retreated—not quite in defeat, as they had gained a month's worth of valuable time for Richmond to fortify and reinforce.

At 0.3 mile, the trail swings away from the reservoir to cross a creek beside the high mounds of the breastworks. When you come to the four-way intersection at 0.4 mile, the pathway straight ahead goes to the campground while the Longmeadow Trail to the left heads back to the reservoir. You need to continue right for 100 feet before making another right and continuing on the Twin Forts Trail, walking on the other side of the breastworks you've been observing.

At 0.8 mile, the route will have returned you to the bridge, where you'll make a left onto the White Oak Nature Trail. People who have been to Florida or the Caribbean may be reminded of mangroves when looking at the vegetation in the shallow waters of the reservoir. On the dry land, the mixed forest of oak, hickory, and loblolly pine has an intermediate story of holly, pawpaw, and

Newport News Park

P Parking

N

0   0.25 mile

0   0.25 kilometer

French Cem

Washingtons
Headquarters
BM 52   Ford
Cem

Creek

Bikeway

Wynn's
Mill Trail

Swamp
Fire
Trail

White Oak
Nature Trail

Beaverdam

Swamp
Bridge

Sycamore
Creek Trail

Longmeadow Trail

Newport News
Park

Campground

Twin Forts
Trail

AQUEDUCT

Overlook

RESERVOIR

all
ide Park

To VA 143
and I-64

Discovery P
Center

Picnic

Golf Course

dogwood, with very little undergrowth. Make a left onto the Sycamore Creek Trail at 1.1 miles, reaching the well-maintained Bikeway at 1.5 miles. To the left, it is about seven-tenths mile to the campground; turn right into a younger forest of smaller trees. Be alert at 1.7 miles, where the Bikeway curves to the right; you want to take the unmarked and ungraveled but wide roadway to the left, where the undergrowth suddenly expands into hundreds of blueberry bushes. A road comes in from the left at 2.6 miles, but you want to keep to the right for a few more feet to make a right onto the

Bikeway and enter a small portion of the Colonial National Historical Park.

The historical park commemorates the battle of Yorktown and the surrender of Lord Cornwallis to General George Washington. (The park is connected by way of the 20-plus-mile Colonial Parkway—passing through Colonial Williamsburg—to the site of Jamestown, the first permanent English settlement in the New World.) Honeysuckle and poison ivy vines are draped over the trees where a road to the left leads approximately 500 feet to Washington's Yorktown headquarters. Continuing on the

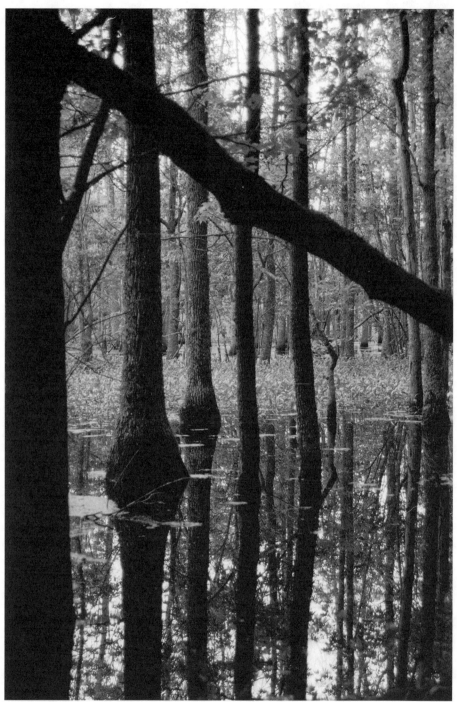

The transition zone, where lake meets swamp

Bikeway, you'll return to the confines of Newport News Park; bear left onto an ungravelled roadbed when the Bikeway makes a 90-degree turn at 3.6 miles.

Turn right onto Wynn's Mill Trail at 3.7 miles, making sure, 100 feet beyond that, to walk on the pathway and not follow the roadbed. The maze of a multitude of breast-works going off in different directions must have required hundreds of hours of back-breaking labor to construct. Coming to the Swamp Fire Trail, turn left, soon crossing a small footbridge. Five-lined skinks are often seen skittering across the bridge in search of insects. The young skinks have five well-defined lines along their backs and bright blue tails, but the characteristics fade and become less obvious with age. As defense mechanisms, the skink has a detachable tail as well as a bite powerful enough to draw blood.

Another section of the Wynn's Mill Trail comes in from the left at 4.5 miles; you want to keep right, heading onto the Swamp Bridge and into a radically different environment of lush summer greenery. Mixed in with the swamp's dense tangle of vegetation is arrow arum, differentiated from other arrow-head-shaped plants by its distinctive long green sheath, or spathe, surrounding tiny flowers that grow on a fleshy spike known as a spadix by botanists. Spotted turtles, aptly named for the yellow dots on their head, neck, and shell, are sometimes seen basking in warm sunshine on logs floating in the swamp. Although they may not appear so as they lei-surely slide into the water when disturbed, spotted turtles are amazingly intelligent crea-tures and have shown an ability to correctly negotiate elaborate mazes.

At the far end of the bridge, make a right; you will soon pass a short side trail leading to an overlook of the swamp. On the main trail at 5.1 miles is an observation platform on the lake. Looking to your right from the platform you'll see where the lake meets the swamp, and it is in this zone of transition that Canada geese, tundra swans, and a variety of ducks make their winter homes. From here, your hike will follow the paved road for a short distance before reentering the woods and coming to an end at 5.6 miles.

If you haven't had your fill of easy hiking on nearly flat tidewater terrain, there are still miles of pathways and fire roads you can use to explore the thousands of acres in a less frequently visited part of the park across VA 105. Personnel at the Discovery Center can supply you with the information you'll need.

3

Belle Isle

Total distance (round trip): 5.0 miles

Hiking time: 2¼ hours

Vertical rise: Less than 30 feet

Maps: USGS 7½′ Lively; state park map

Sadly, as a place that was already deficient in areas in which the public could walk or hike when compared to other parts of the commonwealth, Tidewater, Virginia, lost two of its best trails in 1999. After acquiring lands from the Chesapeake Forests Products Company, the Canada-based St. Laurent Corporation terminated visitor use of a 2-mile nature trail beside the Corrotoman River in Lancaster County. At about the same time, the former company ceased maintaining the Warreneye Nature Trail near West Point in New Kent County.

Earlier in the same decade, Virginians were foresighted enough to see that occurrences similar to this—coupled with the rapid spread of the modern world—threatened their ability to recreate in the natural world. Approving the Parks and Recreational Facilities Bond in 1992, the citizens authorized the commonwealth to expend state funds for the purpose of bringing more acreage into the public domain (and upgrading facilities at existing sites).

Bounded by water on three sides, 773-acre Belle Isle State Park was the first parcel of land to be purchased with the bond money. Archaeological evidence has shown that this small tract along the northern side of the Rappahannock River has been inhabited for at least 11,000 years. The temporary camps of Native Americans who seasonally visited the area became the settlements of Algonquin-speaking peoples who moved inland from the coast. In turn, they were replaced by the Moraughtacunds, part of the Powhatan tribe, who were living in the region when colonists arrived.

Brewer's Point

Mulberry

Belle Isle

Creek

Horse Trail

Mud Creek Trail

Neck Fields Trail

Watch House Trail

Porpoise Creek Trail

Park Office

To VA 683

Belle Isle

Ⓟ Parking

N

0   0.25 mile

0   0.25 kilometer

The newcomers from the Old World soon turned the riverside acreage into a large and thriving plantation. Soon after the Civil War, the land was sold off into several parcels, and by the time of the late 1900s was threatened with the possibility of becoming a waterfront community until the state purchased it in 1993. Still in the development stage, the state park offers picnic areas; overnight accommodations in a Georgian-style mansion and guest house; bicycle, motorboat, and canoe rentals; a motorboat launch, and a car-top launch. Rockfish, croaker, spot, and flounder are found in the waters around the park. The interpretive programs include canoe trips onto the river and into the creeks and marshes. Led by park personnel and volunteer naturalists, the guided paddle journeys focus on the ecology and fragility of the area. Making use of innovative conservation practices to reduce pollution runoff into the Chesapeake Bay, much of the land is still cultivated.

Following old farm roads, a network of trails provides the opportunity to walk by these fields and out to vistas overlooking the Rappahannock River and Mulberry Creek. Most of the pathways are also open to bicyclists and equestrians. Present plans call for more trails to be built, so check at the park office or contact station for the most up-to-date information. A small fee is charged, and pets must be on a leash at all times.

Belle Isle State Park may be reached by driving northward from Kilmarnock (or southward from Warsaw) on VA 3 to Lively. Turn westward and follow VA 201 for 3.3 miles, then turn right onto VA 354. An additional 3.2 miles brings you to a left turn onto VA 683. The contact station is 0.7 mile down this road, the park office is 0.8 mile farther, and the playground area where you leave your car is an additional 0.5 mile.

Initiate the hike by walking from the parking lot to the fence overlooking the broad Rappahannock River, over 3 miles wide at this point. This is a great place to be in early morning as the sun spreads its glow across the water. After enjoying the view, walk next to the woods to begin following the Porpoise Creek Trail, an old road beside a cultivated field.

Turn left onto a small pathway into the woods at 0.2 mile and come to an enclosed blind overlooking a small backwater area of the river. Staying inside this small hut built by volunteers of a local conservation organization, and being quiet as long as possible, increases your chances of observing great blue herons, ducks, geese, and other waterfowl. Small ripples moving across the water in a zigzag fashion could indicate a snake gliding to the opposite shore, while the head of a muskrat may be seen bobbing up and down as it swims to its tunnel home in the bank. Boosted by partially webbed hind feet, these amphibious members of the rodent family are able to swim forward or backward and have been known to stay submerged for more than 10 minutes at a time. Although loss of habitat may be having an impact on their lives, their prolific breeding habits are, at present, unchanged. After a gestation period of about 30 days, the first litter of four to seven young are born in April or May (in Virginia) and are able to fend for themselves inside of a month. By mating again in about 10 days after giving birth, the female is able to produce several litters during the season.

Return to the main trail and turn left, walking between woods and a cultivated field. Pass through a windrow at 0.5 mile and come to a T-intersection beside another field. Turn left onto the Watch House Trail. The Mud Creek Trail comes in from the right a few hundred feet later; keep left on the Watch House Trail—the only bit of dryness separating two wetlands—with a view of the Rappahannock River to the left.

The Neck Fields Trail comes in from the right at 0.8 mile; keep left. Just 100 feet later, turn left onto a mowed pathway. Your perspective onto the Rappahannock River changes as you circle the edge of another cultivated field.

Intersect and turn left onto the Watch House Trail at 1.1 miles, passing through a stand of towering loblolly pine trees and coming to the edge of the river. Over 100 years ago an oyster watch house stood close to 100 feet offshore to ensure that thieves did not sneak in to harvest the fruits of the oyster beds. A later watch house was built on the point of land you are now standing upon. As did those throughout the Chesapeake Bay, the oysters here began to dwindle in numbers in the 1970s due to nonpoint pollution and disease.

Return inland along Watch House Trail to bear left onto the Neck Fields Trail, a wide country lane bordered by loblolly trees, at 1.4 miles. For a bit of a change from walking the old farm roads, turn left onto a mowed pathway along the edge of a cultivated field at 1.7 miles. Tracks in the soft soil attest to an abundance of deer in the park, while the pond visible through the trees may harbor ducks, geese, egrets, and herons. While you may see some great blue herons in Virginia all year long, others fly as far north as Ontario for the summer and migrate to Virginia's Northern Neck—or points farther south—for the winter. Next to the edge of another pond visible through the vegetation at 2.1 miles, begin to circle back on the far side of the field. Songbirds may serenade you in the early morning, while vultures, crows, and hawks wing their way across the open sky.

Intersect the Neck Fields Trail at 2.5 miles and turn left. Passing by a couple of other cultivated meadows (whose mowed pathways along the edges are additional walking options), private homes are visible along Mulberry Creek at 2.8 miles. Be sure to stay on the main route as it continues beyond the farmlands to come to an end on Brewer's Point at 3.2 miles. You certainly deserve a break, so bring the snacks out of the daypack and enjoy the sights and sounds. A small fishing boat may pass by, causing small waves to lightly splash upon the shore, while an osprey may drop to the water, rising a few moments later with a fish grasped in its talons.

When you are ready to return, follow the Neck Fields Trail back to the Watch House Trail at 4.4 miles. Turn left and bypass the Mud Creek Trail on the left at 4.6 miles. (If you wish to extend the hike, you could follow the Mud Creek Trail to another point overlooking the Mulberry River, a round trip of a little more than 0.5 mile.)

Making a right turn onto the Porpoise Creek Trail less than 200 feet later will return you to the playground area at 5 miles.

For a whimsical diversion before heading home after the hike, drive back to Lively and turn right onto VA 3. In Lancaster Court House make a right onto VA 604 for several miles. The Merry Point Ferry, one of the few remaining river ferries in Virginia, will shuttle you across the West Branch of the Corrotoman River. Although this is a utilitarian boat, the ride across the river can be a scenic and enjoyable one as you watch waterfowl and other birds wing their way above the river. To return to VA 3 after the ferry ride, take VA 604 to Ottoman, where you will make a right onto VA 354. Be watching for a right turn onto VA 201 to bring you to back to Lively.

4

Hughlett Point

Total distance (round trip): 1.8 miles

Hiking time: 45 minutes

Vertical rise: 10 feet

Maps: USGS 7½′ Fleets Bay

Like Belle Isle State Park (see Hike 3), the Hughlett Point Natural Area Preserve is a gift Virginians gave themselves by voting positively for the 1992 Parks and Recreational Facilities Bond. The U.S. Fish and Wildlife Service also provided funds to help purchase the 200-acre tract in order to protect the rare northeastern beach tiger beetle and the occurrences of Chesapeake Bay salt marshes, beaches, and dunes.

Enclosed on three sides by the waters of Ingram Cove, Dividing Creek, and the Chesapeake Bay, and rising no more than 10 feet above sea level, the preserve in many places is more marsh than it is dry land. Plants that find a favorable home here include needle rush, salt meadow hay, switchgrass, common reed, cordgrass, and marsh elder. The inland marshes are bordered by wax myrtle, whose berries begin forming in August and develop a white, waxy dust that was used in former times to make bayberry candles. But it is not just the berries that have a pleasant scent; rubbing just about any part of the plant will produce the familiar fragrance. Areas just slightly lower in elevation produce the right conditions for cattails to survive.

Hughlett Point Natural Area Preserve is reached from VA 3 in Kilmarnock. In the main part of town, turn northeast onto VA 200 and follow it for 4.3 miles to a right turn onto VA 606. In another 2.1 miles, make a right onto VA 605. The parking area for the preserve is on the left in an additional 2 miles. No visitor's or parking fee is charged, but be aware that it is a day-use area only. Pets must be on a leash at all times.

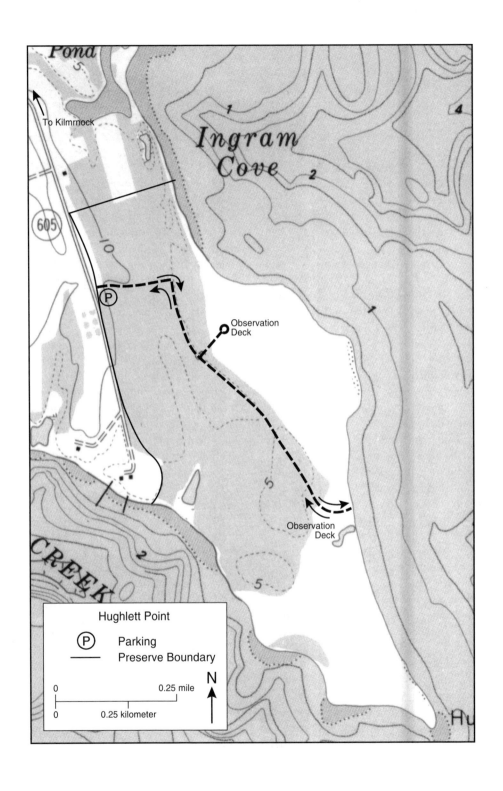

Pond

To Kilmrnock

605

Ingram
Cove

Observation
Deck

Observation
Deck

CREEK

Hughlett Point

Ⓟ   Parking

    Preserve Boundary

N

0   0.25 mile

0   0.25 kilometer

Enter the preserve by taking the boardwalk into a forest dominated by loblolly trees, where you might see a gray fox splashing through shallow, tannin-stained water in pursuit of an early morning meal. The mounds of what appear to be dirt covered by rich vegetation are actually the decaying piles of wood debris left over from the last time this area was logged several decades ago. Look closely and you will find that tracks made by heavy logging equipment are still visible in the soft soil.

Intersect a woods road at 0.15 mile and turn right; the Chesapeake Bay is visible through the vegetation to the left. To appreciate as much of what the preserve has to offer as possible, turn left onto a side trail at 0.4 mile to follow it out to an observation deck overlooking a large marsh and the bay. Note that the deck you are standing upon is built with recycled plastic; maybe one of your old soda bottles contributed to this "lumber" and helped save a tree from being destroyed.

From the vantage point of the deck, the Chesapeake Bay and its accompanying shoreline look much as they did at the time of Captain John Smith's explorations in the early 1600s. Reminders of the modern world may be a large ship passing by on the horizon, or the smoke from the menhaden processing plant in Reedville to the north. A herring that can grow up to 14 inches in length and distinguished by silver sides marked with large dark spots below a bluish upper portion, menhaden are caught in large quantities in the bay. Most often turned into fertilizer, the fish may also be included in pet foods.

Return to the main trail and turn left, soon passing by a small pond on the right at 0.7 mile. The route swings to the left at 0.9 mile, coming to another observation deck. The cattail-lined marsh here has been known to be a good place to watch ospreys and bald eagles on the wing. In addition to providing nourishment and home-building material for muskrats, cattails help stabilize soil along the edge of the marsh.

You will arrive at the beach, the home of the northeastern beach tiger beetle, less than 300 feet later. The beetle begins its life by crawling out of the egg its parent laid in the sand. Spending the first two years of its life in the larval stage, it grows to 5/8 inch in length, has noticeable humps on its back, and large jaws like the adult. It survives by waiting at the mouth of a 4- to 10-inch burrow for prey to come along and be snatched by the powerful jaws. With russet-green heads and black markings on white backs, the adults are only 2/3 inch long. They can often be seen during the warmer months hopping across the sand in search of food. At one time these beetles inhabited much of the shoreline around the Chesapeake Bay, but waterfront development, increased human foot traffic on their sandy home, and the (possible) effects of pollutants have caused their numbers to decrease dramatically. There are only a few places left in Virginia and Maryland in which they are known to exist.

It is time to take a break, so dip your feet into the water (although swimming is prohibited), and sit back to enjoy the sun and the sand. One of the most enjoyable activities in the Chesapeake Bay is to go crabbing by becoming what the locals call a "chicken necker." This is done by attaching a chicken neck (or any other bony piece of meat) to a string and casting it a few feet out into the water. Gradually pull the string in when you feel a tug on it. With luck, a crab will be hanging tenaciously onto the bait and you can slip a net under it before you lift it out of the water. Be careful of the claws when you turn the net over to gently shake the crab out! No license is required for recreational crabbing in Virginia, but I suggest you follow the example of a Maryland law and throw back all crabs less than 5 inches from shell point to shell point.

The public lands of the Hughlett Point Natural Preserve Area stretch to both the north and south of where the main trail meets the bay. You have the option of extending your outing by as much as 3 miles by walking in both directions, enjoying the quiet of your surroundings, combing the beach for hidden treasures, or keeping a lookout for some of the area's wildlife. At one time of year or another, deer, river otter, herons, scoters, egrets, rails, loons, American black ducks, and tundra swans have all been seen along this shoreline.

Follow the main trail back to the parking lot when you are ready to return to your car.

5

Hickory Hollow

Total distance (circuit): 2.5 miles

Hiking time: 1½ hours

Vertical rise: 130 feet

Map: USGS 7½′ Lancaster

The existence of a marked trail system in the Hickory Hollow area of Lancaster County is proof that the efforts of one person can enhance the lives of many people. Although a number of civic and environmental organizations contributed donations and volunteer efforts, county forester Henry Bashore is generally acknowledged as the person who made an idea into a reality. Not only did he help coordinate the groups' efforts and persuade the county bureaucracy to open Hickory Hollow to the public, but he has spent his own time and funds developing, building, and maintaining the trail system. This is surely a lesson to those of us who feel that one person alone cannot make a difference.

From 1780, the first year of recorded ownership, to 1877, the approximately 200 acres of Hickory Hollow changed hands several times and were used for a variety of purposes, notably for timber or farming. In 1877, Lancaster County purchased the property and maintained a poor farm on it until 1905. The process of reforestation has allowed the timber to be harvested numerous times, the last in 1962.

Most of this hike is on old logging roads, making the walk moderately easy. Wildflowers are plentiful. Among them are trout lily, crane-fly orchids, violets, pygmy pipe, and horsetail. Flying squirrels begin their acrobatics in the early evening, and ovenbirds, with their familiar "teacher, teacher, teacher" call, are more often heard than seen.

The trailhead may be reached by following VA 3 for 0.9 mile eastward from the Lancaster County courthouse. Make a left onto VA 604, turning into the parking area on the left in 0.3 mile.

Begin hiking by taking the old road descending into the woods. The large holes in the ground next to the road are known as borrow pits. Soil, rock, and clay were "borrowed" from these spots to aid in building a level roadbed. Walk past the orange-blazed trail to the left in less than 0.1 mile; you will return this way. Pink lady's slippers usually begin lining the roadside sometime in April. Although their numbers may appear to be more than adequate here in Hickory Hollow, this plant is becoming more rare every year in Virginia. Watch your step and, please, don't dig one up to replant at home. Besides, like other orchids, the lady's slipper will grow only when certain fungi are present in its roots. If soil and weather conditions aren't conducive to the fungus, the lady's slipper will not survive. Remember the axiom to follow while on any hike: "Take only pictures; leave only footprints."

Pass by another orange-blazed trail to the left and an old road to the right at 0.2 mile, coming to an intersection in a couple of hundred feet. The Ridge Trail, a shortcut pathway in the trail network, is straight ahead; you want to take the old road to the right, which may or may not be marked as the way to Cabin Swamp. The more-or-less evenly aged deciduous woodland is evidence that this forest was logged in the recent past.

At 0.5 mile, come to a Y-intersection and keep to the right, soon passing by a short side trail to the right leading to a picnic table. Be paying attention at 0.6 mile when the trail leaves the road to the left to make a slippery and steep descent through laurel to cross a small water run in the bottomland. You've reached the Cabin Swamp area. A circular route

spans the wettest sections, so you can be almost assured of getting damp feet. Don't let this dampen your spirits, though. Enjoy this quiet place, which is so intensely green and lush during the warm months that it may make other parts of the forest seem sparse and dull in comparison. Skunk cabbage, marsh marigold, and false hellebore grow among dozens of other wildflowers. Freshwater clams have been seen next to the pennywort in the small streams.

Follow the route through the swamp to ascend back to the road. Retrace your steps to the Y-intersection and turn right (to the left it is six-tenths mile back to the parking lot). Two more intersections are encountered in close succession at 1 mile; keep left at both of them to come into a grove of neatly rowed, carefully planted loblolly pines. Keep right when you come to the next intersection at 1.2 miles. (A left would take you back to your car in about a mile.)

Make a left turn when you come to the T-intersection at 1.3 miles. (A sign says

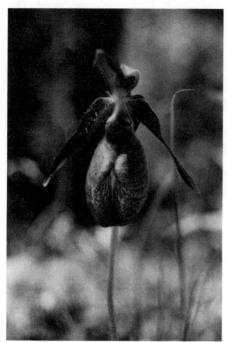

Lady's slipper

there is an overlook in two-tenths mile to the right. The overlook is now overgrown, but you could follow that route for three-tenths mile to explore another section of Cabin Swamp.) Be alert at 1.7 miles, where the trail makes an abrupt descent to the right. It just as abruptly makes an ascent to the left at 1.8 miles. In less than 100 feet, be paying attention—the route leaves the

road and bears right to begin following a pathway. (The road, now called the Ridge Trail, returns to the parking area in 0.7 mile.)

Because you are now on a trail instead of an old road, the hike takes on a more rustic feeling as you walk through an open beech forest next to a creek, passing in and out of laurel tunnels. Heartleaf, running cedar, and partridgeberry make up the groundcover. Come to an intersection at 2.2 miles. The road on which you started this hike is a couple of hundred feet ahead; however, in order to enjoy the walk for a few minutes longer, keep right. The loblolly pines have dropped so many needles onto the understory that it looks to be festooned by thousands of thin brown icicles. Come to the road at 2.4 miles and make a right to return to the parking area in 300 more feet.

You should be aware that in the late 1990s, many residents of Lancaster County (rallied by local citizens Henry Bashore and Ann B. Messick) fought short-sighted government officials who were trying to develop an industrial park on Hickory Hollow lands. The residents' nearly-tireless efforts were fruitful. Grants and donations were raised to purchase and protect the land, which is now administered by the Virginia Natural Heritage Program. If you have enjoyed your hike here, be sure to let the county bureaucrats know.

6

The Northern Neck

Total distance (circuit): 4 miles

Hiking time: 2 hours

Vertical rise: 370 feet

Maps: USGS 7½′ Stratford Hall; USGS 7½′ Colonial Beach South; Westmoreland State Park map

Driving east on VA 3 from Fredericksburg will bring you onto the Northern Neck, a wide peninsula between the Potomac and Rappahannock Rivers. The land took on its present form some 5,000 to 6,000 years ago when glaciers from the last Ice Age melted, raising sea levels enough to form the Chesapeake Bay and cover the Susquehanna River floodplain. The area can be a lesson in the history of America's earlier days, and three sites—one federal, one state, and one private—have trails coursing through them that let you study that time period from a pedestrian's point of view. Fees of some kind are collected at each location.

About 38 miles east of Fredericksburg is the George Washington's Birthplace National Monument. After passing through Oak Grove on VA 3, be looking for a sign directing you to make a left turn onto VA 204 to reach the grounds of the monument in approximately 2 miles. Washington was born on February 22, 1732. The property, once known as Pope's Creek Plantation and now called Wakefield, was Washington's home for the first three years of his life, before his family took up residence at Mount Vernon. Walking the small network of trails past numerous sites will help you gain insight into the life of America's first president and the era in which he lived. The Memorial House, built in the 1930s, is typical of 18th-century plantation homes of the area. Also built in the 1930s, the Kitchen House stands on the site of the original kitchen. Nearby, the Park Service manages some of the more than 500 acres of the monument as a demonstration and working farm, using the agricultural technology of the 1700s. Other portions of the trail network have interpretive signs that discuss the natural, as well as human, history of the land. Pets are required to be on a leash.

From Washington's birthplace continue driving east on VA 3, passing by the entrance to Westmoreland State Park about a mile before a sign directs you to make a left onto VA 214 to arrive at Stratford Hall. Like Wakefield, Stratford Hall was once part of an enormous tract patented by Nathaniel Pope in the 1650s. In 1716, Colonel Thomas Lee purchased about 4,000 acres and built what became home to several generations of one of Virginia's premier families. Among the most famous of the famous to be born here were Richard Henry Lee and Francis Lightfoot Lee, both signers of the Declaration of Independence, and the South's celebrated military strategist, Robert E. Lee. Privately owned,

the 1,500-plus acres are operated as a plantation much as it would have been worked during Robert's lifetime. Livestock graze in open meadows, and fields are cultivated by traditional methods. By taking a 2- to 3-mile circuit hike on a system of interconnecting pathways, you can tour the H-shaped Great House, pass through reforested acres of hardwoods, watch the reconstructed mill grind grains, overlook the broad Potomac River, and visit the spring that supplied water (and a means of refrigeration) for the plantation.

The Commonwealth of Virginia purchased approximately 1,300 acres (at $11.50 an acre) in 1933 to develop Westmoreland State Park, which was once a part of Stratford Hall. The Civilian Conservation Corps (CCC) built most of the still-existing structures and roadways. Westmoreland, one of Virginia's original six state parks, now has rental cabins, several campgrounds, a camp store and restaurant overlooking the river, picnic area and shelters, an Olympic-size swimming pool, and boat rentals available at a dock on the river. Like all of Virginia's state parks, Westmoreland offers interpretive programs throughout the heavy tourist season.

Ever since the park opened in 1936, one of its great attractions has been the fossils found on the river beaches and at the foot of Horsehead Cliffs. Visitors have discovered the skeletal remains of crocodiles, stingrays, porpoises, turtles, whales, sharks, and other marine life that lived in the Miocene Sea some 15 million years ago. In addition to the hike described here, you could walk a little more than a mile along the river from the boat-rental stand to the beach that is part of the Big Meadow Trail, searching for your own souvenirs of these ancient creatures. Be sure to ask about the tides at the visitor center; the river overtakes the beach below Horsehead Cliffs at high tide.

The trails of Westmoreland will bring you into a woods that has not been timbered since the beginning of the 20th century, making the forest a wonderland of exceptionally large-trunked trees towering over sparse undergrowth. Opossums, raccoons, weasels, mink, river otters, beavers, foxes, squirrels and various other rodents, wild turkeys, deer, turtles, snakes, and frogs have all been seen by hikers at one time or another. Yellow Swamp and Big Meadow are good introductions to coastal-plain marshes.

Start from the visitor center after looking at its displays and obtaining the pamphlet for the Big Meadow Trail. Walk through a gate into the field, keeping left to come to the top of Horsehead Cliffs and enjoy the view along the Potomac. Upstream, sometimes hidden by haze, are the buildings of Colonial Beach, while across the 6-mile-wide river is southern Maryland. There is also the possibility of sighting an osprey or bald eagle on the wing.

Swing right and come to the large bulletin board marking the beginning of the red-blazed Big Meadow Trail. Enter the woods on an 1890s logging road where dogwoods and pawpaws are part of the understory. In late fall the pawpaw trees, being some of the last to lose their leaves, add various tones of yellow to an otherwise brown and gray forest. In 0.5 mile you will pass by a large beech tree on the right side of the road; note how the shade from its widely spreading canopy permits very little, if any, undergrowth. Soon you will begin to descend.

At 0.7 mile you need to walk past the boardwalk and continue onto the beach, a great place to learn more about the makeup of the Northern Neck. Being only about 30 miles from the Chesapeake Bay, the Potomac River at this point is brackish. Because of the salinity, creatures that you normally associate with bays or oceans are able to survive here. Blue and horseshoe crabs are often found on the sand. Horseshoe crabs are not really crabs but are more closely related to spiders and ticks. Despite its fearsome appearance, the horseshoe is harmless, mostly using its long, pointed tail to turn itself back over when flipped up onto the beach. Amid deer tracks in the sand you'll probably see lumps of clay that have broken off from the cliffs. The clay was a perfect pottery material for early Native Americans; the attraction for you, though, is breaking open the chunks and maybe finding a shark's tooth millions of years old.

Return to, and turn left onto, the boardwalk, walking through reed grass and rosehips to arrive at the observation tower in Yellow Swamp. If you didn't see them on the river, there is a good chance you will see a few buffleheads plying the stream in the swamp. A small duck, the male bufflehead is easy to identify—it has a nearly all-white body, a black back, and an almost perfectly round black head topped by a

Box turtle

have obviously been around for a long time. Stop for a few moments to pay your respects to these great grandparents of the forest, whose branches are bigger around than most of the trunks of nearby trees. Ascend to swing away from Big Meadow and begin walking on an old road.

The Beaver Dam Trail comes in from the right at 2.1 miles; you want to stay left. Soon the other branch of Turkey Neck Trail comes in from the right; again, you want to stay left. At 2.4 miles the Turkey Neck Trail swings right—you could follow it back about a mile to the park office and then your car. However, keep left on the old road to walk through campground C. Water and restrooms are available in the campground during the season.

Come to the paved park road, cross it, and turn right. In a few feet you will come to orange-blazed Laurel Point Trail, which descends into a holly- and laurel-crowded draw. In 3.1 miles, Rock Spring Pond shimmers emerald as it reflects the evergreen leaves of a laurel thicket. The pond was built in the 1930s by the CCC and now contains a variety of bass and other fish. Continue around the pond to 3.2 miles, where Laurel Point Trail bears left as a pathway to arrive at the boat dock in less than a mile. You, however, will keep right onto the old roadway to follow green-blazed Rock Spring Pond Trail. If you are camped in the park, this wide, level road through the broad valley would make a great moonlight walk before retiring for the evening.

Arrive at the park road in 3.8 miles, cross the pavement, and turn left, soon coming to the restaurant and camp store. Make a right and return to the visitor center at 4 miles.

There are two other short trails in the park. The two-tenths mile River Trail connects cabins 1–18 to the beach area and the half-mile Beach Trail descends from near the restaurant to the swimming pool and beach.

large patch of white. Buffleheads are also referred to as butterballs by duck hunters.

Continue walking beyond the tower, passing by arrowroot, a favorite food of muskrats. In 1 mile come to a T-intersection. The blue-blazed Turkey Neck Trail goes right to campground C; your route takes the trail's left branch, hugging the edge of Big Meadow, where park personnel often report seeing browsing deer and turkeys. At 1.2 miles you will rise to another T-intersection. Yellow-blazed Beaver Dam Trail is a shortcut and will rejoin your route at the 2.1-mile mark. Keep left and continue following the blue-blazed trail, overlooking beaver dams and, maybe, lodges in the swampy meadow. As you walk through the cut of the large tree that has fallen across the trail at 1.4 miles, look on top of it; you will see that it is often used by woodland creatures as a table for feasting on nuts and pinecones. In 1.6 miles you will ascend steps to go by two massive white oak trees that

II

Central Virginia

7

Spotsylvania

Total distance (circuit): 5.3 miles

Hiking time: 3 hours

Vertical rise: 240 feet

*Maps: USGS 7½′ Spotsylvania;
Spotsylvania History Trail map*

During the course of the Civil War, four major battles—those at Fredericksburg, Chancellorsville, Wilderness, and Spotsylvania Court House—were fought in Fredericksburg and Spotsylvania County, and today the National Park Service preserves some of the lands on which these conflicts occurred. The four sites are a short drive apart, each one offering a variety of hiking opportunities.

The battle of Fredericksburg, December 11 through 13, 1862, gave Robert E. Lee what many consider to be his most one-sided victory. The Sunken Road and National Cemetery walks and the 5-mile Lee Drive Trail are within the city limits of Fredericksburg. "Stonewall" Jackson was fatally wounded by his own men a few miles west of Fredericksburg during the battle of Chancellorsville (April 27 through May 6, 1863). The 3½-mile Chancellorsville History and 1-mile Hazel Grove Trails lead hikers past important points of that battle.

After his encounter on May 5 and 6, 1864, with the resolute Confederate forces of General Robert E. Lee at the battle of the Wilderness, southwest of Chancellorsville (the ½-mile Tapp Farm and 2-mile Gordon Flank Trails help put this conflict in perspective), general-in-chief of all Union armies, Ulysses S. Grant marched his forces southward in hopes of seizing the village of Spotsylvania Court House. If the crossroads could be put in Federal hands, the Union would control the shortest route to Richmond. Determined to prevent the North's forces from eventually moving on to the capture of the Confederate capital, Lee

Landrum House Ruins

Bloody Angle

East Angle

McCoull House Ruins

Maryland Monument

N

0   0.25   0.5 mile

Robert E Lee Sch

to Fredericksburg

VA 208

Spotsyl

rushed his troops to the outskirts of Spotsylvania and hurriedly constructed an intricate network of earthen fortifications. The ensuing battle lasted from May 8 to May 21 and included a 20-hour struggle so horrendous that the location came to be known as Bloody Angle.

While all four of the national park sites are worth hiking, I'm going to direct you to the Spotsylvania battlefield because it has one of the longest possible walks through some of the most serene and bucolic scenery. The easy lay of this land in the Piedmont makes the hike a moderately easy one, alternating

between open fields of green grass, sunny meadows crowded with wildflowers, and shaded forests of hardwoods and pine. Before going there, though, stop at the Fredericksburg Battlefield Visitor Center (signs will direct you there from I-95) to gain an overview of all the battles by watching a slide show presentation, visiting the excellent museum, and talking to park personnel. You can also pick up free pamphlets about the trails, so be sure to obtain the ones for Spotsylvania and Bloody Angle (dispenser boxes at the trailheads are sometimes empty).

From the visitor center parking lot, make a right onto Lafayette Boulevard/Business US 1. Stay on the same roadway when the route number changes to VA 208, bringing you to a T-intersection in Spotsylvania Court House. Turning right onto Brock Road (VA 613) and continuing for 1.5 miles brings you to the battlefield entrance on the right.

After studying the exhibits in the shelter, begin the hike by following blue blazes on the left side of Grant Drive past the picnic area. Dogwood blossoms along the road in early spring, and its deep crimson joins other leaves in the mixed deciduous forest to make this an exceptionally colorful excursion in the fall. At 0.6 mile, after walking beside fortifications built by Federal soldiers, cross the paved roadway and enter the woods on partridgeberry-lined Upton's Road. During the afternoon hours of May 10, 1864, Federal colonel Emory Upton brought 12 regiments down this farm road, a move unanticipated by a Georgia brigade entrenched behind the fortifications that you'll cross just before reaching the paved road at 0.9 mile. The element of surprise enabled Upton to take more than 1,000 prisoners, but unsupported by other Federal troops, he was forced to retreat in the face of a Confederate counterattack, losing 1,000 of his own men in the process. Yet immediately after the fighting, Grant promoted Upton to the rank of brigadier general "for gallant and meritorious services."

After studying the old fortifications, known as Doles' Salient, turn left onto paved Anderson Drive, soon crossing over to the right side of the road. At 1.1 miles, pass through a fence stile to where signs mark the site of Bloody Angle. In the present day, the entrenchments may not look like they would have provided much protection, but you must remember that when General Edward Johnson's Confederate division built them on May 8, 1864, the trench was deep enough and the mound high enough that the men could fire their muskets and still be protected. Also, to make it more difficult for an attacking army to overrun them, trees were felled in front of the works, their sharp branches pointing toward the attackers. Passing by the first footbridge over the salient, make a left to cross the ditch on the second bridge and continue walking on a mowed pathway. This peaceful field of wildflowers was in use as a cultivated field on May 12, 1864, but it should be easy to use your imagination to picture the scene when Union forces burst from the woods to quickly capture General Johnson and 3,000 of his men.

At 1.4 miles, turn right onto the gravel road; Union forces built the trenches along this road after the early morning attack. Two chimneys mark the site of the Landrum House (destroyed by fire in 1905), from where General Winfield S. Hancock's Second Corps swept across the open ground toward the Confederate lines. Retrace your steps along the gravel road, returning to take the right-hand pathway mowed through the meadow, passing by several monuments before recrossing the salient of the Bloody Angle at 2.3 miles. Union general Louis A. Grant's firsthand account may best describe the melee and carnage of Bloody Angle: "Nothing but the piled up logs of breastworks separated the combatants. Our men would reach over the logs and fire into the faces of the enemy, would stab over with their bayonets; many were shot and stabbed through the crevices and holes between the logs; men mounted the works and with muskets rapidly handed them kept up a continuous fire until they were shot down, when others would take their place."

The monument to "Uncle" John Sedgwick

Turn left after crossing the footbridge to come to the parking lot behind East Angle. Follow the paved roadway with breast-works to the left, bearing right onto Gordon Drive at the intersection at 2.8 miles. As you come to the edge of a field on your left at 3.2 miles, pay attention, because the route suddenly leaves the road to enter the woods on the right. Running cedar next to the trail fades as the pathway quits the for-est to arrive at the McCoull House site, which, being within the center of the Con-federate salient, served as headquarters for General Johnson. From here, take the mowed trail marked with a sign back in the direction of the paved road. The trail will lead you to the Harrison House site, where Confederate general Richard S. Ewell was headquartered and Robert E. Lee pitched his tent. At 3.7 miles, you'll enter the woods, passing by an incredibly large and intricate maze of winding trenches—Lee's last line of defense, constructed on May 12. Cross the paved roadway, reentering the forest on a blue-blazed pathway. In May, be looking for large tulip tree flowers blooming beside tall and straight loblolly pines.

Take care in crossing busy VA 613 at 4.4 miles to follow the mowed route to the Maryland Monument, marking the spot of the first assault on Southern forces on May

8. Swing right from the monument to gain the high point on Laurel Hill. Having arrived on the run from the battle of the Wilder-ness, the Confederate army had barely enough time to set up defenses before Yankees came swarming toward them. The smell of honeysuckle permeates the air on the edge of the field at 5 miles as you enter the woods and make a right onto dirt Hancock Road. Once again, use caution crossing VA 613. Pass by the monument to Major General "Uncle" John Sedgwick, commander of the Federal Sixth Corps of the Army of the Potomac, struck down by a sharpshooter's bullet on May 9. The exhibit shelter and end of this 5.3-mile hike are just a few feet away.

As in the case of the battle of the Wil-derness, both the Union and Confederate armies sustained tremendous casualties at Spotsylvania—a combined estimated loss of more than 25,000 men. Many historians say the Wilderness conflict ended in a stalemate and that because Grant was unable to capture the crossroads town, he failed to win a decisive victory in Spotsylvania. Yet these were certainly vic-tories of a sort. When Grant pulled his forces away, it was not in retreat. Rather, he continued his relentless drive southward that, in less than a year, ended with Lee's surrender at Appomattox.

Prince William Forest Park

Total distance (circuit): 13.5 miles

Hiking time: 7¼ hours

Vertical rise: 400 feet

Maps: USGS 7½′ Joplin; USGS 7½′ Quantico (VA and MD); Prince William Forest Park map

Just as the mountains to the west in Shenandoah National Park were farmed by unsound practices during the 19th and 20th centuries, so too was the acreage around Quantico Creek. This area, however, was subjected to that form of abuse from the mid-1700s. Two hundred years later, when the federal government acquired much of the land drained by the creek, the soil had become so nutrient deficient that farming was quickly becoming impractical. Tons of topsoil had washed downstream, turning the harbor at Dumfries into a marsh. For nearly a decade, the Great Depression–era Civilian Conservation Corps (CCC) labored to reclaim the area. Their work, and more than half a century of good stewardship by the National Park Service, has borne fruit. A hike through the park reveals a healthy and green hardwood forest bisected by clear-flowing streams filled with aquatic life and providing sustenance for beavers, muskrats, raccoons, deer, turkeys, and more. Herons, kingfishers, and egrets fish the waters, seven different kinds of hawks may be observed year-round, and at least 140 other species of birds have been seen flying by the blackberry thickets and into pine boughs.

The quiet beauty of the park is made all the more remarkable by the fact that it lies less than an hour's drive from heavily populated Washington, D.C. The park, which charges an entrance fee, is located on VA 619, only a few hundred feet from the I-95 exit at Triangle (just south of Dumfries). In addition to approximately 35 miles of trails, the park provides picnic grounds,

Prince William Forest Park

Ⓟ Parking

N

1 mile
1 kilometer

fishing, group-camping cabins, interpretive programs held throughout the year, two campgrounds for tents or trailers, and a backcountry camping area reachable only by foot (required permits and detailed information on current conditions are available from the visitor center). The short Pine Grove Forest Trail is accessible to the handicapped. Because of these amenities and its close proximity to the D.C. metro area, the park attracts many visitors, yet I've always found the trails to be wonderfully underused. In fact, I did this 13.5-mile hike on a Labor Day weekend and saw only five other people, and four of them were within 10 minutes of a picnic area!

Before undertaking the hike, consider walking the Farms to Forest Trail, located next to the Oak Ridge Campground. This 1-mile interpretive loop, along with an accompanying brochure available from the visitor center or at the trailhead, provides a vividly clear example and explanation of forest succession.

Your extended exploration of the park begins in the Pine Grove Picnic Area, where there are two different trailheads of the yellow-blazed Loop Trail. You want to begin on the western end of the Loop Trail, heading northward out of the picnic area. (Be sure to make use of the picnic area's amenities to fill up your water bottles before embarking, as this is your last chance to obtain potable liquids until you return here at the end of your journey.) Enter a hardwood forest with an understory of mountain laurel and azalea. In some spots, partridgeberry is so thick that it forms a dense carpet on the forest floor.

The partridgeberry is such an interesting plant that you might want to take time to look at it on your hands and knees. Two white flowers, which bloom in early summer, fuse together to produce one tiny berry, and a close examination of the berry, which changes from green to red during the cooler months, will show two scars—one from each flower.

Continuing on gently sloping terrain, you'll come to the intersection of Laurel Loop Trail and South Orenda Road where, at 0.4 mile, a footbridge enables you to cross over the South Fork of Quantico Creek. Turning right onto white-blazed South Valley Trail, the route is a pleasant downhill walk next to the stream. Be sure to be paying attention at 1.3 miles, where you'll make a left turn onto the Pyrite Mine Road.

The road receives its name from an operation that existed along the creek from 1889 to 1920. The mine extracted and processed pyrite, which was valued for its high content of sulfur—used to make soap, fertilizer, glass, gunpowder, and a host of other products. Miners were lowered and raised into three main shafts in buckets suspended by 80-foot cables attached to the mine's ceiling. The ore, called fool's gold for its resemblance to that coveted commodity, was raised from the depths and deposited into railroad cars by this same cable system. Due to the great demand for sulfur during World War I, the mine flourished, and the 200–300-man crew was exempted from active duty in the armed forces. But with the discovery of pyrite in places of the world where it could be more easily recovered, the mine closed in 1920, amid the throes of a miners' strike. The CCC dismantled the vacant buildings and used the material to construct many of the cabins, roads, and other developments still in use in the park. When the mine was in full operation, there were more than 70 structures along the banks of the North Branch of Quantico Creek. As part of the process of reclaiming the mine lands, the park service closed the area to the public and covered it with topsoil, grasses, and trees.

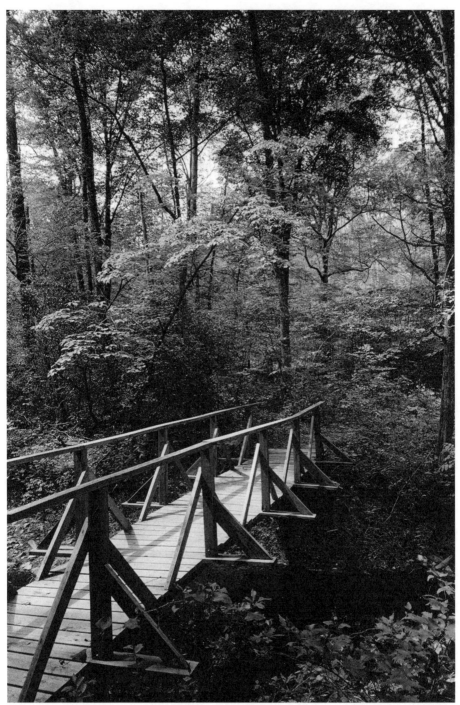

One of many foot bridges in Prince William Forest Park

Continue rising on Pyrite Mine Road to 1.9 miles. At this point you need to make a right and descend along orange-blazed Cabin Branch Mine Trail. At 2.2 miles, turn left onto blue-blazed North Valley Trail where beavers have been gnawing on trees. After you rise above some small cascades at 3.3 miles and drop into a laurel thicket, keep right on yellow-blazed Quantico Falls Trail, forsaking the North Valley Trail for a while.

Quantico Falls and the small cascades you passed just a short while ago are at the fall line, the place where the Piedmont drops onto the coastal plain. While it may not look like much here, the fall line is a major geological feature and, in several places, determined the location of some of Virginia's largest cities. Fredericksburg, Richmond, and Petersburg were all established as transshipment centers on the fall line because their respective rivers became unnavigable beyond those points for large ships bringing cargo upstream from the Chesapeake Bay.

The trail makes an abrupt left from Quantico Falls to ascend past tulip poplars to the four-way intersection at 3.8 miles. Going straight would bring you to parking lot E in six-tenths mile; left goes back to the pyrite mine. Make a right onto blue-blazed North Valley Trail, crossing a water run and coming to another intersection at 4.1 miles. Bearing left on green-blazed Lake One Road would take you to parking lot E in seven-tenths mile; keep to the right, soon following a level route upstream along the North Branch of Quantico Creek. The ironwood in this forest of pines and ferns receives its name from its trunk's resemblance to bulging, sinewy muscles. It is in this wide, isolated valley that you are finally away from the constant dull roar of traffic on I-95. The trail negotiates two low ridges

before crossing the creek where beeches are one of the more dominant trees and beaver obviously enjoy living. At 4.3 miles, the Burma Fire Road goes right toward Travel Trailer Village on the park's northern boundary. You should make a left to rise on the road and cross the paved main park road at 6.0 miles, continuing on the gravel Taylor Farm Road. Gradually descend, accompanied by mountain laurel blossoms in spring and an abundance of blueberries later in summer. Continuing straight, cross Old Blacktop Road—actually made of dirt and a bit of gravel—which runs to the left five-tenths mile to the Turkey Run Ridge Group Campground and to the right one mile to parking lot F.

Arrive at a four-way intersection at 6.8 miles. To the left it's four-tenths mile to the group campground; you want to turn right onto orange-blazed High Meadows Trail. Before leaving the area, do a little exploring around the old orchards, fields, and cemetery of the Taylor Farm site. (If you want to cut the length of this hike by about 3 miles, you should continue straight from the four-way intersection on blue-blazed North Valley Trail for six-tenths mile to intersect the South Valley Trail at the 10.4-mile point of this description.)

From the farm site, your route ascends just a bit before dropping to cross a tributary of the South Branch of Quantico Creek—another good place possibly to see a beaver or two. At one time trapping had decimated the beaver population, but as you've seen, their reintroduction in the 1950s has been successful. Having come to parking lot H at 7.7 miles, cross the paved park road, continuing to follow orange-blazed High Meadows Trail, and soon turn left onto an old woods road with oaks towering above and running cedar hugging the ground. Footbridges bring you across several water runs to the junction with white-blazed South Valley Trail at 8.5 miles.

To the right, this trail takes a winding route of several miles to the Oak Ridge Campground. Make a left onto it, headed down Quantico Creek's South Branch. It can be hard to believe you're only 20-some miles from downtown Washington, D.C., as you walk through this wide, broad, and quiet valley. Like the beaver who use the creek as part of their home and the deer who use it to quench summer thirsts, you might want to make use of the creek's many little pools to cool your feet or take a quick wade. Be careful about wading if there has just been a heavy rain; sand on the pathway shows that the stream can become pretty wild in times of high water. Cross a side stream (the same one you crossed while on the High Meadows Trail) on a footbridge, step across the paved park road, and keep right when the North Valley Trail comes in from the left at 10.4 miles. Cross under the main park road on a most interesting wooden footbridge and

come to a large pool just above the fall line of this branch of Quantico Creek. During the warmer months you may see a snowy egret swishing the water with its feet—its hopes are to stir up some prey to stab with its sharp bill. Switchbacks bring you past three short side trails to the left, successively leading to parking lots C, B, and A.

Cross the paved park road one last time at 12.0 miles and keep right when blue-blazed Turkey Run Trail comes in from the left. Be looking for deer tracks in the soft sand when your trail bears right to continue following white blazes on a woods road. (The roadway to the left is North Orenda Fire Road, leading one and six-tenths miles to parking lot D.) When you come to the next intersection at 13.1 miles, it is time to leave white-blazed South Valley Trail as it continues straight, toward the pyrite mine site. Make a right, cross the bridge, and make an immediate right onto yellow-blazed Laurel Loop Trail, following it back to the picnic area at 13.5 miles.

9

Mason Neck State Park

Total distance (circuit): 3.0 miles

Hiking time: 2 hours

Vertical rise: 50 feet

Maps: USGS 7½′ Fort Belvior; Mason Neck State Park map

Mason Neck, a narrow stretch of land rimmed by Belmont, Pohick, and Occoquan Bays and Gunston Cove, juts out into the wide Potomac River about 20 miles south of Washington, D.C. The first recorded mention of the area was by Captain John Smith as he traveled up the Potomac during his exploration of the Chesapeake Bay and its tributaries in 1608. About 1755, on the northeastern side of the neck, George Mason constructed Gunston Hall, his plantation home, which is still considered one of Virginia's most attractive colonial homes.

As writer of the 1776 Declaration of Rights of Virginia, Mason stated, "All men are by nature equally free and independent and have certain inherent rights . . . namely, the enjoyment of life and liberty, with the means of acquiring and possessing property, and pursuing and obtaining happiness and safety." He refused to sign the U.S. Constitution because it did not oppose slavery nor protect individual rights, but many of his ideas were later incorporated into the Constitution's first 10 amendments and used as inspiration for the French Rights of Man and even the United Nation's Declaration of Human Rights.

It seems somewhat fitting that an area named after the author of a bill of rights for human beings is now largely a preserve for birds, plants, animals, and aquatic life, granting them the most basic of rights, that of survival.

In the 1960s, the Friends of Mason Neck was formed to save the region from encroaching urbanization. Through that organization's zealous labors—and with help from the Nature Conservancy—the Pohick Bay Regional Park, Gunston Hall Plantation, Mason Neck National Wildlife Refuge, and Mason Neck State Park now protect more than half of the neck's approximately 10,000 acres. All of these areas provide good recreational and walking opportunities and will be passed on your way to your hike in the state park.

Take the Lorton exit off I-95 and head eastward on Lorton Road to US 1. Turn right onto US 1, following it to a left turn onto Gunston Road (VA 242). In about 3 miles, the entrance to Pohick Bay Regional Park is on the left. In addition to a 150-site campground, one of the largest swimming pools on the east coast, a picnic area, an 18-hole golf course, and boat-launching facilities, the park has several marked trails (totaling more than 4 miles) that twist and turn through stands of holly and laurel, passing by small inlets covered with water lilies.

Gunston Hall is reached by continuing to follow VA 242 a short distance past the regional park. A 2-mile trail shows off the natural beauties of Mason's homestead. Beyond Gunston Hall, the roadway

becomes VA 600, which you should follow to a sign pointing you to Mason Neck State Park and a right turn onto High Point Road (VA 5783). High Point Road cuts through the Mason Neck National Wildlife Refuge, established in 1969 as the country's first national sanctuary for the endangered bald eagle. A parking area on the left is the access point for the approximately 3-mile Woodmarsh Trail. A brochure (available at the trailhead) provides information on places such as Eagle Point, which overlooks the 250-plus-acre Great Marsh. It is estimated that more than 30 pairs of eagles nest in the refuge over the winter and spring to mate and raise their young.

Continue on High Point Road to enter Mason Neck State Park (visitors with cars are charged a small fee year-round) and eventually arrive at the visitor center. As you should always do when a visitor center offers interpretive displays, spend a few moments here to learn a little bit of the human and natural history of the area you are about to tour. The park is open year-round; somewhat dependent upon the workload of the park's personnel, the visitor center is usually open daily from 10 AM–4 PM.

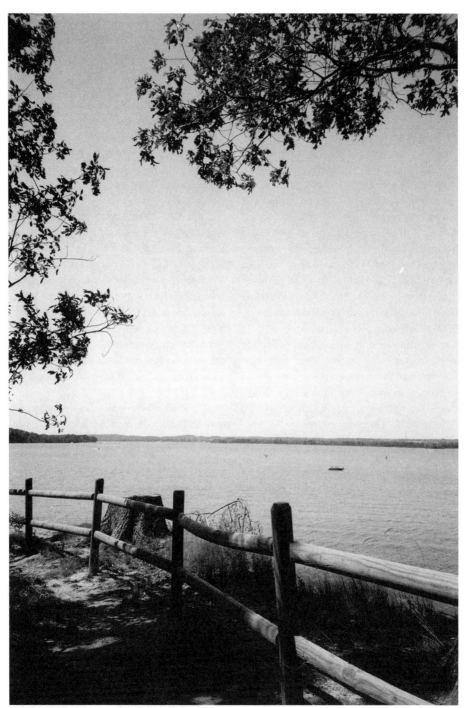

Belmont Bay from near the visitors center

Even though it is far north of the mouth of the Chesapeake Bay, the state park's shoreline is still subject to the rise and ebb of the Atlantic Ocean's tides. This means that the area's marshlands provide the right habitat for saltwater creatures such as an occasional blue crab and attract a wide variety of birds and waterfowl. Despite its proximity to large population centers, this hike can present the opportunity to see, or at least observe signs of, an amazingly diverse array of wildlife. Because of this, and the ease of walking, Mason Neck is the perfect spot to bring city-bound children who have never been delighted by the sprinting leaps of a white-tailed deer, the cry of an osprey flying overhead with a fish grasped in its talons, the gobble of a wild turkey (Ben Franklin's choice for our national bird), or the bark of a red fox calling out to its young. There are, however, copperheads in the park's more remote areas; exercise commonsense precautions.

Begin the hike behind the visitor center by enjoying the sunshine sparkling on Belmont Bay. Turn to your left, walking toward trailheads and picnic areas and passing sweet gums, eastern hemlocks, black walnuts, and red cedars. Drop to a small canoe- and sailboard-launching beach. Cross a bridge over the pond outlet and switchback uphill through pawpaws to the picnic area. The pawpaw's 4- to 5-inch fruit, which resembles a short, fat banana, is at first green but ripens to a purple-brown. Its meat, with the consistency of an overripe banana, was a food source for rural families up to the mid-20th century and is still considered somewhat of a delicacy by many people.

Come to the Bay View trailhead at 0.15 mile; avoid the trail to the left and take the one to the right that goes along the edge of the bay. Cross a wet area on a wooden footbridge and begin walking on a high bank above the bay. The sound of small waves lapping along the shore is bound to have a calming effect on those willing to listen. Use a boardwalk at 0.45 mile to cross a creek that contains northern largemouth bass, black crappie, and bluegill. Take a last glance at the bay as the route swings to the left, using another boardwalk to cross a wide, swampy area of the creek. Here, turtles often use logs floating in the water to bask in the sun.

Leave the boardwalk and follow a pathway lined with laurel as it enters the woods. Look at these woods and reflect back to the time of Captain Smith's ventures in the 17th century. In his journal he noted that, at some places he set ashore, the virgin forest canopy was so thick that direct sunlight almost never penetrated it. Deprived of this nourishment, very little, if any, vegetation grew on the forest floor, and Smith claimed he could peer a mile or more through the trees!

Come to a four-way loop-trail intersection at 0.55 mile and make a hard right. Blueberry bushes abound here. In a couple of hundred feet arrive at a bench overlooking a cattail-lined marsh. Seemingly useless, marshes are one of the most important areas, ecologically, in the world. They produce more organic material than any other area on Earth—almost 10 tons per acre per year. The marshes are dominated by grasses that decay and, along with other material, are washed out to the rivers and bays. This decayed material, known as detritus, is the first link in a food chain that reaches far out into the ocean.

Return to the loop-trail intersection at 0.7 mile and make a hard right, noting a tree trunk scorched by a 5-acre fire in 1986. Leave the Bay View Trail at 0.8 mile and turn right onto green-blazed Wilson

Spring Trail. Undergrowth is not quite as thick here, making it easier to spot some of the park's resident deer or gray squirrel. Walk into a darker forest of beech and holly at 1.2 miles, passing by small, marshlike ponds. Walk over and take a rest break next to one. Many people see eastern painted turtles, one of the most common turtles in the United States, but never know it because they don't look for the reptile's special markings. You'll know if one slides into the pond in front of you because you'll be looking for red markings on the side of its shell and red and yellow stripes on its head, legs, and tail.

Cross the paved park road at 1.4 miles (the visitor center is about five-tenths mile to the left) and continue to follow green blazes through another open area of the forest. In 1.6 miles you will come to the end of the Wilson Spring Trail. The visitor center is to the left; your route goes right onto Kane's Creek Trail. Stay on Kane's Creek Trail until the next intersection, where you bear right to follow a spur trail to Kane's Creek. (This pathway may be closed to the public during peak bald eagle roosting season. If you find it so, go left at this intersection and continue with the hike description from the 2.5-mile point.)

Arrive at the eagle blind on Kane's Creek at 2.2 miles. Kane's Creek is the local late fall to early spring roosting spot for bald eagles. Staying quiet and behind the blind will increase your chances of seeing one or two. If you venture down the unauthorized trails to the water's edge, you not only disturb the wildlife but also add to the erosion problem along the banks of the creek. Don't be disappointed if you fail to see any eagles. Keep a sharp eye out for other visitors to the creek—great blue herons, Canada geese, wood ducks, and an occasional raccoon hoping to catch a frog or dig up some shellfish to include in its omnivorous diet. Muskrat and beaver are often spotted, usually in early morning or early evening, making ripples on the surface of the water when swimming to or from their burrows in the creek's banks.

Retrace your steps to the first intersection and turn right at 2.5 miles, following a different portion of Kane's Creek Trail through a typical Potomac lowland forest of mature oak, hickory, and poplar above an understory of holly and laurel.

Come to a four-way intersection at 2.8 miles. To the left is the Wilson Spring Trail. Straight ahead is the park road. Turn right and arrive at the visitor center parking lot at 3 miles.

10

Bull Run/Occoquan River

Total distance (one way): 11.0 miles

Hiking time: 7½ hours

Vertical rise: 3,180 feet

Maps: USGS 7½′ Manassas; USGS 7½′ Independent Hill; USGS 7½′ Occoquan

Concerned by the threat of urban sprawl in the northern Virginia region, a group of far-sighted citizens banded together in the late 1950s and, along with several local governments, formed the Northern Virginia Regional Park Authority (NVRPA). More than 10,000 acres are now preserved under the auspices of the authority.

Five of the regional parks—Bull Run, Hemlock Overlook, Bull Run Marina, Fountainhead, and Sandy Run—contain 5,000 of these acres along the shore of the Bull Run–Occoquan stream valley. This continuous strip of parkland is a valuable conservation area, preserving marshes and forests and protecting the shoreline of Occoquan Reservoir, the source of water for a large percentage of northern Virginia's population.

Following the winding course of Bull Run and the Occoquan River through four of the five parks, the Blue Trail makes it possible—despite continued, rapid development of the region—to walk more than 20 miles in basically one direction and still be almost continuously on public lands. The shoreline is a nesting place for ducks, geese, osprey, and other bird life. Chipmunks, squirrels, wild turkeys, snakes, turtles, raccoons, foxes, and a large population of deer inhabit lands along the trail. Numerous gnawed trees, especially near and in Hemlock Overlook Regional Park, are evidence of an active beaver community.

The northern section of the Blue Trail begins in Bull Run Regional Park and runs approximately 11 miles to Hemlock Overlook Regional Park. That portion is quite

wet and marshy. Therefore, this hike takes in the more pleasurable southern 11 miles of the trail from Hemlock Overlook Regional Park to Fountainhead Regional Park. Camping is not permitted along the Blue Trail.

For this long, one-way hike, you will need two automobiles in order to do a car shuttle. Fountainhead Regional Park is reached south of Washington, D.C., by exiting I-95 at Lorton. Go westward on Lorton Road (VA 642) to make a right turn onto Ox Road (VA 123) and then a left onto Hampton Road (VA 647). Turn left onto VA 727 to enter Fountainhead Regional Park. Leave one car at the trailhead parking lot, then go back and turn left onto Hampton Road (VA 647). Intersect and turn left onto Henderson Road (VA 643). Continue to the right where Old Yates Ford Road (VA 612) goes off to the left to Bull Run Marina. Bear left onto Clifton Road (VA 645) and watch for the left turn onto Yates Ford Road (VA 615). Cross Kincheloe Road and continue on Yates Ford Road.

Turn into the small trailhead parking area directly across the road from Hemlock Overlook's mailbox (marked 13220 Yates Ford Road). The park is an outdoor education center operated jointly by the NVRPA and George Mason University. In addition to using the park for environmental education classes, "team development" programs make use of an events course located throughout the park. The dining hall, dorms, and events course can be reserved by program participants. The restrooms and trails, however, are open to the public and a trail map is posted at the park's entrance.

From the trailhead parking lot, walk along the pavement toward the park's gated entrance, but in 0.1 mile do not follow the road as it swings to the right through the gate;

rather, continue by entering a hardwood forest directly ahead on an old dirt road that used to be the carriage road leading to Yates Ford on Bull Run.

At 0.2 mile the Horseshoe Trail on the left junctions with the old road. It is possible to take this trail and rejoin your route at the 0.9-mile point of this description. However, you should continue to descend along the road, passing by a plaque to Sol M. Edinin (1920–1981) placed by the Clifton Horse Society, Ltd. At 0.45 mile notice the small rows of circular holes drilled into the inner bark layer of nearby trees. Yellow-bellied sapsuckers drill the holes, sap rises into them, and, true to their name, these woodpeckers feed by sucking the liquid out with long, bristly tongues. Often ants and other insects are attracted by the trees' sweet juices and the sapsuckers can get both "dinner" and "dessert" from just one hole. Pileated woodpeckers also inhabit Hemlock Overlook—the holes they make are large, deep, and almost rectangular.

Arrive at Bull Run at 0.5 mile and turn left through laurel to begin walking on the Blue Trail and paralleling the stream. Several small rock overhangs are located at 0.7 mile and would make great emergency shelters in case of a sudden spring shower.

In a large open area, the Horseshoe Trail joins the Blue Trail at 0.9 mile. Spring flowers such as mayapple, spring beauties, violets, bluebells, and bloodroot are found in profusion here. Dogtooth violet is also abundant later in the spring. Sycamores grow well along this bottomland, reflecting their preference for moist soil as opposed to the rockier, drier ground of the hillsides.

At 1.4 miles, the sounds of a firing range are evident as the trail swings away from the stream to enter a newer forest of cedar and pine. Running cedar spreads itself

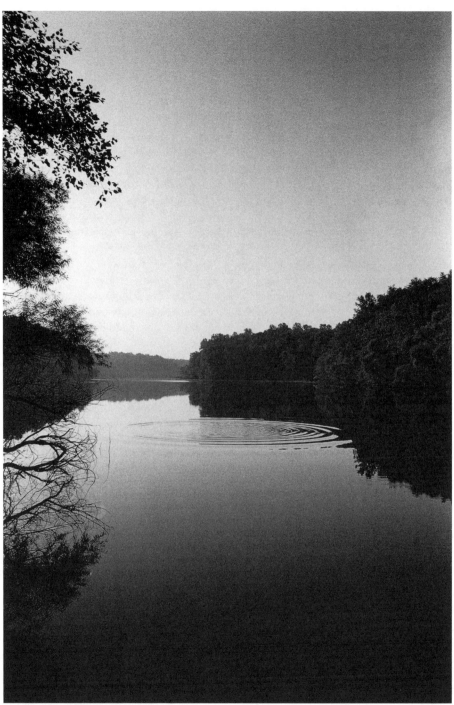

Bull Run near the Bull Run Marina

across the ground, helping to stabilize the soil. Reenter the older-growth forest at 1.6 miles, cross a small creek, and ascend along an old woods road. At the top of the rise at 1.8 miles, you must be alert and take the woods road to the right, not the one to the left. Again, at 2.1 miles, watch for the spot where your route leaves the road. Descend on a pathway to the left. Soon you will ascend to follow another old road through laurel only to descend steeply and begin walking along a creek and another dirt road at 2.4 miles.

The trail leaves the road at 2.6 miles, turns left, crosses a creek, and enters a field. Ducks, Canada geese, and great blue herons are frequent visitors to the backwater area on your right. You may see great blue herons standing motionless in the shallow water waiting for a dinner of fish, snakes, mice, frogs, or small birds to come close enough to be quickly grabbed and consumed. The field is a good place to catch a glimpse of rabbits or deer in the early morning or early evening.

Swing around another backwater area, cross an inlet stream, and at 3 miles walk along the edge of a soccer field, heading toward a parking lot. Just before the lot, turn right, cross a stream, and walk through a rough and overgrown field, aiming for the place where the indistinct trail reenters a wooded area of pines and cedars.

You must be alert again at 3.9 miles as the trail makes an abrupt change to the left to steeply climb the hillside. It drops steeply down and climbs again to begin a series of short ups, downs, and meanderings through a wonderful old hemlock forest. Enter Bull Run Marina at 4.2 miles, passing by a yellow-blazed trail to the left. That trail is a circuit hike of about one mile that rejoins the Blue Trail. Continue to your right, crossing a backwater stream on a footbridge at

4.35 miles, where the yellow-blazed trail rejoins your route from the left. Again continue to the right; ascend to pass by rest rooms, picnic tables, a water fountain, and the boat-launching area in Bull Run Marina.

Take care in crossing busy Old Yates Ford Road. Follow a paved trail a short distance into the woods, but do not follow it back uphill. Continue on a dirt pathway next to Bull Run, which gets wider as you work your way downstream toward the reservoir. Honeysuckle and grapevines wind their way over the trees and across the trail. Watch where you step, as the vines, especially the honeysuckle, could cause you to trip. However, the forest will become more open once you swing around a backwater area. As you walk this upland pathway away from Bull Run, it, unseen by you, is intersected by, and becomes, the Occoquan River.

An orange-blazed trail comes in from the left at 4.9 miles. It, too, is a circular trail of a little more than a mile. The orange-blazed trail rejoins the Blue Trail at 5.1 miles. Begin a series of ups and downs as you meander through the woods close to a housing development. Turn right onto an old road to swing away from the houses and, amazingly, after just having been so close to civilization, enter a wonderfully isolated valley at 5.9 miles.

At 6 miles, ascend out of the valley, cross a low knob, and descend into another small valley only to rise again. Songbirds are especially active here in the early morning as they flitter among the exceptionally large beech trees. You will walk by a few quarter- to half-million-dollar homes as you turn right onto a dirt road at 6.5 miles. There is a T-intersection at 7.5 miles where you need to make a left turn to descend, leaving behind the houses and road noise. One-tenth mile beyond, make a left turn onto a trail following a water run upstream. The creek is deep, murky, and slow-moving, giving the area an almost swampy feeling. Skunk cabbage is one of the earliest plants to bloom here after the first of the year, and if you are hiking in late winter, look for its purple and brown flowers surrounded by broad green leaves. Touch one of the leaves to learn how it received its name.

Cross a stream at 7.8 miles. There may or may not be a log to help you get across. Either way, expect to get your feet wet. After ascending to a T-intersection at 8 miles, turn right and gradually descend to come to your only view of the Occoquan River. This valley was originally inhabited by Native Americans of the Powhatan confederacy, and occoquan can be translated to mean "at the end of the water." The name presumably refers to where the Occoquan empties a few miles downstream into Belmont and Occoquan Bays. Arrive at a four-way intersection at 8.2 miles and turn left to swing around a backwater area and ascend to cross a small creek. Look backward for a few moments to enjoy your last glimpse of the river.

Come onto paved Wolf Run Shoals Road, walking by a cemetery with quite a number of gravestones identifying 1918 as the year of death. Could all of these people have passed away because of the great flu epidemic? A thousand feet beyond the cemetery, you must be alert as your route makes an abrupt turn to the right off the paved roadway to follow a cedar-lined dirt-and-gravel driveway. Soon bear right and descend on an old dirt road.

Cross a creek at 9.1 miles and ascend in a mixed hardwood and evergreen forest. The trail comes to a utility-line right-of-way at 9.4 miles and turns left uphill. Two-tenths mile beyond, turn left away from the utility line. You will cross under another line at 9.8 miles, where you need to make an abrupt turn to the right, soon making another right turn onto a dirt road.

Be alert at 10.1 miles as your route leaves the dirt road, enters the woods to the left, and descends. At 10.4 miles you come to a right turn onto a woods road, where you parallel a small stream. Rock hop a creek at 10.5 miles and ascend steeply, entering Fountainhead Regional Park and soon passing by a horse trail that heads off to the right.

A white-blazed trail comes in from the left at 10.6 miles as you walk through a magical-feeling tunnel of towering hemlocks. On the right, the horse trail rejoins the Blue Trail at 10.8 miles. Stop to look through the late-1800s cemetery.

Reach the trailhead parking at 11 miles. Rest rooms are to your right. The park offers nature trails, a miniature golf course, a picnic area, rowboat rentals, and a boat-launching ramp. A snack shop and visitor center are a short distance down the road to the right.

11

Manassas National Battlefield Park

Total distance (circuit): 5.2 miles

Hiking time: 2¾ hours

Vertical rise: 390 feet

Maps: USGS 7½′ Gainesville; Manassas Battlefield Walking Tours map

The peaceful rolling hills of the broad Manassas plateau were the site of two intense, bloody, and significant battles of the Civil War. On July 16, 1861, General Irvin McDowell marched 35,000 Union troops out of Washington, D.C., in an effort to capture an important railroad junction at Manassas. Most of the Federal forces were 90-day, poorly trained volunteers who had answered President Abraham Lincoln's call to arms after the April 1861 attack on Fort Sumter. Most of the volunteers, the Union commanders, and even Lincoln felt this would surely be a short war.

On the morning of July 21, 1861, McDowell opened fire near Stone Bridge, which spans Bull Run. At first the battle appeared to be going in favor of the Union forces, but as General Thomas J. Jackson held his ground on Henry Hill and fresh units were rushed to his aid, the Confederates eventually forced the Union into a turmoiled retreat to Washington. This first major clash in the War Between the States set the stage for four more years of bitter conflict.

In August 1862, the two forces met once again at Manassas. General Robert E. Lee, now in command of the Confederates and aided by the steadfast forces of General Stonewall Jackson, employed brilliant military tactics to force General John Pope's Union army to withdraw from Bull Run and return to Washington. This opened the way for Lee's first drive into Northern territory and a possible recognition of the Confederate States of America by major European powers.

Manassas National Battlefield Park is reached by leaving I-66 at the Manassas

Exit 47 and following Old VA 234 north. In a little more than 0.5 mile, turn right into the park to arrive at the visitor center. A small admission fee is charged.

To add to your enjoyment of the hike, you should devote at least some time to the exhibits and multimedia programs presented in the center. Several brochures are available that describe the battles, the physical features of the 5,000-plus-acre park, and itineraries for a number of different hiking opportunities.

The circuit hike described here follows a route that touches upon a number of sites relevant to the first battle of Manassas. In addition, it offers a quiet and moderate walk across open meadows, through heavily wooded forests, and along the meandering

and shallow Bull Run. The quiet and peace of this hike is made even more enjoyable when you realize you are only 26 miles from the hustle and bustle of downtown Washington, D.C., and within a couple of miles of its sprawling suburbs.

Begin by walking through the open field from the visitor center to the statue of General Thomas J. Jackson. The Henry House is visible to your left. Ignore it now; your return route will bring you past it. Bear right from the statue, heading toward the cannons. These guns mark Jackson's line of defense on the afternoon of July 21, 1861. It was here that Jackson earned his famous nickname. His troops held their ground while other Southerners dropped back in disarray. Hoping to stop the rout and inspire the brigade under his command, Brigadier General Barnard E. Bee pointed out Jackson's resolute troops and shouted, "There stands Jackson like a stone wall! Rally behind the Virginians, boys!" Although the Confederate forces did rally behind Jackson, Bee was fatally wounded during the battle.

Near the cannons a sign points to a blue-blazed pathway heading into the woods. At 0.3 mile enter the woods where an old road veers off to the left. You should bear right and follow the blue-blazed pathway. (There may be a number of confusing intersections throughout this hike—always take the route marked by the blue blazes.) The dogwood's pink and white leaf bracts color the springtime forest; its red berries dot the woods in the fall, providing food for passing birds.

Cross a yellow-blazed bridle path, descend through a mixed hardwood forest, and at 0.5 mile cross a small, sometimes dry, water run. At 0.6 mile from the visitor center turn left onto old Rock Road, a route used by Confederate troops coming from the south. Honeysuckle, greenbriar, and poison ivy hang copiously from tree branches. Arrive at a four-way intersection at 0.8 mile. Continue along Rock Road, now lined by cedars and other evergreens.

To save you from having to ford Young's Branch, be alert at 0.9 mile, where a pathway bears left from the road and makes an almost immediate right to cross the stream on a footbridge. This shaded place where the shallow, slow-moving waters reflect the trees and sunlight is a nice spot for a rest break. Within a few hundred feet the trail breaks out into the open and your route turns left to rejoin Rock Road.

At 1.25 miles leave the gravel road, follow the pathway to the left, and in 200 feet take care in crossing busy US 29

(Warrenton Turnpike). Pass through a gate and ascend along the right side of an open field. At 1.4 miles you must make an abrupt turn to the right to arrive at a sign marking what was once the site of the Van Pelt House, Avon. Confederates stationed here had a clear view of Stone Bridge and watched as Union forces progressed along Warrenton Turnpike.

There is a confusing intersection of trails at the Van Pelt House site. Trails ahead and to the right would eventually bring you to an intersection close to the Farm Ford at the 2.5-mile point of this hike. However, to continue following this description, make a hard right and, heading southeast, go back in the direction of US 29.

Descend the knoll at 1.6 miles and continue on a boardwalk through a moist bottomland forest dominated by oaks. Ascend steps at 1.9 miles, come to a parking area on US 29, pass through a wooden gate, and arrive at Stone Bridge. Early in the morning of July 21, 1861, the opening shots of the first battle of Manassas were fired nearby. To prevent any further use by Federal forces, the Confederates destroyed the bridge in March of 1862. It was rebuilt sometime around 1880.

Do not cross the bridge. Instead, look for the trail going off to the left to begin paralleling Bull Run. The hike now becomes quieter and more relaxed as you move into the woods and away from US 29. At 2.3 miles you will be near the site Colonel William T. Sherman's troops used to cross Bull Run to join other Union soldiers already engaged in the battle on Matthews Hill.

Come to an intersection at 2.5 miles; bear left. There is another intersection in 200 feet. Here you bear right; a turn to the left would lead back to the Van Pelt House site. Soon, the Stone Bridge Loop Trail comes in from the right. You should continue

Historic Rock Road

along the edge of the woods, eventually cutting through the meadow and crossing a bridle path. Cross a gravel road at 3 miles, enter woods, and ascend along the pathway.

The road levels out at 3.2 miles and soon you will reach a small clearing. Here the curious may wish to do some off-trail explorations. To the left of the pathway you can search for the foundation and remains of the two-story mansion home, known as Pittsylvania, of the Landon Carter family. The family cemetery is hidden by trees and underbrush a little farther into the woods. Now is the time to contemplate the reclamation powers of nature. Note how tall the trees are and how full the forest is. Yet, at the time of the battle, Pittsylvania could be seen easily from the surrounding countryside. The land around the house was open farmland, clear of trees.

Return to the main route and continue following blue blazes along the old woods road. Join up with, and follow, the Matthews Hill Loop Trail. Sixty feet to the left is a marble stone marking the spot where Private George T. Stovall of the Eighth Georgia Infantry was killed as he attempted to carry his brother to safety. There are a number of Park Service interpretive signs along this heavily wooded section of trail. They contain quotes from battle participants and other bits of information. Although it may slow your hiking pace, taking the time to read the signs will add greatly to your understanding and appreciation of your surroundings.

Proceed straight as your route crosses yet another horse trail. At 4 miles the trail breaks out into the open and continues across the field; a line of cannons on your left marks the Union position. Enjoy the clear view across to Henry Hill. In 200 feet you have the option of extending the hike to a full length of about ten miles by crossing

Sudley Road (VA 234) and following the second battle of Manassas itinerary. Consult the visitor center for information on this hike.

To continue following this description, do not cross VA 234, but instead turn left in the field to parallel the roadway. Keen observers may note a number of piles of scat, indicating that raccoons, opossums, and foxes frequent this meadow on a regular basis.

A bench under a tall cedar provides a resting place to enjoy commanding views of Matthews Hill and other points to the west and south. Major General John Pope headquartered his Union forces here on August 29 and 30, 1862, during the second battle of Manassas. Walk downhill a few hundred feet to the Stone House, built around 1848. The Union army used the structure as a hospital during both battles. The house is sometimes open to the public, and living-history demonstrations are presented on an irregular basis. Check with the visitor center for dates and times.

Cross US 29 at the stoplight, follow VA 234, and immediately after using the roadway's bridge to pass over Young's Branch, turn left into the field and then right to walk along the split-rail fence. At 5 miles, near the corner of the field, swing left and ascend to Henry House. Captain James B. Ricketts's forces deployed guns here, but as the battle progressed, Confederate troops drew ever closer and the Northern army began its withdrawal from the first battle of Manassas.

Follow the line of cannons to return to the visitor center at 5.2 miles.

Other nearby hiking opportunities are at Bull Run Regional Park (a sign on US 29 points the way to the park a few miles to the east of the Manassas National Battlefield Park) and the Blue Trail (see Hike 10), which follows Bull Run for more than 20 miles. For hikers desiring to learn more about the Civil War in the state, Virginia contains other Civil War parks with walking opportunities. Among them are Appomattox Court House National Historical Park, Fredericksburg-Spotsylvania National Battlefield Park, New Market Battlefield Park, Petersburg National Battlefield Park, and Richmond National Battlefield Park. All of these sites are identified on the Virginia highway map and are located close to the towns or cities for which they are named.

12

Sky Meadows State Park

Total distance (circuit): 5.4 miles

Hiking time: 3½ hours

Vertical rise: 1,460 feet

Maps: USGS 7½' Upperville; Sky Meadows State Park map

Even from miles away, it's easy to see how Sky Meadows State Park received its name. Large, open, richly green fields dapple vast areas of the hillside as the topography sweeps upward from the rolling Piedmont plain to meet the eastern slopes of the Blue Ridge Mountains.

From the 1700s, most of what is now park property passed through a number of owners. In the 1830s, Isaac Settle, a postman and tavern keeper, built the fieldstone Mount Bleak House, which he gave to his son Abner as a wedding gift. By the 1850s the owners were successfully raising hogs, chickens, turkeys, oxen, and horses and harvesting fields of wheat and corn. The state park is now restoring the farmhouse to its appearance at about that time. Other structures include a carriage barn, summer kitchen, and a log cabin (possibly the original residence on the property).

Sky Meadows is about an hour's drive from Washington, D.C. From I-66 take the Delaplane exit and follow US 17 north to the park's entrance on VA 710 (5 miles north of the village of Delaplane). The park may also be reached by leaving US 50 near Paris and following US 17 south about a mile. A small fee is charged. The park has a picnic area, a visitor center at the Mount Bleak House, a bridle trail, rest rooms, water, and a hike-in campground (with primitive sites, water, and a shelter that was once a farm shed). Permit and payment of a fee are required to camp. Camping anywhere else in the park is prohibited. You may fish in the pond close to US 17 if you have a valid Virginia license.

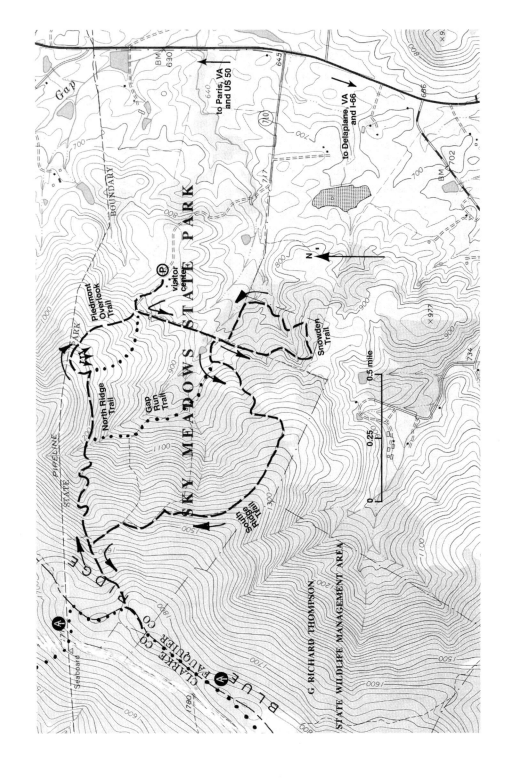

Sky Meadows has one of the best and most active interpretive programs I have ever come across in a state or national park. Among other things, you may find yourself gazing at the stars with an astronomer, making a rag doll, identifying birdcalls while on a morning stroll, or listening to tall tales around an evening campfire. The Mount Bleak House is open for tours. The visitor center can provide dates and times of activities and a park map.

One of the main attractions of hiking in the 1,842-acre state park is that it contains a wide array of plant life, both wild and cultivated. Trees around the mansion include crabapple, plum, cherry, Chinese chestnut, walnut, Norway maple, green ash, sugar maple, forsythia, pecan, dogwood, lilac, and Kentucky coffeetree. The contrast of open meadows and deep forests, coupled with an elevation difference of 1,840 feet as a high point and 640 feet as the low, ensures that wildflower lovers are in for a treat from late winter to midfall. Skunk cabbage could be blooming in moist, wooded areas by mid-February. Bloodroot, cutleaf toothwort, and rue anemone begin appearing on the forest floor about the beginning of April. Shortly thereafter, purple and yellow violets, spring beauties, and star chickweed begin to bloom in the woods. By late April and early May, the wooded areas are at their most colorful—tall wild geranium with its pink blossoms and columbine's drooping, red, bell-like flowers grow above the tiny yellow trumpets of corydalis, while green and purplish jack-in-the-pulpits stick out of moist ground on singular, strong stems.

Sun-tolerant plants line the roadways during the hot summer months. White or violet trumpet-shaped flowers of jimsonweed grow from the poor soil of the roadbanks. Thriving in the pastures are white oxeye daisies and tall, yellow crown-beard. Both of these plants are members of the daisy family, which, according to Roger Tory Peterson, is the largest family of flowering plants and possibly the newest one to evolve on Earth.

Spotted touch-me-not will still be blooming in wet areas in the woods in September and moth mullein adds a bit of yellow to roadsides as late as October.

Animals inhabiting the park include fox squirrels, chipmunks, gray squirrels, skunks, opossums, red foxes, eastern cottontails, deer, and raccoons. It is possible that a coyote may occasionally wander onto park property.

A system of trails wanders through the fields, into the woods, and along small streams; the following hike touches upon most of the highlights to be discovered. It also comes into contact with the Appalachian Trail, furnishing additional hiking opportunities (and primitive camping for those who take it south out of the park).

Begin by following the trail signs from the far end of the parking lot of the Mount Bleak House. In 0.1 mile turn left onto a gravel road. At 0.15 mile you should bypass the turnoff to the North Ridge, Piedmont Overlook, and Appalachian Trails and continue on the road, enjoying the views of open farmlands above and below you. In the 1800s this old roadway stretched for three miles, connecting Paris, Virginia, with gristmills on Crooked Run.

At 0.4 mile bear left onto the white-blazed Snowden Interpretive Trail, one of the newer trails in the park. You could shorten the overall length of this hike by 1 mile by turning right, crossing the fence stile, and following the Gap Run Trail. However, the interpretive trail is an easy walk and will help you further appreciate what you will see and experience on the rest of the hike. Take the time to walk it and absorb

The Mount Bleak House

the information provided about animals of the park and their relationship to their surroundings. Proceed on the Snowden Trail through a mature oak forest along the old roadway built in the 1820s. Bear right at an intersection; you will be returning on the road coming in from the left. Holes in trees mark this as a favorite woodpecker feeding site.

In 0.6 mile the trail turns left off the old road. At 0.75 mile ascend via switchbacks next to a fence line and open field. Deer apparently are quite fond of this section of the park; I counted more than 15 running through the woods, their white tails raised and flashing a warning of my encroachment upon their forest home. At 1 mile descend into an open woods.

The undergrowth becomes fuller and thicker at 1.2 miles as you begin to parallel a small stream that provides nourishment to this lusher vegetation. Turn right onto an old woods road at 1.3 miles. At 1.4 miles

you should turn left onto Edmonds Lane, another 1800s roadway. The builders of the stone wall must have known what they were doing, for even after all of these years, it still lines the road, a testimony to their skill and hard work.

At 1.5 miles return to the loop-trail intersection, bear right, and in 200 feet turn left, cross over the fence stile, and enter a meadow. In 0.1 mile you'll reach an intersection. The orange-blazed Gap Run Trail goes right for two-tenths mile to the campground and seven-tenths mile to the North Ridge Trail, but you should bear left onto the yellow-blazed South Ridge Trail.

At 1.7 miles follow an old road ascending through a wooded area. Pay attention as the trail breaks out into the open—it does not ascend to the bench overlooking the farmland but makes an abrupt turn left and back into the woods. Pass by the site of Snowden Manor. Only the foundation, chimney, and a few stone walls mark where this large, white, frame-columned house stood from the mid-1800s to when it burned in 1913.

At 2 miles bear right and then swing left along the edge of the meadow. Soon, a bench under the shade of a spreading dogwood tree permits you to enjoy a view from the height you have attained. Be careful, though. A large poison ivy vine uses the dogwood as support and is stretching itself along the tree's branches.

Continue ascending, crossing a fence stile at 2.2 miles and entering the woods. Abundant grapevines drape themselves over the trees as you ascend along a nicely graded woods road. If you are the first person to come this way in several days, be ready to run into scores of spiderwebs spanning the width of the road. The webs are even more numerous in the fall, when the spiders work furiously to catch as much prey as possible before the insects disappear with the coming of cold winter weather.

The South Ridge Trail comes to an end as it intersects the blue-blazed North Ridge Trail at 3.2 miles. A descent to the right would lead nine-tenths mile to the campground, but you want to bear left and ascend as the route becomes steeper and rockier, passing through large patches of poison ivy.

At 3.5 miles arrive at a bench and the junction with the Appalachian Trail (AT). The AT runs to the right two and nine-tenths miles to US 50 in Ashby Gap and seven miles to the left to Manassas Gap Shelter. Use the bench to take a well-deserved break in this quiet and isolated place. I have experienced something new and wonderful every time I've visited this spot. I've heard the staccato sounds of a woodpecker to the right of me answered by another on my left, then by one behind me and

again by one in front of me, permitting me to enjoy nature's version of "surround-sound stereo." I've seen turtles mate, oblivious to my presence on the bench. Other times, in late winter, bloodroot had begun to force its way through the hoarfrost-frozen ground, while spring walks a short distance south on the AT have been rewarded with one of the most profuse arrays of trillium ever seen in one area.

From the bench, descend to retrace your steps to the intersection with the South Ridge Trail. This time bear left to continue descending and following blue-blazed North Ridge Trail. The going is rough and rocky as you pass by several crumbling stone walls, evidence that the mountainside was used at one time for the grazing of stock. At 4 miles pass through an area of obvious gypsy moth destruction. Many of the oldest and largest trees are bare and decaying. It's interesting to see, however, how the absence of leaves is now permitting sunlight to reach the forest floor, allowing undergrowth to become lush and full as nature begins the long, slow process of eventually returning the area to a climax forest.

Cross Gap Run. At 4.4 miles is the intersection with the orange-blazed Gap Run Trail. The campground is five-tenths mile and the parking lot one and three-tenths miles along this trail to the right. Bear left to ascend switchbacks on blue-blazed North Ridge Trail. At 4.6 miles, cross a fence to an intersection. North Ridge Trail now goes right, descending to the parking lot in six-tenths mile. You should turn left uphill to begin following red-blazed Piedmont Overlook Trail.

At 4.7 miles break out into the open for what I consider to be one of the best grandstand views in Northern Virginia. From your perch on the eastern edge of the Blue Ridge Mountains, the rolling and flatter lands of the

Piedmont stretch out before you. The meadows directly below slope down to a pond shimmering in the sunlight. Rectangular fields of nearby farms alternate with strips of woodland, turning the landscape into a patchwork quilt of greens, browns, and golds. Vultures soar on rising thermals as clouds float by, leading your eyes to focus on the distance where, on clear days, high-rise buildings of the Dulles-Fairfax area can be seen poking above the horizon.

Descend through the meadow on a mowed route; just before reaching a park residence, descend to the right at 5.2 miles to walk past an old cowshed. In a few steps rejoin the North Ridge Trail, cross a fence stile, and turn left onto the gravel road. Follow the route back to the parking lot at 5.4 miles.

13

Lake Anna State Park

Total distance (circuit): 9.0 miles

Hiking time: 5 hours

Vertical rise: 360 feet

Maps: USGS 7½′ Lake Anna West; Lake Anna State Park map

Every bit of land on Earth has gone through countless changes in its topography, geology, natural history, and uses by the human race. A walk through Lake Anna State Park can provide physical evidence of how past events have shaped the present-day makeup of Virginia's central Piedmont.

Long before humans set foot on this continent, a fault formed in the crust of the earth near what is now Lake Anna State Park. Molten lava poured through this north-south fracture and, as the general lay of the land slopes toward the Atlantic Ocean, the liquid rock spread eastward. Unimpeded, the leading edge of the flow fanned out widely, eventually cooling into a large area rich in iron ore, while behind it the flow was compressed into a narrow band now called the Gold-Pyrite Belt of Virginia.

The Mannahoack Indians, an eastern tribe of the far-flung Sioux nation, lived in the area at the time settlers (or invaders, depending on your point of view) from the Old World began to arrive. Being hunters, food gatherers, and small-plot farmers, the tribe had little use for the mineral riches below their domain and the land remained more or less unchanged throughout their occupancy. Within a hundred years of the newcomers' arrival, though, the Mannahoacks had been forced off their ancestral homes and use of the land began to shift.

Virginia's colonists needed a steady supply of nails, farm implements, and other tools to establish their farms and settlements, and the early 1700s saw the rise of numerous iron furnaces making use of the

VA 7000
to VA 601

Hailey's
Mill site

Fisherman's
Trail

VA 7000

Mill Pond Trail

LAKE ANNA
STATE PARK

Picnic
area

Visitor
Center

Turkey
Run Trail

Cedar
Run Trail

Railroad
Ford Trail

Glenora Trail

Big Woods
Trail

Taylor
homesite

NORTH

Pigeon Run

Anna Creek

Cem

Lake Anna State Park

Ⓟ   Parking

0   0.5 mile

0   0.5 kilometer

N

BM
272

rich ore deposits in what is now Spotsylvania County. Iron mines pockmarked the countryside and logging roads crisscrossed the landscape to enable harvesting of what was known as the Big Woods. The lumber was made into charcoal to fire the furnaces, one of which was on Douglas Run, just east of present-day parklands. By the end of the century, however, most of these furnaces had closed, victims to other furnaces on the more easily navigable James, Potomac, and Rappahannock Rivers.

Agriculture became the region's primary means of livelihood, yet many farmers found that "panning" their water runs resulted in small but profitable rewards. The first recorded gold mine in Virginia was in western Spotsylvania County in 1806, and the Goodwin Mine opened on Pigeon Run in the 1830s. At one time there were at least 23 mines operating in the county, helping make Virginia the nation's third largest gold producer from 1830 to 1850. The California gold rush of 1849 diverted attention from Virginia and the population around North Anna River once again adopted an agrarian way of life mixed with a bit of mineral mining.

Lake Anna was created to fulfill the water needs of the cooling system of Virginia Power Company's North Anna Nuclear Power Station, a short 3 miles from the state park. When the dam across the North Anna River was completed in 1971, the power company gave the lake to the Commonwealth of Virginia. With 8 miles of shoreline, the state park opened to the public in 1983 and offers picnic areas, a boat ramp, excellent nature and history exhibits in the visitor center, swimming in the lake from Memorial Day to Labor Day, a bath house, interpretive programs (one program will teach you how to pan for gold), and concessions. Future plans involve a boat dock and marina and more miles of pathways. There are small fees to use the park.

A network of trails allows you to roam the park's more than 2,000 acres to discover natural secrets and beauties and find reminders of all the human activity that has taken place in the past and continues into the present. The full length of this walk is 9 miles, but there are many intersections along the way that allow you to shorten the walk by taking alternative routes back to your automobile.

The state park may be reached from the south by following VA 208 from the Ferncliff exit of I-64 for 20-odd miles to Lake Anna. (VA 208 also comes from the north from Fredericksburg.) Once the road crosses to the north side of the lake, go several miles to a left turn onto VA 601. Follow VA 601 for 3.4 miles to VA 7000 and the park's entrance on the left. Continue on to the visitor center overlooking the lake.

The Old Pond Trail is an interpretive pathway with numbered stops keyed to a pamphlet available in the visitor center. Pick up one of the pamphlets and use it as you begin walking that trail from the center's porch, soon passing through a tunnel of cedar trees and crossing a wooden bridge over a small creek. In 0.15 mile a bench to the right overlooks the pond, whose muddy edges may be marked by paw prints from opossums and raccoons. In May be looking for the tulip poplars' impressive flowers high up in the trees.

Come to a four-way intersection in 0.25 mile. It is one-tenth mile back to the visitor center to the right, and the Glenora Trail, which you will join up with later, goes to the left. Continue forward on red-blazed Railroad Ford Trail, walking along the shore of the lake, which is lined by cedars and oaks. At 0.4 mile turn away from the lake and into a woods of sweet gum, sassafras, and hickory for a short distance before coming back to the shoreline for a different view of the swimming beach and visitor center.

Before swinging around a point at 1 mile, go down to the edge of the lake. If it hasn't rained hard for a few days, the water is usually very clear and you are likely to see dozens of tiny clamshells just below the surface. Sportsmen may be interested to know the lake contains bluegill, black crappie, channel catfish, walleye, several kinds of bass, and other fish. Check at the visitor center for fishing regulations.

Leave views of the lake for a while and begin walking along an old railroad grade. The railroad was built in 1916 to carry ore from the Valzinco Mine (five miles to the north) to the Allah Cooper Mine (about seven miles to the south), where lead and zinc were extracted and shipped to Mineral, Virginia. These were eventually made into bullets and shell casings to aid the Allied efforts in World War I.

The Railroad Trail ends at 1.7 miles. Green-blazed Glenora Trail goes left for three-tenths mile back to the visitor center; you want to follow this old country lane to the right through a mixed forest of sweet gum, hickory, oak, holly, maple, sassafras, and cedar. Hornets' nests are spotted regularly on this trail, so be attentive. Keep to the right when a road comes in from the left at 1.8 miles. In the mountains of Virginia, hikers are usually slowed down by blueberries in August. Here in the Piedmont you will probably enjoy them by no later than mid-July. At 2 miles you begin to descend gradually and loblolly pines appear in greater numbers.

The Big Woods Trail comes in from the left at 2.8 miles. Continue straight for a short distance to a decaying building

Mountain laurel

slowly being reclaimed by the surrounding forest. This is the only structure still standing from the Glenora Plantation; most of what was once the plantation is now under the waters of Lake Anna. Standing guard over this silent scene is a large, venerable sycamore. Sycamores are generally acknowledged as attaining the most massive proportions of any American hardwood tree. A sycamore's leaves also have the distinction of being the largest single-bladed leaf (4 to 10 inches in length and breadth) native to the United States. Even in a densely packed, mixed forest you can easily spot the sycamores by the gleaming white bark in the upper portions of the trees.

Retrace your steps back to, and turn right onto, silver-blazed Big Woods Trail, an old logging road. (The visitor center is about one and a half miles straight ahead on Glenora Trail.) As you walk next to the lake, look for signs of beaver activity and note how some of the old stumps, especially those of the sycamores, have sprouted new growth. You'll soon cross a wooden bridge and begin to gradually ascend to where the Big Woods Trail ends and meets Turkey Run Trail. Yellow-blazed Turkey Run goes left one mile to the trailhead parking on the Picnic Area C roadway; you should turn right onto it and pass by the Cedar Run Trail to come to a chimney marking the old Taylor homesite (look for the nearby cemetery).

Return to the intersection with Cedar Run Trail at 4.6 miles. Turn right onto it and descend on this white-blazed old country road, walking through fields of running cedar. You will soon cross a wooden bridge (the lake is visible through the vegetation) before swinging around an old homesite on a point of land next to the lake where planted daffodils still bloom in the spring.

Cedar Run Trail ends to meet back with Turkey Run Trail at 5.5 miles. Turn right onto Turkey Run to arrive at the Picnic Area C roadway. Cross the road and continue the hike on blue-blazed Mill Pond Trail. Partridgeberry grows abundantly along this old road. Be watching again, after going under a utility line, for where the trail turns off the road to the left and descends to a cove on Pigeon Run where Hailey's gristmill ground locally grown corn from 1857 to 1889. This is probably the quietest spot you will have been on this hike, so take a break at the water's edge and observe the only industries going on here today—a heron or two trolling the shallow water in search of a meal, a muskrat taking an early evening swim, or a broad-winged hawk surveying its domain. If you are lucky enough to catch a couple of beavers at work you will see some heavy-duty industry in action. Two adult beavers can bring a 3-inch sapling down in about 3 minutes and are able to construct a 12-foot-long, 2-foot-high dam with only two nights of labor.

Retrace your steps back to the Picnic Area C roadway and bear right onto it. When you arrive at the parking area on VA 7000 at 8.2 miles, turn left onto this roadway. You might think pavement is not the best way to end a hike, but enjoy the abundant laurel in bloom in midsummer, the park's almost-tame deer population—which browse in large numbers next to the road—and a great view of the lake that appears at 8.7 miles. The visitor center soon becomes visible, and you'll bend to the left to return to it at 9 miles.

14

Cold Harbor

Total distance (circuit): 1.0 mile

Hiking time: 30 minutes

Vertical rise: less than 100 feet

Map: 7½' USGS Seven Pines; National Park Service Cold Harbor map

After May 23, 1864, and the somewhat stalemated battle of Spotsylvania, Lieutenant General Ulysses S. Grant continued to move in a southward direction in his Overland Campaign to capture the Confederate capital, Richmond. In addition to several other skirmishes along the way, Grant's forces and General Robert E. Lee's Army of Northern Virginia clashed again near the crossroads of Old Cold Harbor. Union soldiers captured the crossroads on May 31, but fortifications, mostly in the form of extensive dirt breastworks built by the Southern army, turned the next 3 days of battle into a standoff. The Federal troops were never able to penetrate the fortifications, while the Confederate army just held its ground, unable to drive the invaders back. From June 4 through 12, the days were filled with minor attacks and occasional sniper fire. Unable to break through the Southern lines, Grant finally withdrew and turned his attention on Petersburg. This successful defense of Richmond is considered Lee's last field victory of the war. Historians say the battle at Cold Harbor influenced the strategies of future wars by proving that well-selected defensives, supported by strong artillery power, are quite invulnerable to direct attack. It certainly turned the rest of the Civil War into a conflict where entrenchments and sieges took precedence over battles of direct assault.

From early 1862 to the city's surrender on April 3, 1865, Union forces engaged in numerous battles in attempts to capture Richmond. Eleven sites commemorating various conflicts and activities are scattered

Cold Harbor

(P) Parking

N

0   0.25 mile

0   0.25 kilometer

RICHMOND
IONAL BATTLEFIELD
PARK

National
Cem

Cold Harbor
Battlefield

Cem

Garthright
House

New Cold Harbor

Old Creek

To I-64
and Richmond

BM
193

GRADE

RAILROAD

throughout the city and surrounding area and make up the National Park Service's Richmond National Battlefield Park. In order to obtain a clear mental picture of Civil War events around Richmond, you should stop in at the Chimborazo Visitor Center at 3215 East Broad Street near downtown Richmond, study the exhibits, and watch the audiovisual presentations. To reach Cold Harbor from the visitor center, take Broad Street to I-95 and follow the interstate north to I-64. Take I-64 east to I-295 and follow that highway north to the VA 156 (North Airport Drive) exit. Continue on

VA 156N for 5 miles, through several twists and turns, to the Cold Harbor park entrance on the right. (The Park Service provides a handout pamphlet describing a circuitous driving tour of the sites of the Richmond National Battlefield Park. Following this tour will also eventually lead you to Cold Harbor.)

In order to add even more background information to your hike, take a few moments to look in on the Cold Harbor Visitor Center. In addition to the usual ethical practices you should follow while on any hike, the Park Service requests that you refrain

These quiet fields were once the site of the Cold Harbor Battle

from removing any relics you may happen to find, park your automobile only in designated areas, and preserve the breastworks by not walking or climbing on them.

Start your hike by walking to the plaque behind the visitor center and continuing on the pathway along the edge of the meadow next to VA 156. You will be crossing the center of the Confederate main line of defense. On June 3, 1864, the Union army launched a massive attack but were soon pinned down by Confederate firepower, and in less than 30 minutes thousands of Union soldiers were killed or wounded. Remember that most of the land you will be walking upon throughout this hike was open farmland at the time of the Civil War; there were few trees or shrubs to hide behind or to use as shields against the showers of bullets filling the air.

Large oak and loblolly pine trees tower above, while sassafras and holly make up the understory as you swing away from the road at 0.2 mile. Holly is very shade tolerant

and is often found flourishing, as it is here, under the canopy of an older and taller forest. Unlike many other trees, hollies are either male or female—thus, they must be in proximity to each other for the female to bear fruit. The berries, which turn bright red in the fall, are a favorite winter food for birds and deer. Wild turkeys are sometimes seen feeding high up in the trees as well as on berries that have fallen to the ground.

At 0.3 mile, cross a footbridge constructed to protect the breastworks. The fortifications here were made by Union soldiers, who, unable to advance or retreat, used bayonets, cups, canteen halves, and whatever other implements would work to dig the trenches in an attempt to escape the unrelenting Confederate artillery and musket fire. This area later became the main battle line for the Federal forces.

The rifle pit you pass at 0.4 mile were dug so that guards could watch for enemy movement but be protected—more or less—from musket fire. Sweet pepper bush is

---

Cold Harbor

now growing near the site, helping to heal the ground's wounds and obscure this little bit of history. In late July, the plant's wildly fragrant white flowers grow in spikes. Stop to smell one and discover how the "sweet" got into the name. The "pepper" portion was given to the plant, possibly, because the dried seedpods resemble small peppercorns. These remain on the plant through much of the year, making it a distinctive plant that is easy to identify.

Cross tiny Bloody Run and the paved park road at 0.7 mile; ascend slightly to continue the hike and pass by a bit of Virginia creeper running along the ground and up some of the tree trunks.

Some of the best-preserved and deepest breastworks and trenches are passed at 0.8 mile. If these trenches and mounds of dirt are still this obvious, just think how deep and tall they must have been more than 100 years ago! Imagine what it was like to be a soldier engaged in this desperate attempt to stay alive. With so many comrades dying around them, men of the Union army wrote their names on bits of paper and attached them to their own clothing in the hope that their bodies could be identified after the battle. It's unfortunate that through the course of history, the human race seems to have expended more energy for hostile actions than for peaceful pursuits.

Swing to the left when you emerge into an open field. Due to the excellent forest-field mixture, foxes have adapted well to living in the rural Richmond area. Very likely the scat that you see on the trail is evidence that one of them has walked the same path you have. Take a stick and break open the scat to find out what the fox has been eating—perhaps there's fur and bones of a mouse, feathers from a bird, wild cherry and grape seeds, or remains of various insects.

The hike comes to an end as you return to the visitor center at 1 mile. (See Hike 11 for information on additional Civil War sites in Virginia.)

15

Willis River Trail

Total distance (one way): 15.3 miles

Hiking time: 9½ hours

Vertical rise: 700 feet

Maps: USGS 7½′ Gold Hill; USGS 7½′ Whiteville; VA Department of Forestry Cumberland State Forest/ Willis River Trail map

After you have traversed several of the Tidewater's and Piedmont's easier and tamer hikes, you may be ready for a change of pace—a walk on the wilder side. The Willis River Trail is a cooperative venture of the Department of Forestry and the Old Dominion Appalachian Trail Club and courses its way for more than 15 miles through many of the lesser-visited regions of the Cumberland State Forest. While club volunteers—who provide most of the labor for construction and maintenance of the route—do an admirable job, quick-growing summer vegetation rapidly overtakes even the best-maintained sections. In addition, there are no bridges to get you across streams or aids to help you climb some of their high banks, and in a few places there is no discernible treadway on the ground. You probably should not attempt this hike until you feel comfortable about being in such situations, but once you've gained that confidence, the Willis River Trail is a highly recommended adventure. Nowhere else in the Piedmont can you feel like you are one of the few explorers to pass through such a concealed countryside yet have the safety of trail blazes showing the way. Bring tackle to try your luck fishing the river for bluegill, crappie, largemouth bass, and pickerel.

Extra time sometimes spent finding your way, and the length of the hike, may make you want to consider doing it as two day hikes. A number of options exist, but as the parking lot of the Bear Creek Market (see below) is a good place to leave one of your automobiles (after asking permission),

splitting the trail into 9.6-mile (6.5-hour) and 5.7-mile (3-hour) segments is the most convenient. The store is also well stocked to provide you with ample lunch and munchies supplies. Water sources should be considered unpotable, so carry plenty. With an abundance of seed ticks and mosquitoes during the warmer months plus ensnaring growths of briars, poison ivy, and other prickly vegetation, long pants and shirts should be your hiking garb here anytime of the year. You will cross a well-developed multiuse trail at one point, but it will be obvious that you want to continue to follow the lesser-used Willis River Trail. Camping options include the designated primitive site at 6.9 miles or the developed campground in 326-acre Bear Creek Lake State Park a little more than 10 miles into the journey. In addition to its campground, the park has picnic facilities, a swimming area, concessions, fishing, and about 4 miles of trails.

To reach the hike, turn off US 60 onto VA 629, which soon becomes dirt. If coming from the west you will make this turn about 12 miles from the US 15–US 60 intersection in Sprouses Corner; coming from the east it will be about 1 mile from the VA 45–US 60 intersection west of Cumberland. Three miles from US 60, a sign identifies Winston Lake, the Willis River Trail's southern trailhead. You can leave a car in the small parking area. Continuing the drive, come to a four-way intersection with the Cumberland State Forest headquarters to the left (obtain free maps of the trail here) and VA 628 coming in from the right. Continue straight on now paved VA 629, passing by the entrance to Bear Creek Lake State Park, 2 miles from Winston Lake. From the state park it's 0.8 mile to a T-intersection and the Bear Creek Market, where you will turn left onto paved

VA 622. Turn right onto dirt VA 623 in 0.4 mile from the market, making a left onto paved VA 624 in 1.7 additional miles. From this intersection it is 2.2 miles to where you bear left onto paved VA 608, which almost immediately becomes dirt. When VA 615 comes in from the right, keep to the left for 0.4 mile to make the last right turn onto dirt Warner Forest Road. Park the car in another 0.5 mile in the small dead-end turnaround.

Do not cross the swinging bridge over the Willis River; instead, look for double white blazes on the southern side of the parking area, which direct you into the woods along a pathway lined by Virginia creeper, mayapple, pawpaw, false Solomon's seal, running cedar, partridgeberry, and a host of entangling vegetation. The partridgeberry is an important ground cover; its roots are shallow but intertwining, forming a compact mat that helps stabilize the soil and keep it from washing away in times of high water. Look for deer tracks and other animal prints as you pass through the damp area just before emerging onto VA 615 at 0.7 mile.

Make a left to cross Reynolds Creek on the roadway's bridge, and in less than 300 feet be looking for double blazes that tell you to make a right onto a probably overgrown pathway beside a swampy area. At 0.9 mile, the trail bears right into the woods and then makes a left along a low ridge before it crosses and ascends out of a gully to the right. When you swing along the edge of a timbered area, it's important to keep a close watch on the blazes as you cross a small water run and bear right on a route that may have no recognizable representation on the ground. Luckily, you will turn left onto an obvious fishermen's trail at 1.1 miles, hiking upstream next to Reynolds Creek and ascending to walk on the hillside. Be alert at 1.3 miles to make an abrupt right across a usually dry water run, and then swing left at a double-blazed cedar tree. Having returned to Reynolds Creek at 1.8 miles, go upstream a few feet and rock hop the creek at its shallowest point. You may need to search for blazes before moving away from the stream. When you come back to Reynolds Creek at 2.1 miles, the trail can be hard to follow, but just stay between the creek on your left and the ditch (which looks almost like it could be an old railroad grade) on your right. Be very alert at 2.3 miles, where ironwood is spread throughout the forest, as the trail swings right to ascend and descend the hillside around a bend in the stream. Deep red fire pinks dotting the woods in spring and summer, the rippling of little shoals, and reflections of large green cedars may be enticements to linger.

The trail crosses a very old road at 2.5 miles and swings to the right, ascending away from the creek to follow a grassy woods road below cedars and loblolly pine trees. At 2.9 miles, make a right onto the dirt Toll Gate Forest Road, walking by an old clear-cut area on the left before going straight across dirt VA 624 and reentering the woods. That patch of wonderfully lush and green vegetation you walk through at 3.7 miles is poison ivy, so tread carefully as you gradually descend next to the small streambank punctuated by animal dens. Sycamores prosper in the wet bottomland you will be walking on once you begin to parallel Bonbrook Creek. The fording of the creek at 4.3 miles may be a little easier if you go upstream a bit. Be careful here if it has been raining hard; Bonbrook Creek has been known to have 10-foot-high flash floods.

At 4.8 miles, make a left onto paved VA 624, following it for 400 feet before turning right onto a gated forest road. Be alert, because your route will take a left off

this roadway in a short distance, descending along a small creek. Make a left to walk upstream next to the Willis River at 5.4 miles. Although the river is slightly murky, its cool, shallow waters would be nice to wade on those hot August days in the Piedmont. At 5.8 miles, make an abrupt turn to the left away from the river, soon entering the 27-acre Rock Quarry Natural Area. The Department of Forestry has reserved several of these natural areas in a number of the commonwealth's state forests. No recreational developments or logging are permitted in them, as these natural areas are intended to be used as laboratories to study the ecology of the areas they preserve.

After crossing a small stream at 6.2 miles, you will follow a defined footpath to a left turn onto a grassy woods road that will, in turn, bring you to a right onto Rock Quarry Forest Road (dirt VA 623 is four-tenths mile to the left). When the road ends in a forest of tall maple and poplar trees, enter the woods to the left, returning to walk along the river, though it is barely visible through the summer vegetation. It is hard for a camera to capture the colorful mixture of groundcover here—the green of running cedar and hundreds of ferns, the crimson red of fire pinks, and the vivid white and yellow of bloodroot. Close to the river at 6.9 miles is the primitive campsite with a fire ring and pit toilet. A bit later, rise from the waterway for a short distance before dropping to skirt a flat bottomland. The vegetation is so lush and quick growing that, even if it receives maintenance on a regular basis, the trail is likely to be quite overgrown and tricky to follow as it returns to the river through twists of honeysuckle vines. At 7.5 miles, once again you must be very alert when, for no apparent reason, the trail makes an abrupt left turn away from the river; be sure to keep a sharp eye out for the

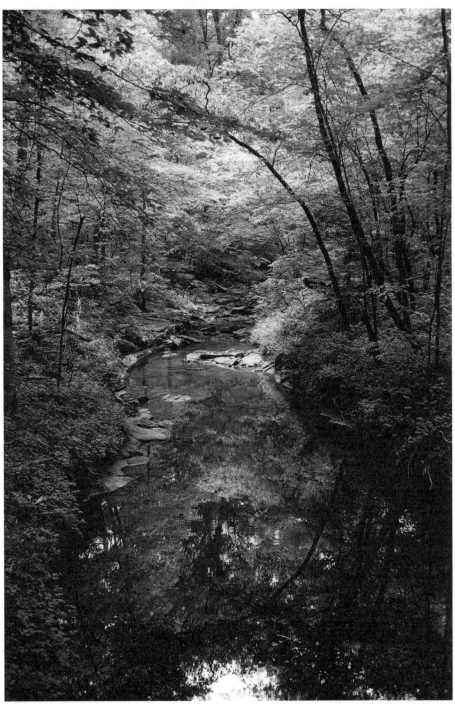

Horn Quarter Creek

blazes (and try not to step on the jack-in-the-pulpits).

Horn Quarter Creek, at 7.8 miles, is quite different from the river. Its clear water and flat rocky bottom, combined with the quiet beauty of the surrounding forest, make this possibly the prettiest spot of the entire hike. Be watching for giant snapping turtles when you cross the creek at 7.9 miles (and be careful crossing any stream around here). They can grow up to 18 inches in length and weigh more than 40 pounds. The one I nearly stepped on as I was fording the creek was well over a foot in size, and it was almost perfectly camouflaged with long fronds of river moss flowing from its back. The turtle's powerful jaw muscles (which it is not reluctant to use) and a belligerent disposition are what give it its name.

After making a left onto an old road, follow the main roadway through the growth emerging after being clear-cut. Just before you enter an older section of woods, make an abrupt right, walking along the edge of the clear-cut area. As the road deteriorates into a creek bed, follow the sudden left onto a faint footpath.

You will soon come onto paved VA 622 (Trents Mill Road), which you should follow past dirt VA 623, the Bear Creek Market, and VA 629 at 9.6 miles. Three hundred feet beyond the intersection, leave VA 622 (across the road from a utility box turnaround) by making a right into a grove of planted loblolly pines, soon to follow an old woods road, and continuing straight past several road junctions. When the woods road ends at 10.1 miles, take the pathway across a small water run. If you have walked the Willis River Trail from its beginning and have had a hard time following its route, you will be happy to know that it will be making use of fairly well-defined pathways from here to the end of the hike.

The grassy road (Forest Trail 24) you cross at 10.3 miles goes right about three-tenths mile to the main road in Bear Creek Lake State Park. The forest is populated by birch, beech, and sycamore trees, some of them especially large along the scenic and winding stream you'll cross at 10.9 miles. Enjoy the walk next to clear-flowing Little Bear Creek with its small ripples, 2-foot-high cascades, and sandy and rocky bottom. Cross over to the other side of the creek at 11.5 miles, continuing upstream amid a garden of mayapple on the ground and pawpaw leaves at eye level.

Pass by a flowing spring, rarer in the Piedmont than in the mountains, under giant grapevines hanging from the trees before crossing dirt Bear Creek Forest Road. After fording Bear Creek at 12.6 miles, bear left onto the grassy woods road with wild rose blooming under the tall pines. A left turn onto dirt Booker Forest Road brings you across paved VA 628 to enter a woods of dogwood and sweet gum.

Descend to cross a stream at 14.4 miles and pass by a walled-in spring (often dry) on your right just before crossing a larger creek; going upstream a bit may help you find a place to rock hop across the water. You are now in the backwater area of Winston Lake, and there are numerous signs of beaver when the trail brings you close to the lake before veering away to ford another tributary. Again, go upstream to find the best place to cross. The ferns and running cedar are a plush carpet from where you look out to the lake and its dam. Descending, you'll make a right onto a handlaid stone pathway, crossing the footbridge to arrive at the Winston Lake picnic shelter and the end of the hike at 15.3 miles.

After having successfully faced the rigors and possible confusions of the Willis River

Trail, you may reach the same conclusion I have: Sometimes it is more interesting and gratifying to hike a route that requires you to use a bit of your own navigational skills rather than one that coddles you with groomed treadways and manicured foliage.

16

Split Rocks/Jefferson's Rock

Total distance (circuit): 6.9 miles

Hiking time: 4 hours

Vertical rise: 850 feet

Maps: USGS 7½´ Harpers Ferry (VA, MD, and WV); Harpers Ferry National Historical Park map

When hiking the Appalachian Trail for the first time, I was so impressed by the view from Split Rocks in Virginia that I spent more than half a day there, etching the scene in my mind. Below the rocks is the Potomac River, punching its way eastward through the Allegheny and Blue Ridge Mountains and meeting up with the waters of the Shenandoah River in front of historic Harpers Ferry. Walking the trail again several years later, I was disappointed to find the AT had been rerouted into Harpers Ferry and away from the rocks. I felt compensated, though, when the trail delivered me to Jefferson's Rock in West Virginia with its different perspective of the same scene. In 1783, Thomas Jefferson was so taken with the view from this point that he described it as "stupendous" and "worth a voyage across the Atlantic."

Thankfully, the old route of the AT is still maintained, and this circuit hike through three different states affords you the opportunity to visit both of these splendid viewpoints. It also provides a chance to explore Harpers Ferry—the site of John Brown's 1859 raid on a federal arsenal and armory—and to walk a distance on the 184-mile towpath of the C&O Canal. Be aware that camping is prohibited on the route of this entire hike because it is all on National Park property. A commercial campground is located on US 340 between Harpers Ferry and Charles Town, West Virginia.

The best, and really only place, to leave your car is in the Park Service parking lot at the end of the bridge immediately after US 340 crosses the Shenandoah River and enters West Virginia.

Start the hike by walking back toward US 340 and turning right to steeply ascend the white-blazed Cliff Trail. Pass by a pathway coming in from the right and the blue-blazed trail to the left (going to the Appalachian Trail Conference headquarters) at 0.3 mile. A trail to the left at 0.6 mile leads to the Park Service training center and the upper town of Harpers Ferry. Just beyond the next trail–going left to the Harper Cemetery–is Jefferson's Rock and the first grand view you were promised.

Folklore states that the flat stone supported by pillars is not the actual rock Jefferson stood upon. Angered by Jefferson's 1800 campaign promise to cut defense spending, a company of soldiers pushed the rock bearing his name over the cliff. Historians generally agree that Jefferson visited this rock formation. Which rock he sat upon, and whether it was the same one that was rolled down the hill, is not known.

You are entering the heart of the city, made a component of the National Park system in 1944. The route is now obviously a tourist pathway, complete with pavement and handrails. As you follow white blazes into town you will pass the ruins of Saint John's Episcopal Church (built in 1852), the interesting Saint Peter's Roman Catholic Church, and the oldest structure in town, the Robert Harper House, constructed between 1775 and 1782. Descend the stone steps that were handcut out of the hillside near the beginning of the 1800s, and turn right onto High Street for a few feet to a left turn onto Shenandoah Street. (A Park Service information center is just up Shenandoah Street. Make a side trip there to obtain additional information about Harpers Ferry; the *Walker's Guide to Harpers Ferry,* available at the bookstore, has additional information on exploring the city.)

A firm believer in individual human freedom, John Brown had hoped to capture the arms stored in the federal arsenal to supply a slave insurrection. You will go by the reconstructed fire engine and guardhouse that he and his men were forced to use as a fort when troops arrived to put an end to his vision.

The peaceful crossing of the Potomac River (and into Maryland) on the footbridge next to the B&O Railroad tracks can become quite exciting if you happen to be on the bridge when a speeding train goes barreling by. Descend the spiral staircase at the far end of the bridge and follow the AT eastward along the C&O Canal towpath. From the late 1700s, individual canals provided water routes around falls and rapids, and by the 1830s, the C&O Canal had linked Harpers Ferry with Washington, D.C. Today the towpath is a National Scenic Trail that can be hiked from the nation's capital to Cumberland, Maryland. A guidebook for the entire route is available at the

Harpers Ferry bookstore. Looking at the perfectly cut stone in the retaining walls of lock number two, at 1.7 miles, and the nearly level route of the towpath, you may find it hard to imagine the intense hand labor that must have gone into building the canal.

Just before going under the US 340 bridge, take leave of the AT by crossing a wooden footbridge over the canal and ascending on paved Sandy Hook Road. Be alert at 2.4 miles! Leave the road and make a left to rise on the blocked-off old access road and follow the US 340 bridge across the Potomac River. The sidewalk is narrow and tractor trailers go whizzing by at speeds that are surely well over the speed limit, so be careful!

Also, use caution as you continue on the narrow shoulder along US 340 (passing by a gas station/grocery store) to turn left onto the Loudoun Heights Trail, identified by blue blazes and a trailhead sign at 3.5 miles. Gradually ascend on an old woods road copiously endowed with growths of poison ivy. The route leaves the roadbed at 3.6 miles, beginning a series of switchbacks. A small break in the vegetation at 3.9 miles provides a hint of the more spectacular view to come. You will reach that view by turning right onto a 50-foot trail at 4 miles to come to Split Rocks. Far below the rocks, shimmering ripples and bits of whitewater in the Shenandoah and Potomac Rivers reflect the light of bright sunny days. Spanning the Potomac River upstream from where the two rivers meet is the B&O Railroad bridge. The attached footbridge is the route of the AT, which you made use of a few miles back. All of Harpers Ferry is spread out before you. Saint Peter's Catholic Church, with its prominent steeple, sits on the cliffs overlooking the Shenandoah, while Hilltop House Hotel,

Handcarved stair steps in Harpers Ferry

high above the Potomac, towers over the historic district. Almost directly north of you are the cliffs of Maryland Heights. (A historical trail makes a circuit route around Maryland Heights, and it is an extremely scenic hike that you should consider doing while in the area. Check at the Park Service visitor center, or in *50 Hikes in Maryland*, another guide in this 50 Hikes series, for more information.)

From Split Rocks, the Loudoun Heights Trail first ascends through hemlocks and then switchbacks into a stand of pawpaw and poison ivy. The utility line right-of-way at 4.5 miles provides additional views, with an increased range to where the AT ascends Weverton Cliffs in the east and continues northward on the ridgeline of South Mountain. The right-of-way again gives a view at 4.8 miles. The trail has now reached the height of the land and will continue with only minor ups and downs on the Virginia–West Virginia border, going by grapevines hanging from oak trees and draping over sassafras. You may have a hard time avoiding poison ivy here; in late summer it reaches more than waist high. The stone foundations you pass at 5.3 miles are the remains of fortifications built during the Civil War.

The Loudoun Heights Trail comes to an end at 5.6 miles. Make a right onto the white-blazed AT, descending into West Virginia and vast fields of poison ivy and going by pits and ditches in the earth, remnants of the charcoal-producing days of the 1800s. Continue the descent into an attractive forest of hardy oaks and maples above an understory of dogwood, soon crossing paved Chestnut Hill Road. The songbirds are especially active in the morning in the newer-growth forest on the other side of the road, while the call of the pileated woodpecker is heard just about anytime of day. Road sounds intrude on the magical feeling of hemlock groves as the trail switchbacks and descends stone steps to come to US 340 at 6.7 miles. Follow the bridge over the Shenandoah River, crossing to the other side of the bridge when there is a break in the heavy traffic speeding by you. Be careful! The hike ends as you return to your car at 6.9 miles.

III

Blue Ridge and Massanutten Mountains

17

Little Sluice Mountain and Cedar Creek

Total distance (circuit): 11.7 miles

Hiking time: 7½ hours

Vertical rise: 2,080 feet

Maps: USGS 7½′ Wolf Gap
(WV and VA); USGS 7½′ Woodstock (VA
and WV)

A look at the Virginia–West Virginia border on a highway map shows large blank spaces between paved roadways. A topography characterized by long, high ridgelines and steeply sloping hillsides permits most modern highways to cross only in the few naturally occurring gaps in the mountains' rugged profiles. At one time, however, dirt logging, mining, and carriage roads carried a bustling variety of vehicles and people up creek valleys and over mountain summits. Those days are gone, but this hike makes use of many of these old roads, most now little more than footpaths, to explore environs that are once again isolated from outside influences. In addition to the seclusion, highlights include possible abundant wildlife, a strong-flowing high-elevation spring, a grandstand viewpoint, and the option of taking a short section of unmarked trail to hone your route-finding skills.

A long walk of nearly 12 miles over rugged terrain, it would be best to do this hike when the daylight hours are many, or as a 2-day, overnight backpack.

Drive to the trailhead by exiting I-81 at Woodstock and following VA 42 westward for about 7 miles to Columbia Furnace, where you turn onto VA 675 for close to 0.5 mile. Make a right onto VA 608, which soon becomes Forest Development Road 88. Keep right on FDR 88 where FDR 92 comes in from the left, pass by the Little Sluice Mountain trailhead 0.5 mile from this junction, and continue just less than 3 more miles to the large parking area at the end of FDR 88. (Depending on the time of year

and conditions, you may find a part of FDR 88 gated or impassable to low-riding vehicles and will have to walk the extra distance to the treilhead.)

Park your automobile and walk back down FDR 88 about 800 feet. The sign for Bread Road Trail {FS 411} may be obscure or nonexistent, but look for faint orange blazes marking an old woods road that ascends into the forest on your right. (The trailhead is directly across FDR 88 from a small car pullout on your left.) The route received its name in the early 1800s when wagons used it to haul food to charcoal makers working on Little Sluice Mountain, producing fuel for nearby furnaces.

In less than 200 feet you need to stay straight when your road crosses another old woods road. Soon the route swings to the left to begin a gradual ascent by contouring around the side of the mountain. The roadway swings right at 0.75 mile, becoming very steep with grades of 30 percent; the footing is rough and rocky in spots. The trail will level out a bit as it enters an obviously older-growth hardwood forest in 1 mile.

The ridgeline of Little Sluice Mountain is reached in 1.3 miles. A small clearing provides a limited view into Stoney Creek Valley and across to Big Schloss (see Hike 18) on the Virginia–West Virginia border. Turn right and gradually descend along the purple-blazed dirt road (open to motor vehicles, well-used, and busy during hunting season, so take proper precautions), which is Little Sluice Mountain Trail {FS 401}. (To the left the road drops down the mountain to FDR 88 in about two miles.)

A low point is reached at 2 miles, where you begin a gentle ascent of about 500 feet to cross a spur ridge whose flat knob would provide a pleasant campsite. A very reliable piped spring is about 60 feet up the dirt road

that comes from the right at 2.3 miles. Continue on the main route, passing by a hunter's camp known locally as Deer Horn Camp. The quality of this spot as a campsite varies widely from year to year, depending on the amount of use or care—or both—that it receives.

Wild turkeys need great expanses of undeveloped, wooded country in order to prosper, and the extensive landholdings of the George Washington National Forest in this part of Appalachia support a large population of these birds. Wild turkeys seem to prefer walking through the forest rather than flying among the trees, and chances are good during the summer of seeing a family flock making use of the same road you're using; the sexes tend to separate during the winter months. Ranging from 2½ feet to 4 feet in size, turkeys are almost constantly hunting for food. Scratchings along the edge of the road may mark where they have been digging for beetles and other insects; searches for their favorite nuts, such as acorns, leave large areas of the forest floor cleared of decaying leaves and other small deadfall. In Virginia, poison ivy makes up about 5 percent of turkeys' diets.

Ignore the old road coming in from the right at 2.5 miles; ascend and descend another spur ridge. Begin nearly level walking at 3.1 miles, passing a small (maybe dry) water run and several good campsites. A riot of ferns adds to the beauty and color of this moist, hidden mountain valley located miles from the nearest paved highway. Be alert at 3.8 miles, where the road you have been following makes an apparent swing to the left; your route makes a hard right to begin following the Tuscarora/Three Ponds Trail {FS 1013}. (Some maps may show this to be FS 405.)

You have crossed into West Virginia,

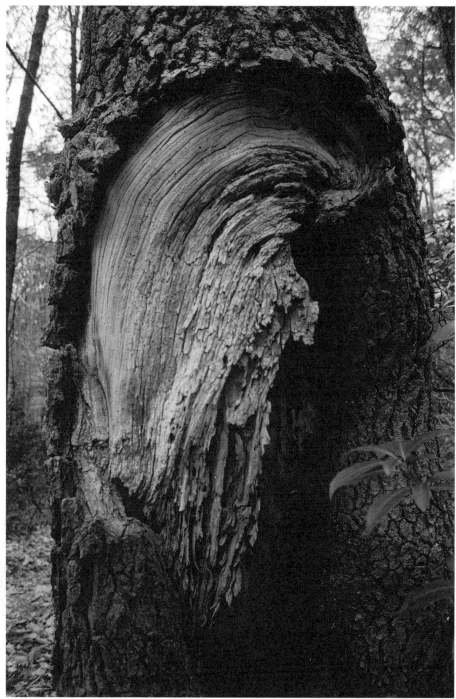
Wound in tree showing growth cycles

and just before cresting the ridgeline at 4.5 miles a small outcropping to the left furnishes a view of Mill and North Mountains and Racer Camp Hollow.

Begin gradually descending, looking for a white-blazed trail (White Rocks Trail {FS 513}) coming in from the right at 5.1 miles. Take this rough, rocky, steep (53 percent grade!), downhill, 1/3-mile path for the best view you'll have on this hike. From your perch high atop White Rock Cliff, the Cedar Creek watershed is below you. Directly ahead, on the Little North Mountain ridgeline, is the obvious depression of Sheffer Gap. The Shenandoah Valley is visible through the gap, while Massanutten Mountain and the ridges of Shenandoah National Park can be seen far to the east.

Return to the main trail, turn right, and continue descending the mountain. Avoid the trail coming in from the left at 6.2 miles, keeping to the right as the treadway becomes softer and grassier. This would be a nice spot for a high mountain campsite. You must be alert again at 6.5 miles—purple-blazed Sulphur Spring Trail {FS 414} is more or less straight ahead, but you need to bear right onto the route that now looks more like a pathway instead of an old road. You have returned to Virginia as you enter a large stand of pines for the first time on this hike. Emerge from the pines at 6.9 miles to descend steeply, soon passing a large outcropping with trees growing out of the rock.

Once again, be alert at 7.8 miles. Avoid the trail to the left; instead, bear right, cross a small water run, and continue to follow blue blazes. It is time for you to make a decision when you step onto gravel FDR 1863 at 8.5 miles. In order to avoid often-wet land near the creek, Cedar Creek Trail {FS 573} was rerouted onto higher ground a number of years ago. You can hike its

present-day route by turning right to follow the yellow-blazed road (which soon becomes a dirt woods road) through the gate and past a few old mine sites. This is the preferred route if you are hiking during high-water times, want to be sure to keep your feet dry at any time of the year, or are uncomfortable about not following a well-marked, obvious pathway. The second choice follows blazes for a short distance before turning onto the old and still discernible (though unblazed) route of the Cedar Creek Trail. It is a good option for those of you who feel adventurous and wish to gain a little confidence in your own route-finding skills. Both choices are about equidistant and join back together at the 10.3-mile point; this description follows the second option.

From where you emerged onto FDR 1863, cross the road and continue to follow blue blazes into the woods. Your route soon joins another road, swings right, and crosses Cedar Creek at 8.7 miles.

Leave the roadbed at 8.8 miles to parallel it on the left. The treadway may be faint, but continue to follow blue blazes to cross a small water run and rejoin the road.

Important! At 9 miles the blue-blazed Tuscarora Trail (some maps and other sources may refer to it by its older name of Big Blue Trail) makes a left turn uphill as it works its way eastward to cross Massanutten Mountain and end in Shenandoah National Park. You need to bear right onto the trail going downhill to recross Cedar Creek in 500 feet.

Looking down so that you can see where to place your feet on the uneven treadway, you will probably see numerous deer tracks in the soil of this moist bottomland. A close examination of these tracks can tell you what the deer were doing when they passed this way. If the points (which point in the direction the deer was going) of the two sections of the hoof are nearly touching each other, then the deer was probably on a "leisurely stroll." When the print shows the two halves splayed, the deer was on the run.

The route may be unmarked, but you can see that you are obviously following an old, sometimes washed-out roadbed as you pass through a wildlife clearing at 9.6 miles and by another one at 10 miles. At 10.3 miles, join up with yellow-blazed Cedar Creek Trail and keep to the left on the old road.

A different old road comes in from the right at 11.2 miles; continue left and pass through another clearing. If you arrive in this final clearing toward the end of the day and don't mind flashlight-walking the last half a mile to your car at 11.7 miles, consider spending the twilight hours in this small field. This is the time of day many forest creatures become active, and you just might see some deer, a raccoon, a skunk, an opossum, or if you're lucky, a bobcat. You are almost guaranteed to hear at least one owl hoot, if not many, as night overtakes day.

18

Big Schloss

Total distance (round trip): 4.4 miles

Hiking time: 2¾ hours

Vertical rise: 710 feet

Map: USGS 7½' Wolf Gap

Big Schloss sits high atop the ridgeline that marks the border of Virginia with West Virginia. A short hike from Wolf Gap along the spine of Mill Mountain will bring you to this sandstone outcropping named by German immigrants. *Schloss* translates as a palace or castle, and once you stand on this natural structure you are sure to be as impressed as the early settlers were. The massive outcropping juts upward from the mixed hardwood forest, rising above the trees to permit a superb view of the surrounding countryside. Luckily, because most of the land surrounding Big Schloss is national forest, the scenery remains somewhat the same as it appeared back in the settlers' days. There are few places like this left in the eastern part of America—your eyes can gaze out upon ridgelines, forests, and valleys that show remarkably few signs of the 20th century.

Big Schloss is reached by exiting I-81 at Woodstock and following VA 42 westward for about 7 miles. In Columbia Furnace turn onto and ascend VA 675 for 6.5 miles to Wolf Gap Recreation Area. Facilities include tent and trailer sites, a hand pump for water, picnic grounds, and pit toilets.

From the large parking area in the Wolf Gap Campground, walk to orange-blazed Mill Mountain Trail {FS 1004}, which is located close to campsite nine. Begin a series of switchbacks at 0.25 mile as the ascent becomes a little steeper.

At 0.75 mile you will reach the ridge, where you should bear left onto a narrower pathway. In winter, your objective—the large rocks of Big Schloss—can be seen directly ahead through the trees. Soon a

Bridge to Big Schloss

couple of rock outcroppings to the right provide excellent views. Rolling out to the distance in the east are Little Sluice Mountain (see Hike 17), the Shenandoah Valley, Massanutten Mountain (see Hikes 27, 28, and 29), and the ridgelines of the mountains along Skyline Drive (see Hikes 19 through 26).

There are several obviously well-used campsites along this ridge. Because this is national forest you could camp just about anywhere you wish. However, you should be conscious that this is a popular hike and that practicing no-trace camping will help preserve the beauty of the area. This means looking for places that have not been impacted already. In addition, although campfires are always nice to sit around in the evening, they are very hard on the land. Fires not only leave charred spots but also destroy nutrients in the topsoil. Some places are so fragile that it could be years before any new growth will appear where a campfire has been. Be kind to the soil and carry a backpacking stove if you plan to do any camping. (The Forest Service has provided fire rings and grates at the Wolf Gap Recreation Area if you do wish to do your cooking over a fire.)

After walking level for a while, you will descend slightly at 1.3 miles only to begin another rise along the rocky crest of the mountain. Pay attention at 1.9 miles as the Mill Mountain Trail continues to the left, connecting with other trails of the George Washington National Forest; you want to bear right and ascend on white-blazed Big Schloss Trail {FS 1004A}.

Arrive at Big Schloss in 2.2 miles, take the wooden bridge across a cleft in the rock outcropping, and break out into the open. Walk all the way to the edge of Big Schloss for your outrageously wonderful reward. To the west is Trout Run Valley and Long Mountain in West Virginia, to the north is Anderson Ridge, while to the east is a repeat of the views you saw from the rock outcroppings you passed earlier. To the south Tibet Knob rises like a cone from Great North Mountain's ridgeline. The first hatching box of the Forest Service's project to reintroduce the peregrine falcon to the area was placed at Big Schloss. If you are extremely lucky, you may see one of these rare birds, also known as duck hawks, flying through the air with strong and rapid wing strokes.

Return to your car by retracing your steps.

19

Marys Rock

Total distance (round trip): 3.6 miles

Hiking time: 2½ hours

Vertical rise: 1,240 feet

Maps: USGS 7½′ Thornton Gap

To a geologist or a geographer, the Blue Ridge Mountains stretch from northern Georgia to central Pennsylvania. Yet in many people's minds, the Blue Ridge is associated with Virginia. In the northern part of the commonwealth, this mountain range is the rampart that separates the rolling topography of the Piedmont from the fertile soil of the Shenandoah Valley. Most geologists believe that about 200 to 300 million years ago the Blue Ridge Mountains were as tall and rugged as the Rockies, and it was the process of erosion that created the mountains we see today. Rock that was once part of a high peak is washed down the mountainside, swept off in rain storms, or carried away by melting snows. Some of those tiny bits of the mountain are deposited in the valleys, raising the lowlands in elevation to form a gentler terrain. Some of the rock particles move on to add minerals and nutrients to Piedmont farmlands, and others continue downstream, eventually reaching the Chesapeake Bay or the Atlantic Ocean.

Encompassing the present-day crest of the Blue Ridge Mountains and its hundreds of attendant spur ridges, which spread in all directions like twisted and gnarled fingers, Shenandoah National Park stretches from Front Royal to Waynesboro, a distance of almost 75 miles and an area of nearly 200,000 acres. Congress authorized the establishment of the park in 1926 but provided no funds for land acquisition. We can thank the Commonwealth of Virginia for making it a reality. The Virginia Assembly appropriated $1 million, and about $1.2 million in donations from various sources (much of it from individual citizens) made it possible to purchase nearly 4,000 tracts of private land, which were deeded to the federal government in 1935. Some of this land was not sold willingly, and there is still a deep-seated resentment of the government by some of the families who were relocated from their ancestral homes. We should not minimize the loss experienced by these families, yet there have been many overall benefits to the land by establishing the park. As the 20th century began, second- and third-growth forests, logged since the early 1700s, covered much of what is now the park. Today, most signs of lumbering, as well as those of grazing and farming, have been largely erased through the growth of the forests. First came shrubs, pines, and black locusts; now 95 percent of the park is nearing a climax forest of oak, hickory, yellow poplar, and other hardwoods. This regeneration is so complete that 40 percent of the park was designated a wilderness area in 1976. Through the years, countless millions of Americans and foreign visitors have been able to enjoy these parklands, which, if they had remained in the hands of a few, would have either continued to deteriorate or, based upon what has happened in other mountain areas of Virginia, been turned into housing developments or high-priced resorts. Today, through law, the park cannot spend any funds to acquire new lands; property can be added to the park only if it is given as a gift.

President Franklin Roosevelt officially dedicated the park in 1936, as men of the Civilian Conservation Corps busily built trails, shelters, fire roads, and various visitors facilities. The 105-mile Skyline Drive was essentially completed in 1939. Today the park has four campgrounds, modern

lodging facilities and a set of rustic cabins, two visitor centers, an information center, and picnic areas.

There are many legends and stories about the origin of the word *shenandoah,* but perhaps the most romantic and beautiful is that it is a derivative of a Native American word meaning "daughter of the stars." When applied to Shenandoah National Park, those words seem more than appropriate, for the park is truly a stellar treasure in the vast system of public lands that citizens of the United States own in common. More than a dozen waterfalls crash down steep slopes, over 200 species of birds, including 35 kinds of warblers, have been recorded in the park, and over 1,200 species of vascular plants can be found within its borders. Turkeys, bobcats, raccoons, and skunks inhabit the region in significant numbers, and you have a chance of seeing black bears on backcountry hikes. There are so many deer that it has almost become common knowledge in Virginia that if you want to see a deer, you simply go to Shenandoah. The best feature of the park for walkers and hikers is that its network of more than 500 miles of trails makes its vast acreage easily navigable. Because the pathways are so well marked, and many of them are graded for gradual ascents and descents, the park is a good breaking-in place for novice hikers.

The majority of the park's trails originate on or near the Skyline Drive, which is accessible from US 340 in Front Royal and US 250 and I-64 east of Waynesboro. US 211 crosses the drive at milepost 31.5 and US 33 crosses it at milepost 65.7. A fee is charged to enter the park.

While hiking, please be sure to obey the regulations instituted by the Park Service in order to reduce the impact of approximately 2 million visitors a year. Wood fires are permitted only in fireplaces in developed campgrounds, picnic areas, and certain trail shelters. No fires are allowed in the backcountry, so bring your backpacking stove if you want any hot meals on your hikes. You must obtain a free backcountry camping permit (available at entrance stations, visitor centers, and some self-registering trailheads) before taking off on any overnight trips. The Old Rag Shelter and the four Byrds Nest shelters are for picnics only and may not be used for overnight accommodations except in the case of extreme weather conditions. Huts along the AT are intended to be used only by long-distance hikers. All dogs must be kept on a leash and are prohibited on certain trails. There are, of course, numerous other regulations, and you will be given a list of the most pertinent ones when you receive your camping permit. In addition, be sure to employ no-trace hiking and camping methods.

The trek to Marys Rock is a good introduction to the park's trails. Using a section of the Appalachian Trail, the hike gains its elevation on a well-graded, switchbacked pathway leading to one of the most easily reached 360-degree views in the park. Along the way you will pass through tunnels of mountain laurel and, except during the coldest months of the year, a grand array of wildflowers. The trailhead is located next to the Panorama Restaurant in Thornton Gap, at the intersection of US 211 and Skyline Drive. One of the parking areas is located on US 211, making the restaurant accessible without passing through the park entrance station.

Enter the woods on a wide trail from the turnaround circle at the end of the parking lot and intersect the Appalachian Trail in a few feet. The AT descends right for one-tenth mile to US 211, but you want to follow it to the left, ascending through a profuse growth of mountain laurel, whose blossoms will burst forth in late spring. A little farther up the trail, stinging nettle can be almost as abundant as the laurel. Brushing up against the nettle will give the tiny, stiff hairs an opportunity to scratch your skin and deposit an irritant that may itch for the rest of the day. One experience of this kind will, no doubt, keep you on the watch for the nettle.

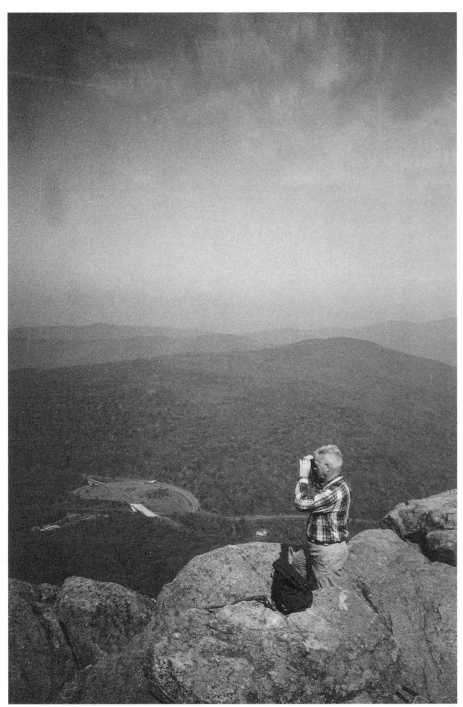

The view into Thornton Gap from Marys Rock

At 0.6 mile, a break in the vegetation provides a view of Thornton Gap and some of the mountains of the park to the north. At 0.9 mile, after switchbacking a couple of times, pass by several overhanging rocks that could become small emergency shelters in case of a rain shower. Cushiony moss growing on boulders along the trail helps soften the look and feel of the rock field you walk through.

Although most of the trail you have been walking on was built by the CCC in the 1930s, the section at 1.2 miles in particular bears the unmistakable signs of the Corps' high-quality handiwork. The pathway rises at a more-or-less gradual rate and is almost wide enough for two people to walk abreast in some places. The rock walls that were built during the Great Depression to shore up this sidehill trail are still performing their duty. Trail crews of today do an admirable job of maintaining, rehabilitating, and reconstructing pathways, but trails of the CCC will still be with us for a long time.

After making a couple more switchbacks, come to an intersection at 1.7 miles. (If you can arrange a car shuttle, you could turn this walk into a one-way hike. After visiting Marys Rock, return to this point and follow the AT southward to a left turn onto Meadow Spring Trail. That trail will drop you to the Skyline Drive at milepoint 33.5. Total distance of the full hike would be about three and a half miles.) Make a right and at 1.8 miles arrive at Marys Rock, made up of granodiorite that geologists believe to be at least 1 billion years old.

Marys Rock is a favorite birders' perch to watch the fall hawk migration. The annual procession may begin as early as August, when one or two hawks a day have been spotted heading south. The watching becomes most spectacular in mid-September through early October as, in some years, several thousand broadwing hawks a day have been seen winging by. Various other hawks, such as the red-tailed and the red-shouldered, keep birdwatchers coming back to Marys Rock into November and even December.

The 360-degree view is obtained by scrambling 80 feet up to the top of the huge rock outcrop—not advisable in wet or windy weather. To the north is the restaurant and road intersection from which you began the hike. Pass Mountain makes up the ridgeline closest to you, and behind it are the Three Sisters and Neighbor, Knob, and Hogback Mountains. Scanning to the east you may be able to make out the gorge of Little Devils Stairs between Little Hogback and Mount Marshall. The Piedmont is clearly visible beyond Oventop and Jenkins Mountain. Southward are the Pinnacle and Stony Man (see Hike 20) while to the west is Massanutten Mountain (see Hikes 27, 28, and 29) rising up to bisect the Shenandoah Valley.

I must admit that, after having visited here countless times, my favorite activity at Marys Rock now has little to do with birdwatching or identifying distant mountains. Rather, it involves picking the perfect-weather day, beginning the hike early in the morning, and carrying a big lunch, gobs of munchies, a quart or two of lemonade, and a good book up to the summit. I pick a nice flat spot on the rock and spend the rest of the day soaking up warm sunshine, eating, reading, and glancing up every so often to gaze upon the serene beauty in which I've enveloped myself. Come here once and you will find that you come here often.

Stony Man

Total distance (circuit): 3.5 miles

Hiking time: 2 hours

Vertical rise: 760 feet

Maps: USGS 7½′ Big Meadows; USGS 7½′ Old Rag Mountain; Shenandoah National Park Whiteoak Canyon and Skyland map

George Freeman Pollock opened his mountain resort, Skyland, to the public in 1888. A carriage road from Luray wound up the western slope of the Blue Ridge, carrying his guests to the lodge sitting below Stony Man. (The road is still in fairly good shape and can be walked from the resort down to the park boundary on the edge of Page Valley.) The resort was an almost immediate success as flatlanders, politicians, and business leaders found it to be a congenial place to enjoy the beauty of the mountains and escape the heat of summers in the cities, valleys, and Piedmont. Yet, unlike many private landowners who, even today, oppose the establishment of federal- or state-protected lands, Pollock was a loyal supporter of Shenandoah National Park and worked diligently to make it become a reality. Today's visitors to Skyland have their choice of nearly 200 rooms (some in cabins) in which to stay, can enjoy their meals in the dining room, and can take guided horseback trips originating from the resort's stables.

Park Service history records show that Pollock first came to the mountains on a scientific expedition to study mammal life on Stony Man for the Smithsonian Institution. Pollock's father had been part owner of a mining operation that had begun around the turn of the 19th century, when chunks of copper were found scattered about the summit of Stony Man. The ore, however, proved to be hard to work and operations ceased by the mid-1800s. Evidence of the mining can still be found, but only by those who are willing to search for it, as the land has had well over a century to hide the scars.

The first part of this hike to 4,010-foot Stony Man, the second-highest point in the park, is an extremely popular one, as you have to gain only about 300 feet in order to reach an Olympian 180-degree view. Most people, though, just follow what is known as the Stony Man Nature Trail (it has signs keyed to a brochure) to the summit and retrace their steps back to the parking area. However, in this hike you will continue northward from Stony Man on the Appalachian Trail (which reaches its highest point in the park on the side of the mountain), leaving the bulk of the crowd behind, to come to another viewpoint on Little Stony Man before following a historic route through a jade forest of evergreens and mountain laurels to return to the point of origin.

You reach the trailhead by driving into the north entrance of Skyland (Skyline Drive mile 41.7) and making a right into the first parking lot. White blazes mark the pathway you want to take as the Appalachian Trail, in addition to a trailhead sign that identifies it as the Stony Man Nature Trail. Pick up a nature trail pamphlet from the dispenser and begin the gradual ascent into an oak forest. (If there are no brochures in the container you can obtain one from the Byrd Visitor Center at Skyline Drive mile 51.)

The silvery-gray logs you see on the ground are all that are left of the once-mighty chestnut trees that used to be so numerous they made up over 25 percent of the trees in Shenandoah's forest. The chestnut blight, a fungus disease accidentally introduced into North America from Asia near the beginning of the 20th century, removed the chestnuts from the landscape of the continent by the end of the 1930s. The chestnut had played an important role in the daily life of Blue Ridge Mountain residents. Being plentiful, the nuts were easily gathered in the fall, providing the mountain people with a supplement to their diet and a quick source of cash when sold by the bushel. The tree's timber was used to build log homes and durable fences to keep livestock from roaming too far. Its bark, rich in tannin, was stripped and sold to tanneries for the processing of hides. The inner bark also contains the tannin, which makes the wood resistant to decay and explains why this wood has yet to completely rot away. The roots and stumps of these fallen trees still produce sprouts that grow for a while before they become fungus-infected and die. The hope is that someday the sprouts will be able to resist the disease or that scientists will develop a strain that will not succumb to the blight.

You will walk in a fir and spruce forest, and this is your chance to learn how to tell them apart. The easiest way is to shake hands with their branches: the balsam fir will feel soft and welcoming to the touch, and while the red spruce's sharp, stiff needles won't puncture your skin, you certainly will not want to give it a firm handshake. Another way to distinguish the two is that the spruce's needles extend out from all sides of the branch, while the fir's needles have two white stripes on the bottom and grow with only two rows, one on each side of the branch.

Come to an intersection at 0.4 mile. To the left it is four-tenths mile to the Skyland road and to the right, six-tenths mile to Little Stony Man Cliffs. You want to continue straight ahead on the nature trail, following blue blazes and keeping to the right at the next intersection to begin the loop trail toward the summit. This is a harsher environment, as evidenced by the stunted trees and those struck by lightning. At 0.5 mile there is a view to the northeast of Nicholson Hollow. According to Pollock, years before the establishment of the national park Aaron Nicholson and his relatives declared the hollow to be a "free state" and not subject to the laws and taxes of Virginia.

Arrive at another four-way intersection at 0.7 mile, where you want to make a right to come to the "face" of Stony Man for a grand view. Below is Page Valley, with Massanutten Mountain on its far side, and the town of Luray, whose nearby caverns are the largest in the Shenandoah Valley. The buildings of Skyland are nearby, while the prominent peak to the south is Hawksbill (see Hike 23). The rocky summit you see to the north is Marys Rock (see Hike 19) and the cliffs closer by are Little Stony Man, where you will be standing a short time from now.

Retrace your steps back to the four-way intersection. Left is the way you came up and right is the horse trail; you want to keep straight, walking by gnarled tree trunks. At 1 mile you'll have returned to the loop-trail intersection, where you don't want to make the hard left but instead keep more or less straight to come to another four-way intersection. Straight ahead is the Stony Man Nature Trail going back to the parking lot; to the right is the horse trail, which leads four-tenths mile to the road. You want to take the AT to the left, descending north through a heavy oak forest. The oak trees became dominant once the chestnuts had been killed by the blight.

Arrive at the cliffs of Little Stony Man at 1.7 miles, where you can look back up to the rock "face" of Stony Man. Switchback down, away from the cliffs. At 1.9 miles the AT goes right for four-tenths mile to the Little Stony Man Parking Area (Skyline Drive mile 39.1); you will go left to begin following blue-blazed Passamaquoddy Trail. The present-day path follows the general route of the original trail Pollock laid out in the 1930s. He evidently named the trail after himself, because he stated that the word means "abounding in pollock" in the language of Maine's Passamaquoddy Indians. You'll soon pass by the lower cliffs of Little Stony Man and begin walking into a grand and deep forest of large oaks and evergreens. When the mountain laurel begins to become abundant, you may find

The Passamaquoddy Trail looking out to lower Little Stony Man Cliffs

it hard to believe there were once mining operations going on in the area.

Pay attention when you come to the intersection at 2.9 miles. Do not continue with the blue blazes, which follow the road four-tenths mile to the Skyland dining room. Instead, bear left onto the yellow-blazed horse trail, still passing through a wonderful evergreen forest. This is one of my favorite spots because it is so quickly accessible from either the dining room or the nature trail parking lot, yet it seems as if almost no one ever walks this portion of the trail. Even horse traffic appears to be light. However, when you come to the next intersection you'll turn right onto a well-used bridle path. Make a left to return to your car, finishing this 3.5-mile walk.

21

Old Rag

Total distance (circuit): 7.7 miles

Hiking time: 6 hours

Vertical rise: 2,300 feet

Maps: USGS 7½′ Old Rag Mountain; Shenandoah National Park Old Rag Trail map

The hike up the Ridge Trail to the summit of Old Rag is one of the most exhausting 3-mile climbs in all of Virginia. Most people who have done the trip also say that it is by far one of the most fun excursions they have ever made. In order to reach the mountaintop, you're going to scramble over giant boulders, slide down bare rocks, crawl through narrow tunnels, and climb a most unique staircase. If you are mentally prepared for these stone formations, you will feel like a kid again, bouncing around on a giant playground. If you view them as obstacles, you'll probably have a miserable time. As a bit of compensation, the route down the mountain is relatively easy, dropping first on a well-graded trail and then descending along gently sloping fire roads.

Be forewarned. This is an extremely popular hike. So popular, in fact, that the Park Service had to build a parking lot—an amazingly large one almost a mile from the trailhead—to keep people from parking on private property or leaving automobiles in the road while the owners went on a hike. A fee, which is paid at the trailhead, is charged to hike this route. Like the Cedar Run/Whiteoak Canyon hike (see Hike 22), I contemplated not including Old Rag in this book because of its heavy use but decided that the mountain is such a wonderful experience that excluding it would be a disservice to you. To avoid the largest crowds I suggest you undertake the hike during the middle of the week and don't even consider it anytime during the autumn "leaf season." Also, to impact this heavily used area as little as possible, please make

this just a day trip and don't camp anywhere along the route. (Park regulations prohibit camping above 2,800 feet in elevation.)

Old Rag is an outlying mountain, not a part of the main crest of the Blue Ridge. The trailhead is reached by taking VA 231 for 12.5 miles north of Madison (coming from the north this would be about 8 miles south of Sperryville); then turn onto VA 602, heading west toward Nethers. There's a small spot next to the road where you can pull off to eyeball the craggy ridgeline of Old Rag as it rises high above fields of planted crops. You want to keep left 0.5 mile beyond the turn (do not cross the bridge) as VA 602 ends and becomes VA 601. A short distance later VA 601 ends and you want to keep left again, onto VA 707. Once more, this time in Nethers, you'll want to keep to the left, now taking VA 600 instead of continuing on VA 707 to the right. At 0.5 mile from this intersection you'll pass the "overflow" parking area. Continue on for 0.8 mile, hopefully to find an open space in the upper parking lot. Even in your car, as you drive up this one-lane road to the trailhead, you'll begin to experience the enchantment of wild places when you see Brokenback Run churning its way over giant boulders and through an emerald forest of hemlocks and ferns.

Take a few moments to read the information on the bulletin board before ascending on the wide and obviously well-used pathway. At 0.2 mile, a nicely flowing spring nurtures patches of chickweed, trillium, and ferns. At 0.5 mile, the hemlocks are replaced by a deciduous forest, but bluets, purple and yellow violets, and bloodroot remain abundant. In 1 mile you'll make a switchback and leave behind the sound of the small creek making its way down the mountain. Continuing with the ascent, you can see, through the leaves and at rock outcrops, the various

hollows—Corbin, Weakley, and Nicholson—north of Old Rag. In the spring, the hillside at 1.7 miles is covered by a great field of trillium just before you step over a water run lined with skunk cabbage.

Your gentle stroll is now over as the trail becomes steeper and the rock scramble begins. The rocks at 2.3 miles allow you to survey the lands in and around Nicholson Hollow where the Hughes River begins its journey from the Blue Ridge to meet the Hazel River in the Piedmont, about 10 miles east of the park boundary. Look above you to see a part of the rugged ridgeline and some of the rock outcrops you'll soon be traversing. A few steps farther on will give you a different perspective on the flatter lands to the southeast. As you continue to ascend, think of the huge boulders that you're going to have to use your hands, arms, legs, knees, and feet to climb over, under, and around as nature's giant "jungle gym." Doing this will keep you from becoming frustrated by how slowly you're now progressing up the mountain. At 2.6 miles, crawl through a 40-foot boulder tunnel and then take a staircase into a narrow cleft. The forces of wind, rain, ice, snow, and sunshine have weathered ages-old hardened lava into these 11 nicely spaced steps.

Advance, with periods of boulder-climbing, until you reach the concrete post marking the 3,268-foot summit of Old Rag at 3.2 miles. Leave the blue blazes and go right to reap the benefits of your labors. Park personnel have told me that they know of only four places in the national park where it's possible to obtain a 360-degree view—and you're now standing at one of them. Just about due west is Hawksbill (see Hike 23) and to the right of it and below Bettys Rock you will see the whitewater of the falls tumbling down Whiteoak Canyon (see Hike 22). Stony Man (see Hike 20) is a little farther to the right, while almost due north you can

The highest rock on the summit of Old Rag

make out the granite bluffs of Marys Rock (see Hike 19). Below you is Weakley Hollow, which you will be following to return to your car. To the east and south is the great expanse of the Piedmont. As your gaze circles back around to the mountains, spot outlying Big Tom and Doubletop Mountains before your eyes come to rest on the green fields of Big Meadows on the main crest of the Blue Ridge.

After enjoying your lunch, wander a bit more on the summit, taking in the various viewpoints and studying the rock under your feet. The Old Rag granite contains peanut-sized bits of feldspar and blue quartz. The quartz erodes more quickly, leaving little bits of the feldspar jutting up from the surface of the rock. Please don't be tempted to take any samples as souvenirs; in any case, rock in the park is just as protected by law as are the plants, animals, and artifacts.

After you have explored the mountaintop to your heart's content, return to the trail, following the blue blazes through mountain laurel on the southwest side of Old Rag where you look down onto Byrds Nest 1. When you arrive at the shelter at 3.8 miles, climb the rock behind it for some additional views. From the shelter you'll follow the Saddle Trail, passing by a place where you can observe Whiteoak Canyon in greater detail than you did from the summit. You will also see the effect of thousands of people a year using the Old Rag Shelter at 4.8 miles. The entire little knob that the shelter sits on is nearly devoid of any undergrowth. Rainwater is unable to soak into the hard-packed, bare ground, meaning the soil will continue to erode away in some areas near the shelter. It is because of this heavy use throughout the Old Rag area that I request that you refrain from camping anywhere along this entire hike route. Perhaps, in order to protect resources, the time has come for the Park Service to dismantle the Old Rag and Byrds Nest 1 shelters and totally ban camping within several miles of Old Rag.

Continue to follow blue blazes, now walking along the Old Rag Fire Road, which is lined by showy orchids in the spring. Also beside the road is running cedar, which resembles tiny hemlock or pine trees. This small club moss can trace its roots back more than 300 million years to when its ancestors grew to be over 100 feet tall. Come to a four-way intersection at 5.2 miles. The Berry Hollow Fire Road descends to the left to go to a parking area on the park boundary. You want to keep straight for just a few feet so that you can make a right turn to descend along the yellow-blazed Weakley Hollow Road. The Robertson Mountain Trail comes in from the left at 6.3 miles, as does the Corbin Hollow Trail at 6.4 miles. Progressing downstream you'll pass by hundreds of wildflowers, eventually returning to the hemlock forest in which you started this hike.

After crossing Brokenback Run and a side stream on wooden footbridges, the hike, sadly, comes to an end at 7.7 miles. It's time to leaf through the guidebook again and begin planning your next walkabout.

22

Cedar Run/Whiteoak Canyon

Total distance (circuit): 8.0 or 9.3 miles

Hiking time: 6 or 7 hours

Vertical rise: 2,320 or 2,560 feet

Maps: USGS 7½′ Big Meadows; USGS 7½′ Old Rag Mountain; Shenandoah National Park Old Rag Trail map

The trails along Cedar Run and in Whiteoak Canyon are so popular that I debated for a long time as to whether or not they should be included in this guidebook. The pathways are worn and eroded from thousands of feet tramping on them year after year, and the crowds during weekends in the summer and fall are so large that it may feel like you're going to a circus instead of taking a walk in the woods. Yet the waterfalls and scenery on this hike are so impressive that it would be gross negligence not to include it in a hiking guide to Virginia.

During the course of the trek, Cedar Run drops about 2,000 feet, creating numerous cascades and pools, while Whiteoak Canyon's six waterfalls are rated to be among the 13 highest in Shenandoah National Park. I have you descending along Cedar Run and, because I believe you can better observe waterfalls when walking up to them instead of looking back at them, ascending Whiteoak Run. When you reach Upper Falls in Whiteoak Canyon you will have the option of choosing one of two different routes. The first option is shorter and follows a dirt road for a distance, making the final ascent a bit easier. The longer option provides a chance to walk among some giants of the forest in a virgin stand of hemlock trees. Be forewarned that no matter which option you choose, the ruggedness of terrain, rough conditions of the trails, slippery footing, and the fact that almost every bit of the vertical rise is accomplished in the 2-mile climb along Whiteoak Run make this a strenuous excursion.

Leave your car at the Lower Hawksbill Parking Area (Skyline Drive mile 45.6) and

cross the road to begin descending on blue-blazed Cedar Run Trail. In less than 100 yards the Skyland–Big Meadows Horse Trail comes in from the right and, in a few feet, goes off to the left. You'll want to keep following the blue blazes. Pass by a spring at 0.3 mile; be careful about any off-trail wanderings, because the stinging nettle is usually waist high by the middle of June. The trail continues to get rougher and rockier. At 0.5 mile you'll begin walking next to Cedar Run as it descends the mountain in a series of small falls, passing by one that drops about 25 feet at 0.7 mile.

At 1 mile you will come to another series of cascades, some with the water spreading out across the full length of the streambed, others channeling the creek through narrow slots in the bedrock. You've walked 1.4 miles when you reach the spot where two streams meet the creek, so you deserve a break. Besides, Cedar Run has leveled out a bit here, and there is a small pebble beach and a deep pool just made for swimming. (Do be careful swimming in any stream. The water may be very cold, the rocks slippery, pools deeper than they appear, and the currents swift.) The large flat rock next to the pool provides a good place to soak up some sun after a quick dip in the cool, clear water.

There is another great swimming hole where you ford Cedar Run at 1.5 miles. You can go downstream a little bit to overlook the largest falls of the run. Return to the trail to ascend 200 feet above the stream before descending steeply, almost straight down, on rough rock steps. By the time you've come 1.7 miles the falls have become so numerous that it is next to impossible to distinguish one from another; just enjoy all of this water dropping down the narrow gorge as the trail climbs high

above the stream once more. Be alert at 2.5 miles, where the trail drops back down to the stream. The route makes a sudden switchback to the left to ford Cedar Run for the final time—avoid the mistake of continuing straight on a pathway that enters private property.

Arrive at an intersection at 2.6 miles, where you will bear left onto the Cedar Run Link Trail. (The Cedar Run Trail to the right goes to the Berry Hollow Parking Area on VA 600. It also joins up with the Whiteoak Canyon Trail, but at a point a little lower than you need to go.) Now that you have swung away from the sound of rushing water, things seem quieter and more relaxed. The trail has only minor ups and downs, woodpeckers chip away at the trunks of hardwood trees, and the songs of other birds can now be heard coming from spots both near and far in the forest.

Come to Whiteoak Run at 3.4 miles, crossing it in just a few minutes to turn left and follow Whiteoak Canyon Trail upstream. (The trail also goes downstream about eight-tenths mile to VA 600.) Remember that camping is not permitted anywhere in Whiteoak Canyon. You have now entered a land ruled by water. Contemplate the steep canyon walls high above you. Thousands of years of water rushing over prehistoric lava beds have carved out this deep and narrow gorge. The stream down here carries the cumulative flow of numerous springs that break forth from their underground flows near the crest of the Blue Ridge Mountains. Even in times of drought, water makes an impact here. The gorge is well protected from direct sunlight, meaning the floor of the canyon is less susceptible to evaporation, enabling plants to survive during times when their counterparts in other portions of the park are struggling to live.

The route going back up to Skyline Drive

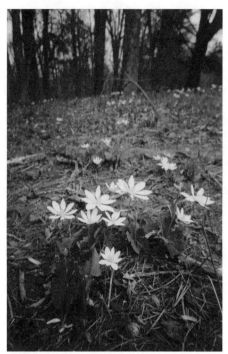
Bloodroot

seems to just ooze out of the canyon walls. In 5 minutes you will be standing at the top of one falls and then, almost immediately, at the base of another. It may sound like the stream is getting larger and noisier as you walk by the large boulder at 5.1 miles. Once you get past it and the sound drops back to its normal level, you'll realize that the face of this giant rock echoes the sounds of the rushing water. Ascend some concrete and stone steps where, once again, the rock walls have water running down them. Come to an intersection at 5.4 miles; take the short side trail to the left to view the largest of the falls, which drop nearly 90 feet into the canyon. If by some miracle you have not met anyone on the hike so far, you are almost guaranteed to do so here. Upper Falls is one of the most popular spots in the park, and the large majority of people who visit Whiteoak Canyon from the Skyline Drive go no farther downstream. Return to the main trail and continue your ascent to a bit of level land at the top of the falls. This place was a popular attraction years before Shenandoah National Park was established. A wagon road extending from Skyland brought in visitors by the hundreds. George Freeman Pollock, who founded Skyland in the 1890s, became known for the fabulous and elaborate picnics he supplied for his guests when they came here to enjoy the falls and take a dip in the stream.

There is an intersection here, and this is the place at which you will have to decide whether to take the longer or the shorter hike. The longer trek is detailed in the final two paragraphs below; to continue with the shorter hike, go upstream a few feet to cross Whiteoak Run on a footbridge. Once on the other side go downstream to turn right and ascend on the yellow-blazed Whiteoak Canyon Road.

At a right-hand switchback at 7.3 miles the road goes one-tenth mile to the Skyline

will be almost as steep, rough, and rocky as the one you descended upon. At 4.1 miles cross over the largest tributary of Whiteoak Run (look upstream to see that it has its own set of small falls) and come to the first of many falls (this one has about a 60-foot drop) you are going to be treated to while on the Whiteoak Canyon Trail. After viewing the falls, negotiate a series of switchbacks and a section that involves some steep climbing. A rock facing permits a view through the canyon and across to some of the mountains along the eastern edge of the park. A few cedar trees are found along this section of the trail, and the ones that grow in the open are gnarled and twisted, reminiscent of trees exposed to the harsh conditions of the high Rocky Mountains.

Pass by another falls at 4.7 miles; so much water is draining into this gorge that the liquid

Drive near mile 45. You want to continue following the yellow blazes by taking the pathway that heads off to the left. At 8 miles you'll arrive back at the Cedar Run Trail. Make a right onto it and stay right at the next intersection to end the hike in less than 5 more minutes in Hawksbill Gap.

If you are doing the longer hike, you will continue upstream from the intersection at the top of Upper Falls to cross Whiteoak Run in a few minutes and ascend along the left side of the creek in a forest of impressive hemlocks. At 7.1 miles you want to leave the Whiteoak Canyon Trail and turn left onto the Limberlost Trail. Slow down and take in the magnificence of this place, as there are few like it left anywhere in North America; the giant hemlocks in this old-growth forest are believed to be 270 to 370 years old. The often-heard cry of a barred owl simply adds to the romance of the woods. Pollock gave the area its name because it reminded him of Gene Stratton Porter's *Girl of the Limberlost.* Pollock was not only the founder of Skyland but also an ardent supporter of the establishment of Shenandoah National Park. He tells his own story in the book *Skyland,* available at the visitor centers. His wife, Addy, purchased the hemlocks to save them from timbering. Sadly, today many of them are succumbing to infestations of the hemlock woolly adelgid.

At the next intersection at 7.5 miles, the Limberlost Trail goes off to the right and you want to keep to the left, ascending on the Crescent Rock Trail. Arrive at Crescent Rock Overlook (Skyline Drive mile 44.4) at 8.6 miles and take the Bettys Rock Trail. Almost immediately turn on to the connector pathway on the left to intersect the Appalachian Trail. Turn left on the AT, passing underneath Crescent Rock and on to the next intersection, where you'll make another left to end the hike in Hawksbill Gap at 9.3 miles.

23

Hawksbill

Total distance (circuit): 2.8 miles

Hiking time: 1¾ hours

Vertical rise: 740 feet

Maps: USGS 7½′ Big Meadows

There is an attraction about the "most" of something that fascinates humans and tends to draw us toward these famous entities. Tourists visit the Sears Tower in Chicago because it is the "tallest" building. We idolize athletes who are the "best" in their chosen sport. Edmonton, Alberta, in Canada, has a mall that draws thousands of shoppers yearly ever since it became known as the "largest" in the world. Spelunkers are always looking for the "deepest" cavern, and, conversely, hikers often have the desire to top the "highest" summit. Hawksbill is not the tallest mountain in the Old Dominion (Mount Rogers in southern Virginia has that honor), but it does have the distinction of being the loftiest peak within the boundaries of Shenandoah National Park.

Unlike the long and involved climbs that you must undertake in order to attain many other paramount pinnacles, the nice thing about Hawksbill is that it may be reached in a moderately easy ascent of less than 700 feet in elevation from where you leave your car. Like Marys Rock (see Hike 19), Hawksbill is a grand spot from which to watch the annual fall hawk migration. The circuit hike is, in fact, a good birder's walk year-round. Evening grosbeaks—not often seen during the warmer months in the mid-Atlantic states—and pine siskins have been spotted fluttering around the evergreens in winter, while ruffed grouse go about their mating rituals in the spring. Warblers and juncos usually become quite common as the temperatures warm up. In the past, the Park Service has used Hawksbill to participate in a program of reintroducing peregrine falcons to the Blue Ridge Mountains. Up until the mid-1950s, these raptors could be seen rocketing about the North American skies at speeds of more than 100 miles per hour. Yet, like the osprey and the bald eagle, they fell victims to the cumulative effects of DDT. The insecticide caused some hatchlings to be born deformed, but more commonly it weakened the shells of the bird's eggs to the point that the eggs simply could not hold together long enough for the chicks to be born. Now that DDT has been banned in the United States, breeding the birds in captivity and then re-

leasing them into the wild has proven somewhat successful in preserving the species.

The hike begins from the Hawksbill Gap Parking Area (Skyline Drive milepoint 45.6), about 15 miles south of US 211 in Thornton Gap or approximately 20 miles north of US 33 in Swift Run Gap. Take the trail from the parking lot, following it to the left as you will be returning on the pathway coming in from the right.

Your route ascends through balsam fir and red spruce, holdovers from another time. The Ice Age's cooler temperatures

---

permitted these trees, more typical of New England and Canada, to begin to compete with, and even gain a foothold against, the traditional southern hardwoods such as oaks and poplars. Once the glaciers receded and warmer temperatures returned, most of the northern plants died out, unable to tolerate a southern climate. However, the cooler temperatures on the higher peaks and ridges of the Blue Ridge, such as Hawksbill, have allowed some of these trees to remain and prosper, separated from their relatives several hundred miles to the north. Look at the range map of a tree identification guide and you will see that a tree mixed in with the evergreens here, the mountain ash, extends itself as far south as northern Georgia only by clinging to the high elevations of the Appalachian Mountain chain.

A side trail to the left at 0.2 mile runs less than 100 feet to a spring that can usually be counted on to flow throughout the year. The trail makes several switchbacks before leveling out somewhat at 0.5 mile; striped maple is abundant in the understory. Its bright yellow flowers, hanging as long-stemmed clusters, make their appearance at just about the time of year when warm temperatures become a daily occurrence. At 0.6 mile enter the no-camping zone, and at 0.7 mile make a right turn at a trail intersection to come to Byrds Nest Shelter 2 and the Hawksbill's summit at 0.8 mile.

Continue to the stone-walled outlook for the almost, but not quite, 360-degree panorama for which you've gained this elevation. Almost directly beneath you are Timber and Buracker Hollows, funneling and dropping East Hawksbill Creek out to the town of Luray, some 3,000 feet below where you are standing. (East Hawksbill Creek, accessible by bushwhacking from Hawksbill Gap, is highly recommended as

a native-trout fishing stream by Harry Slone in his *Trout Streams of Virginia*.) The view westward is of Page Valley, which, except for those who are sticklers for technicalities, is really just the easternmost portion of the Shenandoah Valley. The two sections of the valley come back together near Harrisonburg where Massanutten Mountain (see Hikes 27, 28, and 29), the massive ridge due west, comes to an end. Northward you can see Skyline Drive making a wide swing eastward around a prominent rock outcrop, Stony Man (see Hike 20). To the east is Old Rag (see Hike 21), bristling with its noticeable rocky ridgeline and jagged summit. To the south is Spitler Hill, and closer (to the southwest) is rounded Naked Top.

After your picnic-lunch break at 4,049 feet above sea level, return to the shelter, walking past it to turn right off the dirt road and onto the blue-blazed trail. A few yards down this pathway is another fine view to the west and a new perspective on the southwest. At 1.1 miles you will switchback away from the road, soon coming to small patches of mountain laurel for the first time on this hike (and passing out of the no-camping zone).

Intersect the Appalachian Trail at 1.7 miles. To the left it goes 2.2 miles to Fishers Gap and Skyline Drive milepoint 49.3. You need to make a right, descending and then ascending on the fern-lined AT and listening for the cry of a pileated woodpecker. If you don't know how one sounds, just think of Woody Woodpecker; he and his laugh were patterned after the pileated woodpecker. If, as many ornithologists believe, the ivory-billed woodpecker truly has become extinct, then the nearly 20-inch pileated has inherited the status of being North America's largest woodpecker. At 2.2 miles you will swing around a large rock promontory to cross a series of rock slides,

. . . and it's still alive!

or talus slopes, whose openings in the forest canopy can provide limited views of Stony Man to the north. For the second time on this hike, mountain ash trees are part of the forest. Not really an ash but, rather, a member of the rose family, its red berries usually hang on the tree well into winter, providing food for grosbeaks and other birds. People of the southern Appalachians used to make a tonic from the juice of the berry to treat a variety of ailments.

You will soon begin a quick switchbacking descent along a spur ridge to arrive at an intersection at 2.7 miles. The AT keeps to the left and reaches Stony Man in 2.7 miles. You want to make a right turn and go 500 feet to return to the parking area in Hawksbill Gap.

24

Rapidan Camp

Total distance (circuit): 7.4 miles

Hiking time: 5 hours

Vertical rise: 1,480 feet

Maps: USGS 7½′ Fletcher; USGS 7½′ Big Meadows

Shortly after he was elected president in 1928, Herbert Hoover sent his personal staff on a search for the perfect site for a weekend retreat. He stipulated that it had to be within a day's drive from Washington, D.C., and, in order to be an escape from the heat of summer and as free of mosquitoes as possible, above 2,500 feet in elevation. Being an ardent angler, Hoover's most stringent requirement was that the site had to contain favorable trout-fishing streams. The location of Rapidan Camp on the eastern edge of the Blue Ridge Mountains next to the Rapidan River met all of these requirements, and Hoover, declining to use federal funds or offers of assistance from the Commonwealth of Virginia, purchased the land and building materials himself.

The Marine Corps, as part of a training exercise, constructed roads and 13 buildings, completing the major portion of Rapidan Camp in 1929. Hoover and his wife, Lou, came to the camp often during his term to escape the rigors of being America's First Family, but the president also used the retreat to meet with high-level government officials and foreign dignitaries. Probably the most memorable of such meetings was with the prime minister of Great Britain, Ramsey MacDonald, in which world armaments and limits on naval power were discussed. Upon losing a bid for reelection in 1932, the Hoovers donated the camp and 164 acres to the Commonwealth of Virginia for inclusion in the proposed Shenandoah National Park, which was established in 1935. He had hoped that future presidents would

continue to use his camp, but Franklin Delano Roosevelt could not negotiate the topography and established a new retreat in Maryland.

Interpretive tours of the camp are available during the season. Check at visitor centers for the latest information.

The grounds of the camp are open to the public year-round and can be reached by way of this circuit hike. The trip takes in the two streams that come together at the camp to form the Rapidan River, the short interpretive trail winding through the camp while giving bits of information about the area, and a lush stand of mountain laurel.

If you have two cars and wish to shorten the hike by 2.0 miles, you can leave one automobile at Booten's Gap (Skyline Drive mile 55.1). To begin the hike leave your car in the Milam Gap Parking Area (Skyline Drive mile 52.8), cross the drive, and enter the woods on the AT. In a few hundred feet you will want to take the blue-blazed Mill Prong Trail, which heads off to the left and passes through an overgrown orchard. Amazingly, despite this spot's proximity to the road and all of the developments around Big Meadows Lodge, I have twice seen black bears lumbering around these old fruit trees. Bears are omnivores, and vegetative matter is the largest part of their diet, so these bears may have been enjoying fruit from trees that were planted in the 1920s or earlier. Actually, it seems like bears will consume just about anything, including twigs, leaves, roots, nuts, insects, carrion, and berries. They tear the bark off a tree in order to consume the cambium, or the living inner bark of the tree. Everyone knows that bears love honey and the honeycomb, but they will also eat the bees and their larvae. Most of the animal protein in their diet comes from grubs, ants, termites, beetles, and other insects, with fish and small mammals, such as mice and voles, comprising the bulk of the small amount of meat they do consume.

At about 0.5 mile, hemlock trees begin to appear; you will cross Mill Prong at 0.7 mile. At 1.1 miles, cross a sidestream and come to a T-intersection. The trail to the left goes about eight-tenths mile to the Rapidan Fire Road and then two and two-tenths miles to Big Meadows. You, however, want to bear right, following the trail, which at this point is open to horses and is identified as such by being blazed yellow. You will soon be walking along Mill Prong, where in times of plentiful rainfall there are small cascading waterfalls and pools that may entice you to soak your feet for a while. Stinging nettle and jewelweed, as they often do, grow side by side. In the fall you can find out why jewelweed is also known as touch-me-not. When its seedpods are good and ripe, just touching them will cause them to explode open, casting the seeds in all directions.

At 1.5 miles you will begin a switchbacked and quick descent, entering a no-camping zone. A couple of minutes later you'll cross Mill Prong a few feet below 10-foot Big Rock Falls. Continue descending in this pretty little green stream valley of moss, boulders, hardwoods, and hemlocks. The Rapidan Fire Road comes in from the left at 1.9 miles, where you'll bear right to arrive in Rapidan Camp. Three of the original 13 buildings are still standing. The one in the middle is the President's Cabin, and the Prime Minister's Cabin (where MacDonald stayed during his visits) is on the right. President Hoover's guard, secretary, and manager, Larry Richey, and the president's physician, Dr. Joel T. Boone Jr., stayed in the Creel Cabin, the smaller building to the left. Take the signed interpretive trail through the grounds, and perhaps you can recapture the days when

A hemlock forest

government policy was decided while casting fishing lines into the water and international politics were discussed while sitting on an old log. Just behind the cabins, Mill Prong and Laurel Prong meet to form the Rapidan River. The Rapidan flows eastward to join up with the Rappahannock River a few miles northwest of Fredericksburg. In turn, the Rappahannock continues the march, becoming miles wide before it finally deposits the water you see flowing past you at Rapidan Camp into the Chesapeake Bay.

Finishing the interpretive trail, walk away from the camp on a gravel road, the yellow-blazed Laurel Prong Trail. At 2.2 miles the road forks—take the one to the left and not the one going directly uphill. You will soon begin a slight ascent into a hemlock forest—lover's paradise. At 2.5 miles the road becomes Fork Mountain Trail and heads off to the left. You will need to follow the now blue-blazed Laurel Prong Trail to the right as you leave the no-camping zone. After crossing Laurel Prong, come to a zone of transition at 3.5 miles.

The hemlocks give way to hardwoods, and mountain laurel appears in abundance for the first time on this hike. The ascent also becomes a bit steeper.

At the top of the ridgeline, at 3.8 miles, arrive at a T-intersection. To the left, Cat Knob Trail goes about half a mile to meet the Jones Mountain Trail. Bear right, continuing on Laurel Prong Trail to a break in the vegetation that permits a view of Booten's Gap and the Shenandoah Valley beyond. There is some interesting-looking rock tripe on the rock formations you pass at 4.2 miles. While tripe is not the best-tasting of foods, stories abound of people lost or trapped in alpine areas who have survived for days by eating nothing but lichen such as this. (Please don't taste the rock tripe here. Remember, it is against the law to pick any vegetation in the park.)

You will come to another T-intersection at 4.9 miles. If you have been able to arrange for an automobile at Booten's Gap (Skyline Drive mile 55.1), you can turn left to follow the AT to end the walk in half a mile. To continue on the circuit hike, bear right and follow the AT up the southern flank of Hazeltop Mountain to the 3,812-foot summit at 5.4 miles. This is a totally different environment from that at Rapidan Camp. The soil is drier, the forest is almost exclusively hardwoods, the rocks of the ridgeline are uplifted and tilted, and there are gooseberries and fields of cow parsnip. Pass through a grove of hawthorns on sloping land at 6.2 miles. Because of the complexity and difficulty of distinguishing one type of hawthorn from another, there is no agreement as to how many different kinds there are throughout the world. Some botanists say 120, other declare there are more than 1,200. Be that as it may, the heavy foliage and sharp-tipped thorns of the trees provide a well-protected nesting site for many different species of birds. Arrive back at the Mill Prong–AT intersection at 7.3 miles, where you'll turn left to return to Milam Gap and the Skyline Drive to finish the hike at 7.4 miles.

The Byrd Visitor Center is less than 2 miles to the north on Skyline Drive and is certainly worth a visit now that you're in the area. You can obtain information on various aspects of the park, pick up a backcountry camping permit, study the exhibits showing the human and natural history of the area, and watch movies or attend ranger-led programs about the park. Books, maps, and more are sold here, and if you want more information on Rapidan Camp you can pick up a copy of Darwin Lambert's *Herbert Hoover's Hideaway*.

Adjacent to the visitor center is the Big Meadows complex, containing a lodge, picnic area, campground, and wayside camp store and restaurant. In season, interpretive programs are given in the amphitheater, and if you're lucky, you might happen to catch a lap dulcimer concert or a bit of mountain music in the lodge's tap room.

25

Brown Mountain/Rockytop

Total distance (circuit): 20.0 miles

Hiking time: 2-day backpacking trip

Vertical rise: about 4,000 feet

Maps: USGS 7½′ McGaheysville; USGS 7½′ Browns Cove

The Big Run watershed is the largest in Shenandoah National Park—1 inch of rainfall translates into 200 million gallons of water falling into the drainage system! A rugged topography—made up of Brown Mountain, Rocky Mountain, Rockytop, and the main crest of the Blue Ridge—encircles Big Run and invites exploration, but there are so many miles to cover that it is best to plan an overnight hike to have enough time to enjoy yourself. As you go to sleep, snug and comfortable in your tent, you will have the satisfaction of enjoying peace and quiet because the great majority of backcountry hikers in the park overlook this area as a camping destination. Carry plenty of water and be sure that you have obtained information about and know the current park regulations concerning backcountry campsites.

Having obtained a backcountry camping permit at an entrance station or visitor center, you can reach the beginning of the hike by turning off Skyline Drive at the Loft Mountain Wayside (mile 79.5) and taking the service road to the campground. Leave your car in the auxiliary parking area just above the camp store. This way you will be able to have a junkfood feast at the camp store just before, and after, the hike. If you are doing the hike at a time of year when the campground is closed and you are unable to gain access to the parking lot, probably the best place to leave your automobile, and begin and end the hike, is the Doyles River Parking Area (Skyline Drive mile 81.1), which is at the 18.7-mile point of this hike. Either way, when you obtain your backcountry permit be sure to tell park personnel where you will be leaving your car.

From the parking lot, walk to the camp store, take the pathway behind it for a good view of the Piedmont, and follow the trail out to the Appalachian Trail. At 0.4 mile, come to and turn left onto the AT, whose open areas continue to give views to the east. Butter-and-eggs, a European flower that has spread from cultivated gardens, blooms throughout the summer months. During the fall, when the thistle is in flower, the unmistakable seedpods of milkweed cover a large percentage of these open fields. Enter a wooded area where some grand, old, gnarled trees deserve your respect for being able to survive year in and year out in this harsh upland environment.

At 1.5 miles the Frazier Discovery Trail comes in from the left. You will keep right, soon coming to an outcrop on the left to present you with a view of the Big Run drainage, the area into which you are heading. At 1.6 miles the Frazier Discovery Trail takes leave of the AT to go left six-tenths mile to the Wayside coffee shop. Once again, keep right, this time beginning a long, switchbacked descent. After an open area where you can enjoy blackberries in season, you will enter the woods and descend more rapidly to intersect a trail at 2.5 miles. This one goes left about two hundred yards to Ivy Creek Spring and six-tenths mile to the Wayside. Stay to the right on the AT.

By the time you cross Ivy Creek at 3.2 miles, it will have become large enough to have a small cascade and pools. Take a break and look into the water to find a few small trout and maybe even a crayfish or two crawling from one submerged crevice to another. Tiny, harmless ring-necked snakes sometimes take advantage of the flat rocks to warm themselves in the bit of sunshine that manages to make it through

the forest canopy. After you have gobbled down a few handfuls of gorp and several swigs of water, you'll begin to ascend through a typical Virginia woods of mountain laurel, pines, and blueberries.

At 3.7 miles you will have a view that takes in Rockytop, whose heights you will be standing on later in the hike, and Trayfoot Mountain. Descend to come to the Ivy Creek Overlook at 4.6 miles (Skyline Drive mile 77.5), where you leave the AT to walk northward on the grassy shoulder of the drive. As you walk along the roadway you can survey what is going to be your domain for the rest of the day and part of tomorrow—Rocky and Brown Mountains, Rockytop, and the numerous tributarial hollows of Big Run. At 5.2 miles come to the Brown Mountain Overlook and begin to follow blue-blazed Brown Mountain Trail along a narrow ridgeline that often carries the tunes of various songbirds.

Come to an intersection at 5.9 miles where the Rocky Mountain Run Trail descends left for two and seven-tenths miles to the Big Run Portal Trail. Ascend to the right, slabbing a hillside whose heavy undergrowth and dead and dying trees are a sign of gypsy moth infestation. The gypsy moth was brought to Massachusetts in 1869 from France for experimental crossbreeding with silkworms. Unfortunately, some escaped and the moth has now spread throughout much of North America, with some being found even as far away as California and Washington. It is when they are in the larval, or caterpillar, stage that they feed on the leaves of trees and other foliage, sometimes completely defoliating vast acreages. A healthy tree can usually withstand one or two consecutive years of defoliation, but any more than this and the tree will probably die. There is some hope that natural forces, such as the

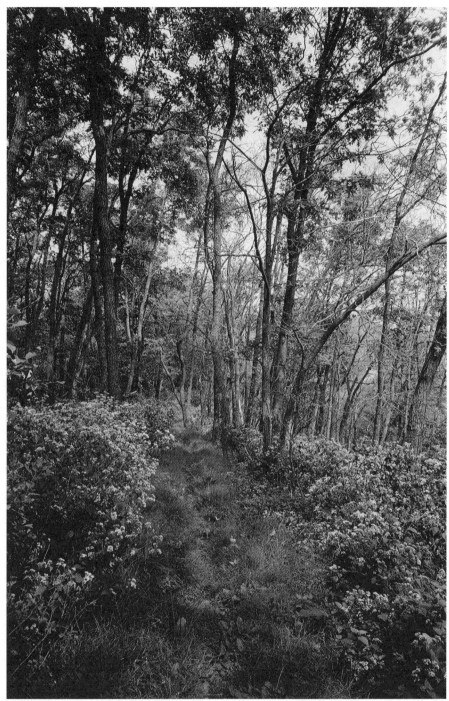
Flowers along the Appalachian Trail

nucleopolyhedrosis virus and the gypsy-moth fungus, can help bring the moths under control. One thing is certain, though: Just as surely as the chestnut blight cleared the way for oaks to become one of the dominant trees in the southern highlands, the gypsy moth is changing the look of our forests once again. It will be interesting to see what the vegetative cover of the Blue Ridge Mountains will be in decades to come.

After going up and down and back and forth along the undulating ridgeline, you'll reach the 2,800-foot summit of Rocky Mountain at 6.8 miles for one heck of a view. The whole Big Run watershed is laid out below you and across the valley is Rockytop with Trayfoot Mountain behind it. You can make out your route back along the entire ridgeline you have just walked from Skyline Drive. Look at the rock beneath your feet and you can see the fossilized bore holes of the skolithos, a worm believed to have lived 500 million years ago. Be looking for these signs of ancient life just about any time this hike passes by rock outcrops or talus slopes.

As you resume the gradual downward trend along the ridgeline, you will begin to notice the effects of a 1986 fire that burned 4,775 acres and was the result of a camper's gasoline stove getting out of control. The trunks of some of the pines are scorched, but the trees live on. The pathway alternates between being soft and spongy from years of fallen pine needles and a narrow and rough treadway of rocks and boulders. You attain the summit of Brown Mountain at 8.2 miles for a view much like you had from Rocky Mountain, except that the valley floor appears much closer. The descent is now via switchbacks, and breaks in the vegetation will give you an interesting perspective on the very southern peak of Massanutten Mountain to the northwest.

Intersect the Big Run Portal Trail at 10.3 miles and turn left so that you can make a right turn in just a few more feet. There are some great swimming holes when you cross Big Run. As I was beginning a hike once in mid-May, a ranger jokingly dared me by saying, "You'll be a real man if you take a dip in one of those mountain creeks!" By the end of July the water should have warmed up enough that just about anyone can enjoy submersing themselves for a while. Just remember, in addition to cold water, any mountain stream is likely to have deep holes, slippery rocks, and swift currents. (After your swim, it is worthwhile to take a short walk downstream a few hundred yards to Big Run Portal, where the stream impressively rushes through a narrow ravine in the bedrock.)

From the bridge, ascend along the rocky trail, veering away from the stream. Be paying attention at 10.9 miles, where the trail continues ahead for two-tenths mile to the park boundary; you want to make a left and begin the long and sometimes switchbacked ascent of blue-blazed Rockytop Trail. Looking out through the vegetation you should be able to make out Brown and Rocky Mountains and mark your progress as you rise from the valley floor. At 12.6 miles, cross one rock field, and soon after, another. Above you is the highest peak on the ridge—the one that most people refer to as Rockytop, although USGS maps give another knob farther up the trail that distinction. The view you have is to the west, most notably Lewis Peak. It is estimated that there are anywhere from 300 to 600 black bears at any given time in the park, and judging from the amount of scat I've seen when crossing these talus slopes, the Big Run watershed must provide food for quite a few of them. The scat is usually cylindrical, somewhat like that of a dog's, and often contains remnants of what the bears have eaten—seeds, leaves of grass, rodent bones and fur, and nutshells. During the time of year when the bears are gorging themselves on the abundant variety of berries in the park, the scat is no longer solid but resembles a large, black or dark blue, liquid cow pie.

The Lewis Peak Trail takes off to the right at 14.2 miles, so you want to keep to the left. Walking sticks (the insects, not the hiking aid) are so perfectly camouflaged that you have to keep a sharp eye out to spot one even though thousands feed on the park's foliage. You'll now be making minor ups and downs on the ridgeline, walking in and out of patches of turkeybeard, pokeweed, and wild rose, until you come to the Austin Mountain Trail going off to the right at 16.1 miles. The Rockytop Trail ends at a four-way intersection at 16.5 miles. The Madison Run Spur Trail makes a hard right to descend to Madison Run Road in about three-tenths mile. Big Run Loop Trail descends left to Big Run. You want to go straight toward the Skyline Drive and the AT, which you will intersect at 17.2 miles. Turn left and follow its white blazes, descending to cross the Skyline Drive (mile 82.2) and then walking on the rocky backbone of a ridge, passing by some interesting rock formations. Shallow remains of trenches built during the Civil War are overgrown with trees and underbrush on the right side of the pathway.

Hike by the Doyles River Overlook (Skyline Drive mile 81.9) and descend to the intersection with the Doyles River Trail at 18.7 miles. A parking area and the Skyline Drive are 120 feet to the left; you want to continue straight and ascend on the AT, but be on the lookout for poison ivy overtaking the pathway. A rock outcrop will present you with a view of just about every place you've been on this hike—Loft, Brown, and Rocky Mountains and Rockytop. Here, on Big Flat Mountain, the apple trees you walk under are evidence of an old orchard. Deer are attracted to this area and you will no doubt see a few close to where you leave the AT at 19.6 miles to make a left onto the Loft Mountain Nature Trail. With the large number of deer seen in the Blue Ridge Mountains, it is hard to believe that the population near the turn of the 20th century was almost decimated. Some historical accounts say that domestic dogs ran down and destroyed (as they still do today in many rural and suburban areas) almost as many as were killed for human consumption. Loss of habitat from farming and timbering only compounded the decline in numbers. To rectify this assault on the natural order of things, white-tailed deer were reintroduced into the park in 1934 and it is estimated that 6,000 now live within its borders. When you come to the campground's amphitheater you'll want to make a right to ascend to the road and your car, ending the hike at exactly 20 miles.

The camp store, with its cold liquid refreshments and shelves of high-calorie snacks, is only a few hundred steps beyond the parking lot.

26

Riprap Hollow

Total distance: 9.6 miles

Hiking time: 6 hours

Vertical rise: 2,260 feet

Map: USGS 7½′ Crimora

Hot summer days are not meant for working in office buildings or for toiling in the bright sunshine. They are better spent peering off into the distances while standing on lofty ridges with soft breezes blowing through your hair, having picnics with family and friends in quiet shady groves, or walking into narrow ravines to take dips in cool mountain streams. A hike into Riprap Hollow can provide you with places to experience all of this and more. It therefore provides the perfect excuse for you and a few compatriots to chuck work for the day, fill up the daypacks with sandwiches, gorp, and other goodies, and go wandering about in the southern section of Shenandoah National Park.

You could just as readily start this circuit hike from the Riprap Parking Area (Skyline Drive milepoint 90), but I have you beginning and ending the hike from the Wildcat Ridge Parking Area (Skyline Drive milepoint 92.1). I've done this so that after you have made the 1,300-plus-foot, 2.7-mile climb out of Riprap Hollow, you won't face 2.8 more miles of ups and downs in order to reach your automobile. If you have two cars, you could completely eliminate those miles (making it about a 7-mile hike) by first leaving one car at Wildcat Ridge and then beginning from Riprap parking. After obtaining your backcountry permit and obtaining current camping regulations, you could make this into a backpacking trip easily walked in 2 days.

Take the trail from the Wildcat Ridge parking, which is about 15 miles north of US 250 and I-64 in Rockfish Gap. In 0.1 mile, come to a four-way intersection where

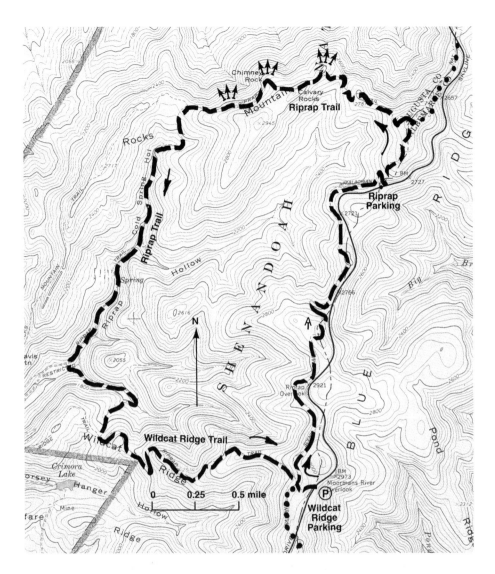

the Wildcat Ridge Trail is straight ahead (you will be returning on it) and the Appalachian Trail runs left and right. You want to turn right onto the AT, walking through an understory of mountain laurel, sassafras, and azalea. Azalea, like mountain laurel and rhododendron, is a member of the heath family and grows well throughout the mountains of Virginia. The national park seems to have more than its fair share of azaleas, and if you are lucky enough to be walking in the woods during that short period of the year (usually late May and early June) when it and the mountain laurel are both in full bloom, your eyes will have a visual color feast. The laurel's clumps of white to rich pink flowers mix nicely with the azalea's deeper pink blossoms.

The Riprap Hollow area was the scene of three wildland fires during the 1990s; the

---

portion of the AT you are now walking upon was burned in 1999 when ashes from a controlled burn by national park personnel were rekindled by strong winds. Within a week, the fire grew to 3,200 acres, and it took 500 firefighters, aided by engines, helicopters, and air tankers, to control the flames. Luckily, it was mostly just undergrowth that burned along the AT (the effects of the fire might not even be noticeable by the time you walk here), but the interior area of Riprap Hollow sustained major losses. The large number of gypsy moth damaged trees was a major factor in the fire's rapid spread, and you may see a number of dead trees when looking onto the lower elevations from some of the hike's viewpoints. You may also find a number of downed trees along the length of this outing that were felled to prevent the fire from spreading by aerial embers and to remove fire-weakened trees along the pathways.

At 0.7 mile, low growth permits a view of the Shenandoah Valley and of the place you are eventually going to enter, Riprap Hollow. Pass by an occasional rhododendron shrub as you gradually rise to cross a flat ridge and begin descending on switchbacks at 1.2 miles. Repeat this up-and-down process a couple of times until, at 2.4 miles, you can spot the ridgeline you will use to descend into the hollow. At 2.7 miles the Riprap Parking Area is a few feet to the right; you want to stay left, continuing on the AT, to come to another intersection at 3.2 miles. Leave the AT and make a left onto blue-blazed Riprap Trail as it descends with limited views of the valley created by Paine Run. The rocks to the right at 4 miles provide a wonderful grandstand view. North is Horsehead Mountain and beyond it is Trayfoot Mountain, but the most spectacular view is of the Shenandoah Valley as it stretches north and south and west. From here it is obvious why the wide, rolling expanse of the valley, bordered on the east by the Blue Ridge Mountains and on the west by the Allegheny Mountains (somewhat hidden here by Massanutten Mountain), was the natural conduit for early settlers as they made their way to southern Virginia and points westward from Pennsylvania, Maryland, and northeastern Virginia.

By the time you reach Chimney Rock at 4.4 miles, you have lost more elevation and the valley will appear much closer. Gaze back up to your right and you can see the Skyline Drive near the crest of the mountains—that's how far down you have come since you turned off the AT. The hillside trail you continue to descend is well graded and wide; keep looking through the vegetation and you'll be able to monitor the progress of your descent in relation to the surrounding mountains. The next rock outcrop at 4.8 miles gives a completely unobstructed view of the Paine Run watershed. The very southern peak of Massanutten Mountain is visible to the northwest as it juts above the ridge of Trayfoot Mountain. You are so close to the floor of the Shenandoah Valley that it seems as if you could be walking on it in just a few minutes. In addition to the wind rustling the leaves, your ears should now be able to make out the sound of the stream dropping into Cold Spring Hollow.

You may also have noticed that landscape you have been passing through for the last half-hour or so was impacted by the Calvary Fire of 1998. This burned 1,430 acres, taking in the northern one-third of the Riprap Trail and burning down to Paine Run and Riprap Hollow.

Drop quickly into the hollow, where the trail becomes rough and rocky in this exceptionally beautiful gorge. Don't take the old, washed-out path going left and downhill after you've passed the small falls at 6.1 miles. Rather, you should ascend up to the right and then drop back down to cross the stream.

Riprap Falls

You have entered Riprap Hollow when, after 6.3 miles of walking, you reach what many consider to be one of the prettiest spots in the park. The water of the stream has worn a large, deep hole into the bedrock, creating an absolutely lovely swimming pool where you can relax, propped up against smooth rocks, while the waters of a small falls massage tired muscles. A more perfect place to while away a few hours would be hard to find. The silvery water drops around soft-looking, moss-covered boulders, sunlight is filtered through thousands of hemlock needles, and the pool mirrors the evergreen leaves of mountain laurel and rhododendron thickets. Although catawba rhododendron can often be found in abundance almost anywhere else in the mountains of Virginia, this is one of the very few places in Shenandoah National Park that it thrives in great numbers. Something else to contemplate while you are relaxing here—about one mile beyond the park boundary, this stream disappears from the surface of

the earth, joining Shenandoah Valley's subterranean water system.

Unfortunately, no matter how lovely this spot is, you are eventually going to have to leave. At 6.5 miles cross over to the west side of the stream, beginning to follow the old fire road. Burn spots from the 1991 Riprap Fire are still evident around the forest. It is interesting to note that, if you were to look at a map, you would find that the three wildland fires of the 1990s almost fit together like the pieces of a jigsaw puzzle.

Be sure to be paying attention at 6.9 miles, because the fire road continues straight, but you want to make a left to cross the stream and begin to rise out of Riprap Hollow on the Wildcat Ridge Trail. You will first ascend on an old road, crisscrossing a side stream before the road ends and you ascend steeply to obtain the ridgeline in 7.8 miles. If you have ever had the pleasure of walking through a field of bear grass in the northern Rockies, you'll be excited to see turkeybeard scattered about. While it doesn't grow quite as tall as its western relative in the lily family, the turkeybeard's cluster of tiny white flowers at the top of its stem can be almost as large and impressive.

The use of this sidehill trail makes for a more gradual ascent to where you come into a gap to cross over to the other side of the ridge for a view of the cliffs and talus slopes near the summit of Turk Mountain to the south. Take in your last good view of Shenandoah Valley from the trail. From here you will crisscross the ridgeline a few times, coming to the intersection with the AT at 9.5 miles. Cross the AT and continue straight to the Wildcat Parking Area at 9.6 miles.

Aren't you glad you didn't go to work today?

27

Signal Knob

Total distance (circuit): 10.4 miles

Hiking time: 7 hours

Vertical rise: 2,220 feet

Map: USGS 7½′ Strasburg

A walk to Signal Knob can bring you into a natural world of clear, flowing springs, succulent blueberries, deep woods, and quiet mountain streams. The walk can also help you appreciate the methods by which humans communicated in days before telephones, televisions, space-age satellites, and the Internet created the worldwide, almost-instantaneous exchange of information.

Drums, in the form of hollow logs beaten with wooden sticks or stones, were probably the first means of long-distance communication. Once humans discovered how to make and control fire, smoke signals were employed. Later, as written languages became more precise and established, humans learned to use single symbols to convey concepts that would have taken many words to describe. Thus, flags came to be tools for signaling messages. Using flags, people could relay information from point to point, over and over again, to get the messages across great distances.

During the Civil War, the Confederacy used 2,106-foot Signal Knob, which overlooks a sweeping panorama of the Shenandoah Valley, to spot Union troops moving south from their encampments in Winchester and other places to the north. Information on these movements was signaled by flag to points farther south and then relayed numerous times, sometimes all the way to Richmond, the capital of the Confederacy.

You can reach the beginning of the Signal Knob hike by taking I-81 to VA 55 (Strasburg exit) and following VA 55 through Strasburg,

Strasburg
Reservoir

MOUNTAIN

AQUEDUCT

Signal Knob

Airway Beacon
2106

N

0   0.25   0.5 mile

Massanutten
Trail

VALLEY

SIGNAL KNOB TRAIL

Shenandoah Valley
Overlook

Tuscarora
Trail

Meneka
Peak   2393

Massanutten
Trail

Buzzard Rock
Overlook

Bear
Wallow
Trail

Meneka
Peak
Trail

MOUNTAIN

Fort Valley
Overlook

To Waterlick

Spring

P

GEORGE   WASHINGTON

Campground

VALLEY

BM 747

628

Ruins   Elizabeth Furnace
Recreational Area

Massanutten Trail

Amphitheater

Picnic
Area

Campground

to Strasburg

BM
757

CREEK

Shawl Gap

continuing from town about 5 miles to a right onto VA 678. Driving 3.5 miles on VA 678 will bring you to the Signal Knob parking area on the right. (See Hike 28 for directions to this hike from other points.)

A white-blazed trail comes into the parking area from the left. As you will be returning via this route, ignore it now and take orange-blazed Massanutten Trail (some maps and other sources refer to it by its older name of Signal Knob Trail {FS 402}), leaving the parking lot to the right. Trail builders and maintainers have made your walking easier by doing a good job of removing boulders from the path, yet the treadway is on-and-off rough and rocky for the first 2.6 miles of the ascent. Despite the ruggedness, Signal Knob has become a popular mountain-bike destination, so be prepared to have to move aside at any moment.

Pass a Forest Service cabin (closed to the public) at 0.25 mile. In 0.4 mile, when you cross a small water run, look uphill a few feet for its source—a spring emanating from a stone-walled box. A rock slide, causing a break in the vegetation, gives a limited view to the southeast of shimmering Passage Creek in the valley directly below. Plan on abundant and irresistible blueberries at this spot in July and August to slow the forward progress of your hike.

Buzzard Rock, a prominent outcropping to the east, is visible at a natural overlook in 1.5 miles; the mountains of Shenandoah National Park are to the southeast. A burn area at 1.6 miles provides additional views. Small circular holes in the trees are an example of how nature makes use of the results of such fires: the holes were made by sapsuckers in search of the insects that invaded the trees in order to feast on decaying wood. Swing around a spur ridge at 2.2 miles to another overlook, this one of

bucolic Fort Valley nestled between the eastern and western ridges of Massanutten Mountain. Kennedy Peak is the prominent point on the eastern ridge.

Shenandoah Valley Overlook Trail, no longer maintained, heads off to the right at 2.9 miles. You have just about reached the ridgeline and will be walking more or less level for a while. White-blazed Meneka Peak Trail {FS 427} goes off to the left, crosses the peak, and rejoins this hike in about one and one-half miles at the 6.4 mile point; keep right. Greenbriar and sassafras are beginning to crowd out the rest of the undergrowth. Pass by the transmitter—the present-day means of communication that utilizes the mountain—and keep to the right to follow yellow blazes when a trail comes in from the left.

The far-reaching, commanding view of Shenandoah Valley from Signal Knob at 4.4 miles makes it easy to see why the Confederates used this vantage to observe Federal troop activity. With a little searching, remains of the stone fortifications they built can be found on the knob. The Southern army planned its strategy for the battle of Cedar Creek in 1864 from this point. Because of this advantage, the battle at first appeared to be going in their favor, but Federal forces eventually rallied, forcing the Confederates under General Jubal A. Early's command to beat a hasty retreat southward. The Union wanted to ensure the valley would no longer be useful to the South, and the destruction by General P. H. Sheridan's troops was so complete that, in his words, "a crow would have to carry his rations if he flew over it." Turkey vultures are often seen hovering over Signal Knob, riding thermals rising from the valley.

Around the Signal Knob area is a trail that heads back to the transmitting towers. You need to look for the wide, descending,

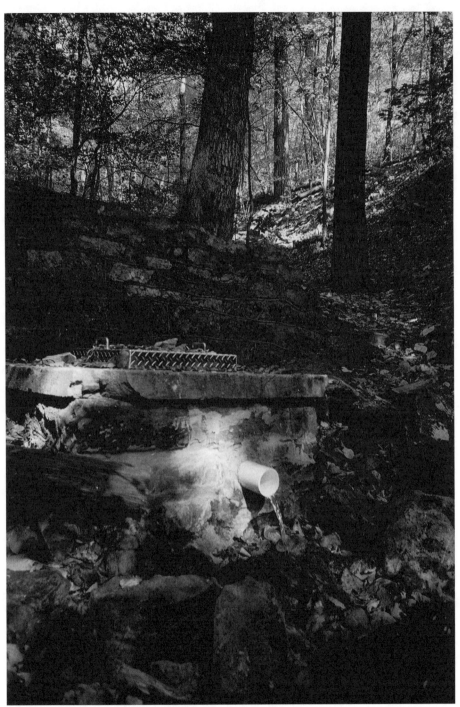
A box spring near the beginning of the trail

orange-blazed Massanutten Trail (some maps and other sources refer to it by its older name of Massanutten Mountain West Trail {FS 408}), which will bring you to the headwaters of Little Passage Creek at 5 miles. In this valley is Sand Springs, the source of water for the troops on Signal Knob. Nearby is the grave of an unnamed soldier from Georgia. Upon finding a rotting headboard with only the words "A Georgia Volunteer," Mary Ashely Townsend was moved to write:

What fights he fought, what wounds he
    wore,
All are unknown to fame;
Remember, on his lonely grave
There is not e'en a name!
That he fought well and bravely, too
And held his country dear,
We know, else he had never been
A Georgia Volunteer.

Continue downstream to a four-way intersection at 5.7 miles. Orange-blazed Massanutten Mountain West Trail continues straight and the Tuscarora Trail (still identified on many maps and other resources by its older name of Big Blue Trail) is to the right. Take a left to cross Little Passage Creek and ascend the switchbacking, blue-blazed Bear Wallow Trail {FS 405}, which is also a part of the Tuscarora Trail at this point. The Tuscarora Trail is a marked long-distance pathway of more than 200 miles. Its southern terminus is a junction with the Appalachian Trail a couple of miles north of Elk Wallow Gap in Shenandoah National Park. The trail crosses the Shenandoah Valley and continues through Virginia, West Virginia, Maryland, and Pennsylvania, where its northern terminus junctions with the AT just north of Donnellytown, Pennsylvania.

A trail to the right at 9.2 miles leads to the Elizabeth Furnace Recreation Area; keep left, cross a stream, and slab the hillside, following the blue and orange blazes. Larger trees, now making up a greater percentage of the forest, give the woods a deeper and darker feeling. Ascend a short distance to cross a spur ridge and descend through forest showing the scars of a 1984 fire and years of gypsy moth invasions. A break in the vegetation lets you look out over the same farmland you observed from the Fort Valley Overlook, only now, with your lower elevation, you are able to make out more detail. Continue the descent, which is gentle at times but makes use of switchbacks at other spots.

A trail to the right at 9.2 miles leads to the Elizabeth Furnace Recreation Area; keep left, cross a stream, and slab the hillside, following the blue and orange blazes. Pine trees are conspicuous in their absence in this lowland forest. Slowly healing pits and depressions in the earth are evidence of old charcoal hearths and iron-ore mines that furnished materials for the nearby Elizabeth Furnace while it operated throughout much of the 1800s.

The Tuscarora Trail bears to the right at 9.9 miles; continue left to return to your car at 10.4 miles. A right turn out of the parking area onto VA 678 for a drive of less than a mile will take you to two short (0.25-mile and 0.5-mile) interpretive trails in the Elizabeth Furnace Picnic Area. See the end of Hike 28 for additional walking opportunities in the nearby area.

28

Woodstock Observation Tower

Total distance (round trip): 0.3 mile

Hiking time: 15 minutes

Vertical rise: less than 50 feet

Map: USGS 7½′ Rileyville

This little jaunt is so short it can barely be considered a hike. Nevertheless, if you are in the area, you shouldn't pass up the chance to walk to the Woodstock Observation Tower. It is so easy that even those who are out of shape can handle it—an excellent introduction for someone you are taking out on a hike for the first time. There are very, very few places in Virginia where you can reap such a marvelous and rewarding payback for the small amount of energy you will expend and the few minutes of time you will invest walking to this destination.

The drive to the trailhead is also simple and pleasurable. Take the Woodstock exit off I-81, heading eastward to town, and turn left onto US 11. Despite the usual, modern-day strip of several service stations, motels, and restaurants next to the interstate, the town proper has retained much of the look of a previous era. The Shenandoah County Courthouse on Main Street, built in 1792, is the oldest courthouse still in use west of the Blue Ridge Mountains, and the inside of the building has been restored to its original design. Even having a meal in Woodstock can take on a historical aspect—one restaurant is in a former gristmill built in 1848 and another in a log cabin decorated with early American artifacts and antiques.

Take VA 758 east out of town, entering the rich green, fertile, rolling pastoral landscape that has given the Shenandoah Valley much of its fame. Stay on VA 758 through several intersections, soon crossing the Shenandoah River. Observe and remember what the river looks like close up, for soon you will be treated to an aerial view that takes in many miles of its course. The road eventually turns to dirt and makes numerous switchbacks up the mountain, enabling you to use fossil-fuel power instead of leg muscles to gain the elevation necessary to reach the ridge on Powell Mountain.

Leave your car at the signed parking area and ascend a few stone steps on the right side of the road. Coming into intimate contact with a mountaintop environment of boulders, pines, and oaks, cross the white-blazed Wagon Road Trail {FS 552} in 200 feet. Wagon Road Trail drops approximately one mile to the left to the Little Fort Recreation Area (a Forest Service campground and picnic area). A resort used to operate at Seven Fountains in Fort Valley (to the east). Most of its guests arrived in Woodstock by train from the metropolitan areas around Washington, D.C., and a stagecoach carried them from Woodstock, over the mountain, and to the resort. Wagon Road Trail actually follows the old stage route, and a meadow near the Little Fort Recreation Area was used as a picnicking and rest stop.

Continue on the ridgeline of the mountain to arrive at the Woodstock Observation Tower at 0.15 mile. Construction of the tower in 1935 was a cooperative effort by the Civilian Conservation Corps and the Woodstock Chamber of Commerce.

The 360-degree view from the tower is absolutely stunning. To the west, rising out of the wide, emerald expanse of Shenandoah Valley, are Little Sluice Mountain (see Hike 17), Mill Mountain (see Hike 18), and the higher Allegheny Mountains in West Virginia. At the base of Powell Mountain are the world-famous horseshoe bends of the Shenandoah River. The meandering course of the river between Edinburg and Strasburg is almost 50 miles, but a straight distance between the two towns is only about 15! To the north and

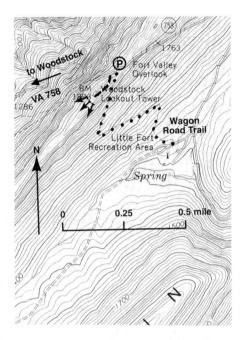

south are the ridgelines of Powell and Green Mountains, which, along with the eastern flank of Massanutten Mountain, completely surround Fort Valley, giving it the appearance of being a large volcanic crater. This "natural fort" was named by George Washington, who would have used the valley as a retreat had he been defeated at Yorktown. Farther east, beyond Massanutten Mountain and across Page Valley, are the Blue Ridge Mountains of Shenandoah National Park.

Let your eyes feast on this restful, visual treat. Maybe, just maybe, you shouldn't worry about the history of the area. Perhaps you shouldn't even try to pick out specific landmarks. Just relax and enjoy the splendor of this moment, a moment that you have been picked by the fates to experience and possess.

The Massanutten Mountain area is rich with additional hiking opportunities. Continuing to drive east on VA 758 from the observation tower brings you into the heart of Fort Valley and to the intersection with

Woodstock Observation Tower

VA 678. Making a left turn onto VA 678 for several miles will bring you to the Elizabeth Furnace Recreation Area for two short interpretive trails and the Signal Knob hike (see Hike 27). A right onto VA 678 from its intersection with VA 758 and then continuing south via VA 675 and FDR 274 will take you past the Duncan Knob hike (see Hike 29), the Lion's Tale Trail–an interpretive trail for the visually handicapped–and the Massanutten Story Trail, a 0.5-mile paved pathway suitable for wheelchairs. Another paved trail and several other pedestrian routes emanate from the Massanutten Visitor Center in New Market Gap, where FDR 274 meets US 211.

29

Duncan Knob

Total distance (circuit): 8.75 miles

Hiking time: 6 hours

Vertical rise: 2,240 feet

Map: USGS 7½′ Hamburg

At an elevation of 2,803 feet, Duncan Knob sits atop Catback Mountain, which is actually just one of the many ridges that make up 50-mile-long Massanutten Mountain. Standing alone and bisecting the Shenandoah Valley, Massanutten Mountain prevents the north and south branches of the Shenandoah River from meeting each other until the mountain comes to an end near Strasburg. The hike to Duncan Knob allows you to become familiar with the ridges and valleys of this great mountain and to gaze out upon a large expanse of land to see how the mountain has helped shape the surrounding topography.

This walk, which involves a short stretch of unmarked trail and a bit of scrambling up a rocky slope for a few hundred feet, can be easily accomplished as a day hike. However, because the hike is all on public land where camping is permitted, you might want to consider an overnight trip. Not only would this prolong your time on, and enjoyment of, the mountain, but it would also put you in position to be on top of Duncan Knob at the times of day when its view is best appreciated—early morning or early evening. It is at this time that rays of the sun strike the earth at just the right slant to produce a golden, glowing landscape—a great time to take photographs. Campsites are plentiful, especially in the first 3 miles or so. Just be sure to carry enough water, as sources may be scarce at the flattest or most choice sites.

(By the time you hike here, trail names and the color of blazes may have changed. However, the description and route of the hike will continue to be correct.)

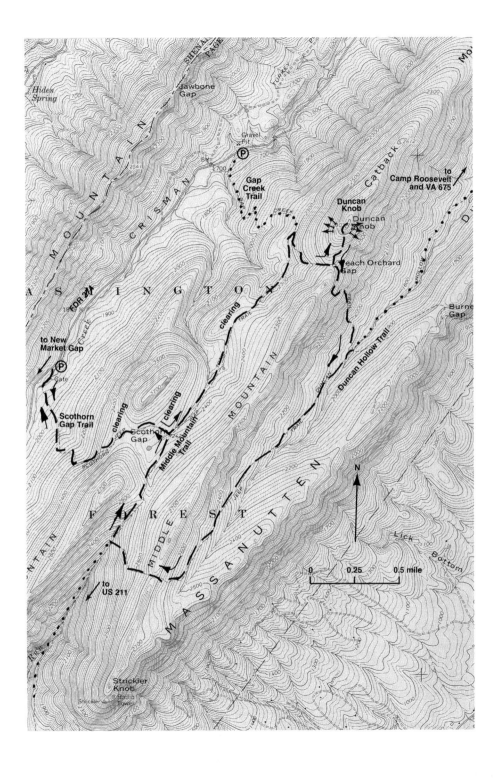

Exit I-81 at New Market and follow US 211 eastward for less than 10 miles to a left turn onto FDR 274 in New Market Gap. If you come to the Forest Service's Massanutten Visitor Center on the right side of US 211, you have gone just a few feet too far. (But before turning around, chat with the center's Forest Service employees or volunteers about the vast number of hikes that can be taken in the Massanutten Mountain area.) Once on FDR 274, follow it past Massanutten Mountain Story Book and Waterfall Mountain trailheads to arrive at the Scothorn Gap Creek Trail {FS 555} on the right in 4 to 5 miles.

Begin the hike by crossing Passage Creek and ascending the old red-blazed road. In 0.4 mile the road makes a little zigzag and ascends at a steeper grade; in one spot there are several switchbacks to modify the grade a bit before the road resumes the steep ascent. Mountain laurel becomes more dense and maple and sassafras leaves add dashes of red to the forest in the fall. Level out on the ridgeline, passing through a wildlife clearing at 0.9 mile. Clearings such as this can be found in almost all of America's national forests. Usually they are not naturally occurring open spaces but are created by the Forest Service (many are remnants of old logging operations) to provide food or shelter sites for particular types of birds or animals. By designing the lay of the land and planting certain trees, shrubs, grasses, and flowers, a variety of wildlife, such as deer, turkeys, grouse, squirrels, and quail, can be attracted to an area. Camp in the woods next to a clearing, be quiet and still, and odds are—especially at dusk—you will be able to watch several birds or animals as they go about their daily activities. Take the proper precautions, though, as these clearings are popular hunting spots during the season.

Skirt the corner of another clearing at 1.3 miles and bear to the right, looking for the red blazes as your route reenters the woods to junction with yellow-blazed Middle Mountain Trail {FS 555A} coming in from the right. You will return on this trail. Turn left now and descend along the old woods road. At 1.8 miles an unmarked trail to the right leads to a small pond that can provide wildlife with water during dry seasons. In 2.1 miles skirt the right side of a clearing and continue to descend, sometimes quickly. The forest you are walking through must be home to a great assortment of wildlife, judging by the wide variety of scat seen on rocks. At 2.6 miles the route crosses a small draw and ascends slightly, becoming more of a trail than an old roadway.

Scothorn Gap Creek Trail ends as you come to blue-blazed Gap Trail {FS 409} in 2.8 miles. Part of this trail drops to the left for about a mile to FDR 274, but you want to follow it uphill to the right. Come onto the ridgeline in Peach Orchard Gap in 3.1 miles. At the high point in the gap is an unmarked, faint, but discernible trail off to the left. Follow this trail (if you lose it, just keep going uphill) through the woods for a little more than a thousand feet to come to the rock scree facing of Duncan Knob. Scramble up the rocks (going a bit to the left is the easiest) to the knob. Take a well-deserved break on top; the Olympian view more than makes up for the few calories you've burned to reach here.

Directly southwest is Middle Mountain—you have just walked along its western flank and will soon explore its eastern side. To the west are rocky outcroppings on Kerns Mountain and beyond is I-81 winding through the Shenandoah Valley. Southeast and almost directly below are the oxbow bends of the South Branch of the

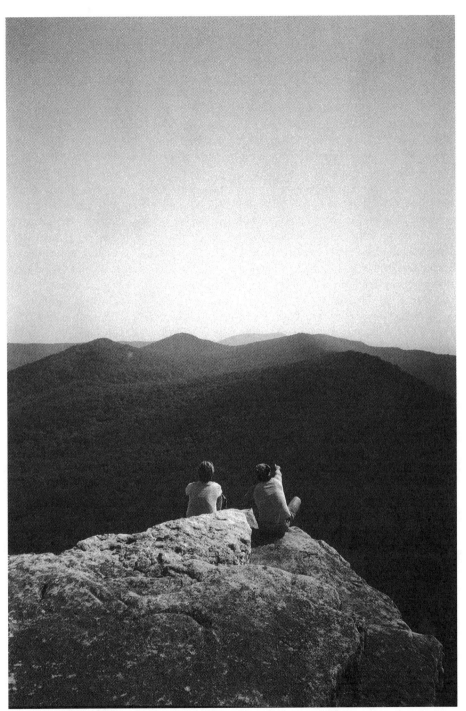

The view of Middle Mountain from Duncan Knob

Shenandoah River. On the eastern horizon, across Page Valley, are the Blue Ridge Mountains of Shenandoah National Park.

Return to the Gap Creek Trail and turn left (eastward) to descend a rocky pathway through abundant sassafras. Gap Trail ends as it meets up with orange-blazed Duncan Hollow Trail {FS 410}. To the left it is about three miles to Camp Roosevelt (site of the first Civilian Conservation Corps camp in America; building foundations still exist) and VA 675. You need to make a right and gradually ascend. Despite the presence of an old roadway, Duncan Hollow is a wonderful valley, showing few signs of human activity and isolated from traffic noise and other sounds of modern society. The hollow also supports a luxuriant growth of mountain laurel, especially beautiful from May to June when the clusters of rich pink to white flowers contrast with deep green leaves.

Be looking for small, cone-shaped holes made by ant lions in the sandy soil of the roadbed. These enterprising larvae make use of the "angle of repose" by crafting the sides of their dens at about a 30-degree angle, the steepest slant at which dry sand can sustain a slope. Unsuspecting insects stepping onto this sand steepen the slope by just a degree or two and are sent tumbling into the clutches of the lion hiding in the sand below.

Ascend more quickly at 4.7 miles for a short distance before the road mellows again and you pass through a forest of large oaks and maples. Several trees bear the scars of violent lightning strikes. In 6.1 miles the road deteriorates into a rough and rocky pathway that swings to the right and ascends steeply to attain the boulder-strewn and mountain laurel–covered ridge of Middle Mountain at 6.4 miles. If you are hiking in the fall, stop to examine the small capsules on the mountain laurel. Break open one of these capsules, which were the plant's flowers earlier in the year, and you will discover what looks to be brown dust. Each dust speck is actually a seed of the mountain laurel and is so small that more than 1,000 of these seeds could easily fit into something about the size of a pea.

At 6.8 miles the Duncan Hollow Trail goes off to the left to descend to US 211 in a little more than three miles. Your route is now to the right, following yellow-blazed Middle Mountain Trail as it rises at a gradual, almost imperceptible grade. Soon, though, you will descend to intersect Scothorn Gap Trail at 7.4 miles. Bear left, following the red blazes to the left of the clearing to make the final descent, retracing your steps on the same old road on which you began this hike and arriving back at Passage Creek and your automobile at 8.75 miles.

See the end of Hike 28 for additional walking opportunities in the nearby area.

30

Ivy Creek Natural Area

Total distance (circuit): 5.0 miles

Hiking time: 3 hours

Vertical rise: 500 feet

Maps: USGS 7½′ Charlottesville East; Ivy Creek Natural Area map

Like the Blue Trail that follows Bull Run and the Occoquan River (see Hike 10), Ivy Creek Natural Area is an example of the benefits that occur when a group of concerned citizens band together. The natural area is a buffer zone protecting a part of the South Rivanna Reservoir, a major source of water for Charlottesville. The nonprofit Ivy Creek Foundation was formed in 1979 to assist local governments in planning, expanding, and operating the area in an ecologically sound manner.

The organization has done an admirable job of preservation. Fall hikers will walk pathways lined by blossoms of pokeweed, cardinal flower, moth mullein, and dayflower. Spring flowers include hepatica, shadbush, pennywort, and rue anemone. Canada geese, herons, and ducks can be found at the reservoir. The area's topography contains fields, streams, marshlike backwater areas, tree-covered ridges, and habitats appropriate for a wide variety of animal life. Be looking for groundhogs, rabbits, deer, raccoons, turkeys, opossums, foxes, and maybe even a mink.

The layout of the natural area's trails is a marvel in its own right. With only 215 acres to work with, trail designers have made possible hikes of 5 to 6 miles with a minimum of backtracking. To reach the area, follow US 29 north through Charlottesville, turning west onto VA 743. Stay on VA 743 through some tricky intersections and name changes for 2.3 miles to the natural area's entrance on the left.

From the parking lot take a paved trail to a kiosk with bulletin boards, which provide route comes into a field. After about 30 feet, make an abrupt left turn into the woods. At 0.17 mile, come to an intersection where you bear right and descend to continue on the blue trail.

At 0.25 mile, pass by an old stone-walled spring and descend to a large beech tree and view of Martin's Branch estuary. Continue on the blue trail up through the woods and back across the field to the same intersection as at 0.17 mile. Make a hard right to proceed onto the one pathway that you have yet to walk upon, following the route near an old fence line. Two hundred feet beyond, make a right onto the red trail. Continue descending, passing by a bench and bearing right.

Come to Martin's Branch in the low-lands area of the forest, continuing to follow the red trail. Take the short side trail leading to an overlook of Martin's Branch estuary and the reservoir. During summer and fall, the 3-feet-tall showy monkey flower grows prolifically in the muddy soil near the edge of the water. Its violet, yellow, and white blossoms make it almost impossible to misidentify. Retrace your steps and turn right onto the red trail, skirting the reservoir.

Ascend and, at 1 mile, swing away from the reservoir. Stop to admire a magnificent 200-year-old white oak, the largest tree in the natural area. Something to reflect upon: This tree was already a teenager when Abraham Lincoln was born in 1809! There are many other impressive oaks in this portion of the forest. Some scientists believe that, if not subjected to timbering, insects (gypsy moths do extensive damage), or disparate mishaps, white oaks may be able to live for 600 years.

Bear left at the next intersection to begin following the brown trail. Skirt a field, which is maintained as an open area to

detailed information. Trail maps and brochures may, and should, be picked up here. Leave the pavement and walk behind the barn and in front of one of the most unique rest rooms you are likely to see anywhere. The "clivus multrum" was built in 1982, making it the first composting toilet at a public facility in Virginia.

Begin following the blue-marked trail by descending into a mixed pine and hardwood forest. In 0.1 mile be alert when the create habitat variety. Reenter the woods at 1.2 miles and go right at the intersection, staying on the brown trail. A bench under a grand old beech is a convenient resting spot.

Turn right at 1.25 miles and continue on for a few feet to another right onto the red trail along the edge of a clearing. Come to a four-way intersection at 1.5 miles. Continue straight to follow the lesser-used orange trail into a forest of many dogwoods. Descend through mostly hardwoods and ferns with good winter views of the reservoir.

There is a major intersection at 1.6 miles where you need to turn right onto the P (Peninsula) Trail. In a section of laurel, bear right at a loop-trail intersection for sundry views of the reservoir. As the trail swings around the peninsula's point, a pathway drops right to the bank of the reservoir. Although you can see beaver activity all around the peninsula, it is especially obvious at 2.1 miles; you might also witness a great blue heron rise from the reservoir, taking flight on its 70-inch wingspan.

Return to the loop-trail intersection at 2.2 miles, bear right, and, 0.1 mile beyond, return to the major intersection. Make a hard right onto the orange trail. Soon cross a (usually) dry water run on a plank bridge and ascend a short distance along an old road through open hardwood forest. Reach the height of the land and descend.

Swing left at 2.6 miles. Stay left again at 2.8 miles, as the trail to the right merely leads to a pipeline right-of-way. Turn right onto the OL (Loop) Trail at 3 miles to skirt the edge of another clearing being reclaimed by the forest. At the next intersection, keep left; the trail right is a shortcut to the red trail. Having returned to the orange trail at 3.1 miles, turn right onto it. At 3.2 miles you will have come back to the same intersection as the 1.25-miles intersection.

Avoid both trails to the left and continue on your route along the red trail.

There is a confusing intersection at 3.3 miles. Do not go through the crumbling stone walls, as this will bring you back to the OL (Loop) trail. Instead, stay on the red trail to cross a small tributary of Martin's Branch.

Cross the pipeline at 3.4 miles, leave the red trail, and bear right onto the green trail. (The red trail is shorter and rejoins your route at the 4.1-mile point.) Reenter the woods through dogwoods and pines.

Cross a stream. You are on the border of the natural area, and private homes may be seen through the vegetation. Use a wooden footbridge to cross the stream and at 4.1 miles rejoin the red trail. Martin's Branch is crossed one more time, at 4.2 miles, as you continue to follow it downstream. In a few hundred feet step over another tributary of Martin's Branch and bear left onto the white trail. The red trail to the right is a shorter way to rejoin your route at the 4.8-mile point.

You will encounter three intersections within the next 0.2 mile. Keep right at each of them. The first is where you'll make a right onto the well-used pathway of the red trail. Continuing straight at the next intersection would bring you to the barn and rest rooms. A left at the third intersection goes to the rest rooms.

By now, if you have been able to negotiate the maze of intersections correctly, you will be following the SC (School) Trail through the woods.

Cross a small water run and ascend on the School Trail. Have you ever wondered what tulip poplars, red maples, red oaks, black oaks, black gums, black cherries, white pines, Virginia pines, American hornbeams, or American beeches look like? These trees, and others, are labeled

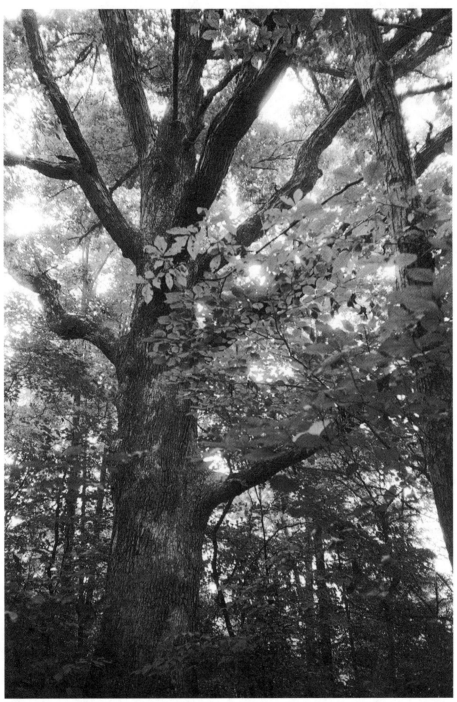

White oak

here, permitting you to make close-up observations of the bark texture, leaf shape, kind of seed or flower, and other identifiable characteristics of each species.

At 4.8 miles, cross under a utility line, walking onto the red trail. Bear left at the next junction, coming into the succession field and walking toward the parking lot. (A right would have gone onto the fainter yellow trail, which loops back to the red trail near the 4.2-mile point of this hike description.) Return to your automobile at 5 miles.

Except for special events, the natural area is open only during daylight hours. A short wheelchair-accessible trail is located close to the barn. Camping and pets are not permitted. Picnicking is allowed, but no tables are provided. Entrance is free; donations accepted.

31

White Rock Falls and Slacks Overlook Trails

Total distance (circuit): 5.0 miles

Hiking time: 3 hours

Vertical rise: 1,050 feet

Map: USGS 7½' Big Levels

Shenandoah and the Great Smoky Mountains National Parks, two of America's most-visited and scenic national parks, are linked via another beautiful and popular component of the national park system, the Blue Ridge Parkway (BRP). Meandering along the crest of the mountains for more than 469 miles, the parkway provides an opportunity to become intimately associated with the natural and human histories of the southern Appalachian Mountains.

In 1933, President Franklin Roosevelt made an inspection tour of the first Civilian Conservation Corps camp to be established in Virginia. Roosevelt not only enjoyed the beauty of Shenandoah National Park but was well pleased with the progress and potential of the Skyline Drive. Prodded on by local politicians (who realized its economic benefits) and naturalists from Virginia, North Carolina, and Tennessee, Roosevelt approved the idea of the parkway and development began on September 11, 1935. With the construction of the Linn Cove Viaduct on the eastern flank of Grandfather Mountain in North Carolina in 1983 and several more years of joining together "missing link" sections, the task was accomplished. On September 11, 1987, a ceremony on the viaduct officially declared the completion of the parkway, exactly 52 years after the project was started.

There are more than 100 Park Service trails along the parkway and dozens of Forest Service, state park, and private pathways that either connect or come in close contact with it—in other words, there exist ample occasions to experience and explore the mountains. In addition, the world-famous 2,000-mile Appalachian Trail parallels the parkway for more than 100 miles in Virginia. Also, the ambitious and soon-to-be famous Mountains to Sea Trail, which someday will stretch 700 miles from Clingman's Dome high atop the Great Smokies to the white sand and rolling surf of Nags Head on the Outer Banks, criss-crosses the parkway in western North Carolina numerous times. If you desire any more information, *Walking the Blue Ridge: A Guide to the Trails of the Blue Ridge Parkway* contains detailed information on each and every trail along the full length of the parkway.

The Blue Ridge Parkway may be reached by exiting either US 250 or I-64 in Rockfish Gap a few miles east of Waynesboro. Follow highway signs for a very short distance and turn south onto the parkway.

Before hiking the White Rock Falls and Slacks Overlook Trails, I suggest you walk two short pathways that will provide you with enough knowledge and insight to make your future ramblings in the Blue Ridge Mountains more enjoyable.

The Algonquin, Delaware, Iroquois, Catawba, Shawnee, and Cherokee Indians

---

were living in, or making use of, the Blue Ridge Mountains when European-based explorers first arrived in the New World. Traveling southward from Pennsylvania or westward from the coast of North Carolina, settlers began arriving in the early 1700s. Their numbers gradually increased to the point that by the end of the Revolutionary War small communities were established throughout the mountains. Isolated from urban centers, these settlers became quite self-sufficient.

An excellent introduction to the lifestyle of these hardy folks is provided by the Mountain Farm Trail located at BRP milepost 5.9. The Park Service has reconstructed a typical mountain farm of the early 1900s along this 0.25-mile pathway. Signposts explain the uses of various structures such as log cabins, gear lofts, and weasel-proof chicken houses. Here you will learn how a maul and frow, beatlin block, or ash hopper was used. A garden is planted for the growing season and live demonstrations are presented during the spring, summer, and fall. Check at the visitor center for times and dates.

The 0.2-mile (circuit) Greenstone Trail is located at BRP milepost 8.8. Signs along the oak- and hickory-lined trail explain the volcanic origins of the northern Blue Ridge Mountains. Although this is a very short trail, the information learned on it will add greatly to your appreciation of the mountains as you drive and walk through them.

The White Rock Falls Trail is located at BRP milepost 18.5 in White Rock Gap. However, there is only a small grassy parking area here, and the trail sign is hidden below the roadway. Therefore, be on the lookout for the parking area and a tree blazed with an orange diamond. White Rock Falls Trail was built by the Youth Conservation Corps in 1979 and is now

excellently maintained by volunteers of the Tidewater Appalachian Trail Club. (In fact, in recent years they constructed a new series of well-built switchbacks to eliminate the former steep climb up from the falls and back toward the parkway.)

To begin the hike, leave your car, cross the roadway, and gradually descend on the trail, which is lined with wintergreen and covered over by towering hemlocks. Farther on you may run across mayapple, trillium, and wild geranium in early to late spring. Within the first 0.2 mile you will cross three small footbridges above jumbles of large boulders in the valley below. Pass by old, crumbling stone walls that were probably, at one time, "hogwall" fences used by farmers to keep their razor-back pigs from wandering too far. At 0.5 mile the pathway joins an old roadbed, but be alert because it soon makes an abrupt turn to the right, off the road, to gradually ascend through mountain laurel and pine. Sassafras is particularly abundant here.

Some of the older trees on this route bear the markings of successful feedings by, evidently, quite a number of woodpeckers. Continue with gradual ups and downs and at 1.2 miles cross a small stream. The spot is an ideal relaxation point. Ascend, steeply at first, but then on well-graded switchbacks. Continue in a ravine rich with hemlock.

Reach a trail intersection at 1.6 miles. Three hundred feet to the right along the rock wall leads to White Rock Falls—a most magical place. Admittedly, when compared to other falls, White Rock is not all that spectacular. However, the attractions here are that you have reached such a nicely isolated spot while expending such a little amount of energy to do so, and now you are able to enjoy the small but exceptional rocky gorge the water has carved out of the mountainside. The sun, beaming through

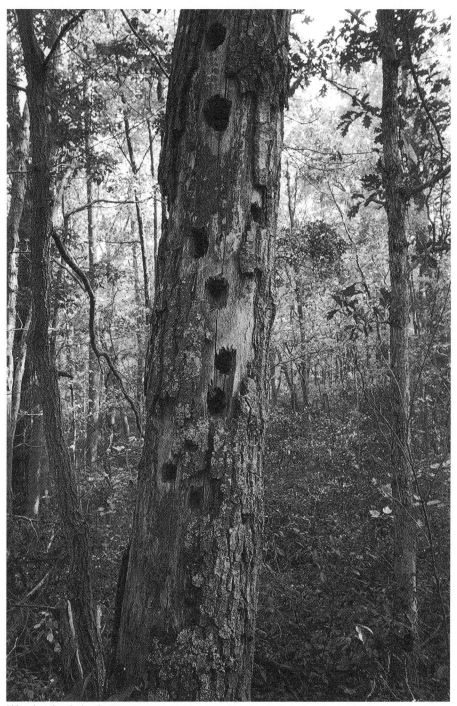
Woodpecker holes in a tree

hemlock and mountain laurel, creates shadows that dance about on the steep walls as the water cascades 30 to 40 feet through the boulders. After a stop at this enjoyable spot, return to the intersection and begin the climb back to the parkway.

At 1.9 miles reach a sort of ridgeline and descend slightly. A few rocks to the right afford good views of the valley just before you cross a footbridge and gradually ascend. You must be alert at 2.2 miles, for no matter how inviting that cool hemlock grove looks, the trail does not continue straight into it. Rather, make an abrupt right across the creek and ascend. Cross another footbridge and at 2.7 miles arrive on the parkway at milepost 20.

Continue by bearing left, crossing the parkway, and turning onto the unmarked trail past the picnic tables at the northern end of the Slacks Overlook parking area. In 250 feet, at the intersection of two unmarked trails, turn left downhill and intersect the Slacks Overlook Trail {FS 480A}, marked with blue diamonds. The Slacks Overlook Trail opens up a number of options for further hikes. A left turn onto the Slacks Overlook Trail would lead you to several paths descending into the Saint Mary's Wilderness (see Hike 33) or to other trails that drop down to the Forest Service's campground on Sherando Lake (see Hike 32). However, your present route does not go left, but rather right, and slabs the hillside. From here on out it is a pleasant walk through a mountainside environment of hardwoods, mountain laurel, and berry bushes. In fact, it is more or less downhill from here until the last half a mile.

Berry bushes are abundant as you walk onto and begin following a spur ridge at the 3.1-mile mark. Two-tenths of a mile beyond, begin a gradual and then more rapid descent. Turn left onto an old roadbed at 4.3 miles. At 4.5 miles you reach the intersection with the orange-blazed White Rock Gap Trail {FS 480}, which drops to the left for about two miles to Sherando Lake. Turn right and ascend through hemlock. Pass by an old homestead site where raspberries should be plentiful (and delicious!) in season before coming to a sign identifying a spring as the headwaters of North Fork Back Creek. Continue to ascend.

Arrive back in White Rock Gap on the parkway having completed the 5-mile circuit.

32

Sherando Lake

Total distance (circuit): 1.6 miles

Hiking time: 1 hour

Vertical rise: 280 feet

Maps: USGS 7½′ Big Levels; Sherando Recreation Area map

Sherando Lake is one of George Washington National Forest's largest recreation areas. It may be reached by taking the Waynesboro-Lyndhurst exit off I-64 and following VA 624 to Lyndhurst. After 2.5 miles bear left onto VA 664 for 7.5 miles to the entrance road on the right. Sherando Lake is a U.S. Fee Area.

Attractions at the site include a sand beach, snack-vending machines, a visitor center with interpretive materials, a picnic area, and a campground; the recreation area can accommodate close to 900 people. The 24-acre lower lake was built by the Civilian Conservation Corps in the 1930s, while the upper lake of 7 acres was built in 1958 for flood control. Both lakes reportedly have good fishing of largemouth bass, bluegill, and catfish. Trout are stocked in the spring and fall.

With so much to offer, and because it is located within a few minutes' drive of the Blue Ridge Parkway, Shenandoah National Park, and the cities of Waynesboro and Staunton, the recreation area is exceedingly popular and is usually busy almost every summer weekend.

This hike is a fairly easy and pleasant stroll next to the lake and to an elevated viewpoint. The whole family should be able to enjoy the walk, which will help you escape the hustle and bustle of a noisy beach or crowded campground.

From the beach and picnic-area parking lot, take the paved trail right, walking to the front of the large bathhouse and visitor center. Make note of the chairs on the porched breezeway of the rustic but rather elegant stone and log structure. After your walk, this would make a nice spot to relax and enjoy the lake—framed by mountains in the distance—and the pleasingly manicured and landscaped lawn in front of the breezeway.

Continue on pavement around the beach and ascend stone steps onto a pathway (Lakeside Trail {FS 300}) entering the forest. The trail is more or less level as it continues just above the shore of the lake, passing by abundant blueberry bushes, mountain laurel, and rhododendron.

The farther you get from the noisy beach area, the more likely you are to spot a belted kingfisher make a swooping dive into the

lake in search of food. If successful, the bird will emerge a few moments later with a fish in its beak, sometimes emitting its distinctive dry rattle as it flies off to consume the meal.

An ancient Greek tale is the basis for a modern-day term and tells of the origin of kingfishers. Halcyone, daughter of the King of the Winds, threw herself into the sea to drown upon hearing of the death of her husband. She did not die, but rather she and the spirit of her husband were turned into kingfishers—birds having the power to calm tumultuous waters. Thus, our use of the phrase "halcyon days."

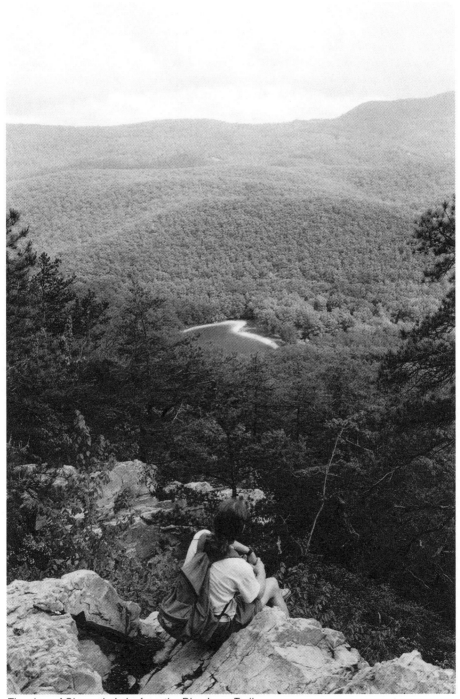

The view of Sherando Lake from the Blue Loop Trail

Reach the far end of the lake at 0.5 mile and make a left across the earthen dam to a trail along the spillway. During times of heavy rain and high water a descent on the short pathway (stay behind the fence for safety) can be exciting. Large volumes of water come rushing through the concrete canyon, loudly swishing and swirling, to make patterns and designs that exist momentarily, only to be replaced by others.

Retrace your steps to the other side of the dam and turn onto the Cliff Trail {FS 301}. Thanks to a series of switchbacks and the pathway's enterprising use of the natural lay of rock formations, the less-than-300-foot climb to the ridgeline is accomplished moderately easily.

Torry Ridge, the sloping valley formed by the north fork of Back Creek, and much of the lake can be seen from a viewpoint at 1 mile. The trail now begins a gentle descent along the ridgetop, where blueberries and sassafras are the dominant understory.

Identifying sassafras can be difficult at times. Its leaves may be one of three different shapes—three lobes, two lobes (resembling a mitten), or a single lobe. Just one type, or all three, may be present on any given tree.

Sassafras bark can be used to make a delicious tea, and its dried and crushed leaf buds are used in gumbo filé. At one time, sassafras root is what gave root beer its distinctive taste. Today, of course, most root beers are flavored artificially.

A trail comes in from the left at 1.4 miles; keep right and continue with the gradual descent. Walk past the beach and bathhouse and return to the parking lot at 1.6 miles. Better yet, pick up a cool drink, settle into one of the chairs on the bathhouse porch, read a good book, and look up occasionally to savor the scenery and the end of your halcyon day at the lake.

A myriad of hiking opportunities fan out from the Sherando Lake campground. The Blue Loop Trail ascends to the Torry Ridge Trail, which, in turn, can be used to ascend Bald Mountain and connect with trails in the Saint Mary's Wilderness (see Hike 33). The White Rock Gap Trail goes upstream along the north fork of Back Creek to White Rock Gap on the Blue Ridge Parkway (see Hike 31). A handout map, available at the entrance station, shows the small network of trails located close to the lake and within the confines of the campground.

33

Saint Mary's Wilderness

Total distance: 17.5 miles

Hiking time: overnight hike

Vertical rise: 2,400 feet

Maps: USGS 7½' Vesuvius; USGS 7½' Big Levels; US Forest Service Saint Mary's Wilderness map (recommended)

In a farsighted move, the United States achieved permanent protection for certain tracts of public land with the passage of the Wilderness Act in 1964. Within a few years, over 90 areas and more than 11 million acres had been brought into the National Wilderness Preservation System.

It soon became apparent, however, that the system was not as far-reaching as its proponents had hoped—all but four of the wilderness areas were west of Wichita, Kansas. The law's definition of wilderness, with phrases such as "the area generally appears to have been affected primarily by the forces of nature, with the imprint of man's work substantially unnoticeable," prohibited almost any area east of the Mississippi River from being included in the system. Recognizing that the East, with its earlier settlement and heavier population concentration, had more disturbed land than the West, another law was passed in 1975. This one permitted places where the evidence of human activity was gradually being reclaimed by natural processes to fit within the definition of a wilderness. That law (and hard work by wilderness proponents) has given Virginia more than 160,000 acres of officially designated wilderness.

Saint Mary's is a prime example of a spot that would have been excluded from the system before 1975. Railroads snaked into the river valley and onto some of the surrounding hills to transport the manganese ore and iron ore that was mined from the turn of the century to about 1917. Activity, with much more elaborate methods of

surface mining, began again during World War II and continued until the mid-1950s. Vegetation has begun to obscure some of the scars upon the land, yet, when explored with a historical mien, these reminders of bustling mining days can actually become a highlight of a hike.

The landscape this hike passes through is varied. The Saint Mary's River and some of its tributaries are native-trout streams, but due to several factors (one thought to be acid rain), the number of trout is declining. It is hoped that efforts by the Forest Service, such as liming the streams to neutralize the acid, may stop or slow the rate of decline. The hike begins rather gently by following one of the old mining roads (now soft and grassy in some places) along the environs of Saint Mary's River. Less than 4 miles into the trip, the route swings away from the river and into several areas of former mining activity. You leave the mines behind by making a stiff climb of about a mile to upland forests on Big Levels and Bald Mountain. From the high point, the hike descends into small stream valleys (providing secluded camping spots) before dropping back to Saint Mary's River for the return back to the trailhead. If you hike it in two days, as suggested, even with the considerable change in elevation, it is a trip of only moderate difficulty.

Saint Mary's Wilderness is reached by following VA 606 east from the Raphine–Steeles Tavern exit off I-64/81 for 1.5 miles to Steeles Tavern. Make a left onto US 11 for only 0.1 mile before making a right onto VA 56. In 1.1 miles is a left onto VA 608. Drive 2.2 miles from that intersection, watching for when VA 608 curves right to go through a railroad underpass. Three-tenths mile from the underpass, turn right onto FDR 41 and continue 1.4 miles to its terminus at the trailhead parking area.

(Please note that the Forest Service is no longer blazing trails in the wilderness. At some point in time, the paint that is there will begin to fade and references noted in other books or maps to colored blazes will no longer be valid. Do not worry, however, as the route of the trails is obvious and will still be maintained.)

Begin hiking at the far end of the parking lot where the Saint Mary's River Trail {FS 500} enters the wilderness area next to the river. Look up to your right to see the open talus slopes on the mountainside about 1,000 feet above you. Virginia creeper vines twist along the ground and onto tree trunks, as does a bountiful amount of poison ivy. Much of the time you will be walking on a rough and rocky pathway whose mud-caked stones reveal that it is actually a floodplain streambed. You'll pass a flowing spring at 0.6 mile before coming into small patches of rhododendron and mountain laurel 0.8 mile from the trailhead. The route crosses to the other side of Saint Mary's River at 1.2 miles. Periods of low water often permit rock hopping, but high water sometimes makes for a nasty, and possibly dangerous, ford.

The Saint Mary's Falls Trail {FS 500B} goes off to the left at 1.4 miles. (A walk of less than 30 minutes, one way, will bring you to the 20-foot falls.)

Keep right on Saint Mary's Trail and ascend into the hollow that the Sugartree Branch has created between Long Drive and Mine Bank Mountains. All too often, we hikers get caught up in the movement of the hike and fail to really see what we are walking through. You deserve a rest break, so stop for a while and gaze upon your surroundings. Don't look up, down, or even sideways. Look straight ahead and you will be amazed at how many things are located just at eye level. The angular twists and turns of a dogwood branch; the distinctive look of birch bark on the trunk of a tree; the two narrow, whitish strips highlighting the bottom of hemlock needles; shiny ever-green rhododendron leaves (which provide deer with nourishment in the winter); the sparkling water of the creek rolling over boulders in small cascades—all of these, and more, crowd your sight, almost de-manding that you focus on them, that you take in all their various textures, shapes, and hues, so that this special little spot in the world will still be with you long after you leave the wilderness.

A wide, deep swimming hole beckons you to linger even longer at 1.6 miles, for soon you will cross the stream, ascend somewhat steeply, and be away from the sound of water for the first time on this hike.

While doing some off-trail exploring in the old mining area at 2.1 miles, you will find the remains of an old surface mine—concrete and steel blocks, pits dug deeply into the earth, scraps of sheet metal from former storage sheds, and bits of iron slag hidden in the underbrush. Small pathways head off in many directions here so you need to look for the main route in order to swing to the left and descend around a gi-ant pit that opens up a view of Cellar Moun-tain to the north.

The rhododendron and mountain laurel become thicker where the route crosses a small stream on a culvert at 3 miles. An-other water run is crossed before the Mine Bank Trail {FS 500C} comes in from the right at 3.6 miles. Keep to the left, continu-ing on Saint Mary's River Trail.

Cross Bear Branch at 3.8 miles and come into another area bearing the scars of mining activities. Once more you can wander off the trail, closely inspecting crumbling founda-tions, large pits, and small mounds of dirt

covering old equipment and mining waste products. When you are ready to continue, return to the main route, taking the trail around a number of pits and piles through numerous dogwood trees. Rhododendron has become noticeably more abundant. At 5.2 miles, the old roadway begins to rise steeply—so steeply that the route sometimes leaves the road for short switchbacks to make the as-cent a little easier. Enter Big Levels at 5.9 miles—the name aptly describes the terrain you are now walking upon. The area was cre-ated hundreds of millions of years ago during the Paleozoic era when shifting continental plates caused the first uplifting of the Blue Ridge Mountains. Afterward, geologists be-lieve, stream erosion carved out deep and narrow canyons into the uplift. As water wore away the ridges, they became more rounded and, as the streams deposited more silt into the ever widening valleys, a gradual equaliz-ing of ground elevations occurred, creating this high mountain plateau.

At 6.15 miles, a bulletin board marks the wilderness boundary. Directly ahead is Green Pond. Walk the few steps to ob-serve this mountaintop swamp of boggy soil and water-inundated trees. Follow the grassy road from the bulletin board, swing-ing left around Green Pond. Pay attention at 6.2 miles because your route makes a sudden right off the road and onto a path-way. Follow the path to FDR 162. Turn right to soon begin ascending, by way of switch-backs, this four-wheel-drive roadway. (The Kennedy Ridge Trail {FS 479}, which goes about three miles to FDR 42, is the dirt road across FDR 162.)

During the month of June, FDR 162 is the place to be to see, possibly, the best display of rhododendron blossoms in the George Washington National Forest. Rounding each bend in the road, you are treated to different multitudes of flower petals ranging in color

---

Saint Mary's River

from pure white to bright pink to dark pink to rich shades of purple.

Descend after crossing the summit of Flint Mountain at 7.6 miles, but rise again in less than half a mile. The amount of rhododendron continues to delight the eyes, even when not in bloom, and 9.1 miles of walking delivers you to a clearing on the left for the only wide-open vista of the hike. Directly in front of you from the clearing is Torry Ridge, with the Blue Ridge Parkway and houses of the Wintergreen Resort just behind it. To the east is Three Ridges with the Priest (see Hike 35) visible in the south to the right.

Continue along FDR 162, bypassing the road to the left at 9.5 miles (which leads three-tenths mile to the top of Bald Mountain). In order to turn onto the Bald Mountain Trail {FS 500E}, you need to watch for it coming in from the right at 9.8 miles. The path is somewhat obvious, but the trail sign is hidden about 20 feet into the woods.

The Bald Mountain Trail receives very little traffic, so there is a good possibility of not seeing anyone while walking its full distance.

Descend and, at 10.3 miles, switchback into the head of a small valley, which feels well isolated and virtually unused. Cross and begin paralleling a hemlock-lined creek on a rocky, descending pathway. Cross the creek again as the valley opens up. You have reached your evening's destination. Find a good campsite somewhere within the next 0.4 mile, set up the tent, and watch, or at least listen, for wild turkey or ruffed grouse while enjoying your well-deserved dinner.

Begin the next day by leaving the creek and rising along an old roadbed at 10.8 miles. You need to be alert once more because at 11.7 miles the route leaves the road to make an abrupt right turn onto a trail hedged by azalea and sassafras. Shortly, intersect and turn right onto the Mine Bank Trail {FS 500C}. (The Blue Ridge Parkway, milepost 23, is about 300 feet to the left.)

Descend, sometimes somewhat steeply, through a forest of oak, maple, and black gum. Mountain laurel is at about eye level and Indian cucumber root, a member of the lily family, attains a height of 1 to 3 feet. It is an intriguing-looking plant that rises on a single stem to a whorl of leaves about halfway up its length to continue on to a second whorl on top. The uppermost leaves hide a small, dangling, yellow flower that blooms in May and June. The underground portion of the plant is edible.

In June, the beauty and plethora of rhododendron blossoms at and near the creek crossing make the 12.5 miles you have walked worthwhile. When you cross the stream again, appreciate the yellow birch, which provides browse for deer and whose catkins (flowers) are a favorite grouse food. Cross the creek several more times until the valley becomes a narrow gorge at 13 miles where the stream drops quickly and your route now follows an old road.

You will negotiate delightfully green rhododendron tunnels before the terrain levels out for you to intersect the Saint Mary's River Trail at 13.9 miles. Turn left to descend along the trail you came up yesterday. Eventually you will cross the river again, return to FDR 42, and come to the end of your 17.5-mile hike in the largest national forest wilderness in Virginia.

34

Crabtree Falls

Total distance (round trip): 5.8 miles

Hiking time: 4¼ hours

Vertical rise: 1,520 feet

Maps: USGS 7½' Massies Mill; Crabtree Falls Trail map

Amusingly, five different sources completely disagree on what makes the five cascades of Crabtree Falls, which drop from the northwestern face of Pinnacle Ridge, so special. One calls them the highest falls east of the Mississippi River. Another claims a total drop of 1,200 feet, while a third authority states the cascades have a combined descent of 1,080 feet. A book on the geology of Virginia gives the overall drop of the falls as only 500 feet. A fifth reference quotes no distance on the falls but proclaims them the highest cascading falls in Virginia.

For the hiker, there is no real need to be concerned with the exact distinction of Crabtree Falls. Suffice it to say that, often, you must go on an extended, arduous journey in order to reach and appreciate a waterfall of any significant or true scenic value, but not in the case of Crabtree Falls. In fact, you can reach the first of the impressive cascades by a relatively easy walk of less than 10 minutes from a trailhead located off a paved roadway. From there, the Forest Service's first-rate pathway of graded switchbacks and wooden staircases winding over and around giant boulders helps ease the burden of gaining about 1,000 feet in 1.5 miles to reach the top of the upper falls. Observation decks of native stone and timber, overlooking different portions of the falls, seem to appear at convenient spots—just at about the time you are looking for an excuse to pause and catch your breath.

This moderately strenuous hike may be reached by taking the Raphine–Steeles

Tavern exit off I-81/64 and heading east on VA 606 for 1.5 miles to US 11. Turn left onto US 11, but leave it in less than 0.1 mile by making a right onto VA 56. A 9.2 mile drive on this narrow, twisting road will bring you across the crest of the Blue Ridge Mountains and to VA 826, which comes in from the right. If you have four-wheel-drive vehicles or ones with high clearance, you could take VA 826 (which quickly becomes dirt) several miles to leave one of the vehicles at the Crabtree Meadows parking area and turn this into a one-way hike. Continue on VA 56 2.8 miles beyond VA 826 to the Crabtree Falls Trail parking lot on the right. Outhouses are located adjacent to the parking area.

Due to the fragility of the area and the popularity of this hike, camping is not permitted within 100 feet of the south fork of the Tye River or within 500 feet of the trail.

Follow the blue-blazed trail from the parking lot and in 200 feet cross the south fork of the Tye River on a wooden bridge. Stop for a moment or two to admire the effort, expense, and engineering expertise the Forest Service has expended in order to permit you to continue the hike with dry feet. This is not an ordinary, built-on-site, rough, split-log trail bridge. It was constructed in one laminated arched span, transported by way of the narrow roadway you drove to reach here and then lifted into place by cranes.

After admiring the handiwork of human beings, take a few more moments to "hear the river tearin' the mountain on down," as singer-songwriter Walkin' Jim Stoltz puts it. Some geologists believe that at one time the Appalachians were at least as high as the present-day Himalaya Mountains, only to be eroded by wind and, especially, water. Most often, the rivers and creeks slowly wear away small bits of rock and soil.

Sometimes, though, the erosion can take on cataclysmic proportions. In August 1969, Hurricane Camille, in combination with another storm front, dropped somewhere between 2 and 3 feet of rain onto the Tye River Valley in less than 6 hours. The swollen streams—uprooting trees and sending house-size boulders crashing down the mountain sides—destroyed homes, bridges, and roadways and took a large toll in human life. Enough soil was stripped away to reveal granite rock that had been hidden for hundreds of millions of years.

Moisture-laden air coming from the creek along with shade provided by the rich forest should make you notice a slight drop in temperature as you come to the first falls overlook in 0.2 mile. The water dropping in front of you makes a picturesque scene, but be sure to look upward to appreciate the full length of the falls you are viewing. Hemlocks and moss-covered logs keep the area looking richly green throughout much of the year.

Indian cucumber root and wild bleeding heart grow along the trail as you switchback uphill. At 0.4 mile you'll reach another platform, followed a short distance away by an excellent view of an approximately 70-foot cascade. Another vantage point, this one looking downstream, is reached at 0.7 mile. The falls and cascades seem to get taller and more impressive the farther you progress along the route. Violets, wild geranium, and jewelweed are now common.

Poplar and hemlock line the creek where it drops down a smooth vertical rock face at 0.9 mile. You will soon get a short breather where the trail levels out onto a shelf and the stream descends over boulders in a series of small cascades. Ferns, the dominant green undergrowth, share the forest floor with jack-in-the-pulpits and

Upper Crabtree Falls

false Solomon's seal. Distinguishing false Solomon's seal from Solomon's seal is best accomplished at either flowering or fruit-bearing time. The Solomon's seal's little bell-shaped flowers hang down from the stem, while the tiny, starred blossoms of false Solomon's seal extend from the end of the stem. Later in the year, Solomon's seal's fruit is a dark blue (almost black) berry, easily differentiated from the red berries of false Solomon's seal.

At 1.5 miles you reach the base of the upper, and certainly most impressive, falls. The water splits and takes many different paths down the rocks, so be sure to walk around as much as possible (remember to stay on the path, though) to gain various perspectives on the falls.

Come to the top of the upper falls at 1.7 miles. The water drops at such a precipitous angle that it is hard to really see any great portion of the falls. For safety reasons, don't be tempted to walk to, or on, slippery rocks in order to peer over the edge in hopes of obtaining a better look. Rather, continue on a few feet and take the footbridge across Crabtree Creek to follow a side trail out to an observation platform. You still won't be able to see the falls from here, but you can tell how much elevation you have gained by gazing down into the narrow valley carved by the south fork of the Tye River. Fork Mountain is on the other side of the valley.

Retrace your steps, cross the creek, and continue upstream. Be paying attention at 1.8 miles, where a trail on the left goes just a few feet to the side of the creek; you want to bear right onto the trail that ascends a short distance and then levels out. From here to the end of the hike, there is very little gain in elevation, so enjoy the easy walking through hemlocks and mountain laurel.

Make a mental note of how the pathway looks as your route intersects and turns right onto a woods road at 2.1 miles. Be watching for this spot on your return trip, as it is easy to overlook and make the mistake of continuing to walk down the road. (If the road leads you to a crossing of the creek on your return hike, go back until you find the trail turning off the road.) Mayapple, violets, wild geranium, and cinquefoil add their touches of colors and shapes to the undergrowth near the road.

An old road comes in from the left at 2.7 miles; keep right. Arrive at the end of the trail and the parking area on VA 826 in 2.9 miles. Outhouses are located in the woods to the right.

Across VA 826, gnarled old crab apple and apple trees grow in the field (known as Crabtree Meadows), where camping is permitted (water can be obtained from Crabtree Creek). During the 1930s, a sawmill operated, and a number of people lived, on these acres of relatively flat land located between 4,040-foot Maintop Mountain and the 4,063-foot summit of the Priest. The Appalachian Trail (see Hike 35), which goes over both of these mountains, can be reached by following VA 826 uphill for about half a mile from the end of Crabtree Falls Trail. Unless you did a car shuttle, it is time to retrace your steps back to your car at the lower parking area.

35

Appalachian Trail

Total distance (one way): 26.1 miles

Hiking time: 4 days, 3 nights

Vertical rise: approximately 7,000 feet

Maps: USGS 7½′ Montebello; USGS 7½′ Massies Mill; USGS 7½′ Big Levels; USGS 7½′ Sherando; USGS 7½′ Horseshoe Mountain

The Appalachian Trail follows the crest of the Appalachian Mountains for more than 2,100 miles as it makes its way from Springer Mountain in Georgia to Mount Katahdin in Maine. Every year approximately 200 to 400 pairs of hearty, boot-clad soles are employed by their owners to complete the full length in 4 to 6 months, but the majority of people make use of the trail for a few hours, a day, or a weekend. Benton MacKaye's 1921 proposal for a long-distance trail in the Appalachians resulted in volunteers constructing the first few miles in New York during 1922. Fifteen years later the final link was completed in central Maine. Much of the beauty of the AT stems from the fact that almost every mile of it was, and still is, built and maintained by volunteers, whose love of the outdoors leads them to invest their time and hard labors so that you and I can enjoy a walk along America's premier National Scenic Trail.

Virginia contains over 500 miles of the AT, about one-quarter of its full length. This backpack trip along it and one of its side trails has almost everything that makes hiking worthwhile in central Virginia. The trek never drops below 3,200 feet for the first two days, and it crosses the 4,060-foot summit of the Priest on the third day out. From the Priest it plummets more than 3,000 feet, just to regain most of that elevation along a waterfall-studded creek. These up-and-down efforts are amply rewarded. There are magnificent views, rhododendron-lined native-trout streams, remote forest glens, open fields of green grass, wildflowers by the thousands, and ample opportunities for quiet, isolated, and scenic campsites.

This portion of the AT—well-built, marked, and maintained by the Natural Bridge and Tidewater Appalachian Trail Clubs—is heavily traveled, especially in May and June when the bulk of thru-hikers (people hiking the AT's entire length) pass through. It is instructive and entertaining to be on the trail at this time, but no matter what month, carry a tent in the event a shelter becomes overcrowded. For a more solitary experience, hike at a different time of the year or camp at the numerous pretty little sites you will pass instead of staying in shelters. Water is available near the shelters and from several other sources. There are planned relocations for the AT, but the route will not be significantly altered nor will any great distance be added or subtracted.

The easiest way to reach the two ends of the hike is to make use of the Blue Ridge Parkway. Exit I-64 in Rockfish Gap, a few miles east of Waynesboro, and drive southward on the parkway to Reeds Gap, BRP milepost 13.7. Parking for your ending trailhead is just to the left, off VA 664. Continue south on the parkway to exit at milepost 45.6. Follow US 60 east for 4 miles to the left turn onto VA 634. Make a right onto VA 755, which becomes dirt FDR 48. Along the way is wonderful Wiggins Spring; every day, gallons of water bubble up from its underground source. Past the spring in 0.5 mile is the trailhead parking for the AT in Hog Camp Gap. (Hikes over Cold Mountain [see Hike 37] and Pompey Mountain and Mount Pleasant [see Hike 36] are nearby.)

First Day:
Total distance: 7.7 miles
Hiking time: 5 hours

Almost immediately you begin to reap the rewards of this hike by gradually ascending north from Hog Camp Gap in open meadows along the ridgeline of Tar Jacket Ridge. A better view unfolds with every upward step, culminating with the wide vista from Tar Jacket's summit at 0.5 mile. Turn around to see the AT working its way over open Cold Mountain and continuing southward into the forest of Bald Knob. East of Cold Mountain are the 4,000-foot summits of Pompey and Pleasant Mountains. The exciting thing, though, is to face the direction in which you are headed, for visible in front of you is the terrain you'll be traversing for the next couple of days. Closest is Rocky Mountain, and then Elk Pond Mountain. You will be coursing along their easterly facing slopes before ascending to the summit of Maintop Mountain. That large massif to the northeast is the Priest, the high point of your multiday trek.

Dropping from Tar Jacket Ridge, the AT enters the woods and crosses FDR 63 in Salt Log Gap at 2.2 miles. At 3,250 feet, this depression in the mountains is the lowest point you will hit until you drop into the Tye River Valley the day after tomorrow. The route ascends and passes a viewpoint on the side of Rocky Mountain looking back at Tar Jacket Ridge; cross FDR 246 at 3.4 miles and Greasy Spring Road at 3.9 miles. (From Greasy Spring Road you have the option of leaving the AT to hike an alternate pathway for a while. You may even decide to camp somewhere along it. Blue-blazed Lovingston Spring Trail {FS 731}, a former route of the AT, goes left over the crest of Rocky Mountain to Lovingston Spring in

9.0 mile, an excellent water source and good campsite. From here it continues 2.6 miles to rejoin the AT at the Seeley-Woodworth Shelter.)

Continuing on the AT from Greasy Spring Road, you will walk through a woods representative of the typical forests of the southern Appalachians, with dozens of hardwood trees showing off their luxuriant summer foliage. Wolf Rocks Overlook provides a view of Spy Rock and the Priest at 4.9 miles. Wind in and out of small hollows and groves, crossing the headwaters of the north fork of Piney River at 5.8 miles and one of its tributaries, Elk Pond Branch, at 7.0 miles. Your first day's walk is over after you turn right onto the blue-blazed side trail at 7.7 miles and arrive at Seeley-Woodworth Shelter in 500 feet. Drop the pack, unlace the boots, and kick back to enjoy the restful sounds of owls hooting in this relatively young forest.

Second Day:

Total distance: 7.2 miles
Hiking time: 5 hours

Because you don't have to invest any time in driving to a trailhead and have to do only a few hours' worth of walking, it's okay to be lazy and not get moving by the crack of dawn on your second day out. Use the early morning hours to sleep in, to cook a big breakfast, or to just watch the minutes of the day unfold in front of the shelter. The nocturnal activities of the shelter mice cease when the grainy, gray atmosphere of twilight retreats. New sun rays shine on the forest, bringing leaves, tree trunks, and underbrush into sharply defined, three-dimensional focus through the interplay of shadows with light.

Having finally packed up and walked back to the AT, make a right onto it. After descending and crossing a dirt road at Porters Field, you may huff and puff a little as you ascend through a hemlock grove, passing by some good views to attain the high point of Porter's Ridge and dropping to Fish Hatchery Road at 2.3 miles.

Take the blue-blazed side trail to the right at 2.8 miles, following it about 0.1 mile to scramble up Spy Rock, which will unquestionably present you with the best vista of the hike. Maintop Mountain is to the north, while behind it and to the west, on the other side of the Blue Ridge Parkway, is Whetstone Ridge. To the northeast, east, and south you are almost surrounded by the entire Religious Range—the Priest, Little Priest, the Friar, Little Friar, and the Cardinal. Southwestward are the miles you have walked since leaving your car yesterday—Elk Pond and Rocky Mountains and Tar Jacket Ridge. With less than 5 miles left to reach the evening's destination, you have time to dawdle; a good, long break is in order for the top of dome-shaped Spy Rock.

Return to the AT and ascend to the summit of 4,040-foot Maintop Mountain (no view), soon passing into mountain laurel groves at 3.9 miles and using a trail relocation constructed in 1991 by members of the Natural Bridge Appalachian Trail Club and volunteers of the Appalachian Trail Conference's Konnarock Crew. This relocation swings around a knob, adding a pleasant vista from Cash Hollow Rock of a number of ridgelines in the Religious Range. Continue with minor ups and downs over small ridges and into gaps where the twisted mountain laurel and rhododendron grow and cross dirt Cash Hollow Road at 5.4 miles.

After another up and down over a ridge, you will reach Crabtree Falls Road (VA 826) at 6.2 miles. If you did get an early start on the day and are feeling particularly

energetic, you might want to take a side trip to Crabtree Falls. The Crabtree Falls Trail (see Hike 34) can be reached by following dirt VA 826 left for five-tenths mile.

Continuing on the AT, the climb from VA 826 is the final effort for the day, as the route gains about 600 feet of elevation to where you will turn right onto the blue-blazed pathway at 7.1 miles. Reach the Priest Shelter and a spring 0.1 mile beyond the intersection. This shelter, sitting nearly 4,000 feet above sea level, has a special feel to it. By now, thru-hikers, who started their journey 800 miles ago in Georgia, will have a few good memories and stories that they're willing to share—if not in person, then by their entries in the shelter's register. After dinner, when conversation is on the wane, places such as this are the best settings in which to read books recounting other people's adventures on the AT. David Brill's *As Far As the Eye Can See* and Cindy Ross's *A Woman's Journey* are two of the best.

Third Day:

Total distance: 9.5 miles
Hiking time: 7½ hours

Rise early today! You have an appointment with the sunrise to watch its alpenglow slowly spread pinkish gold tinges across the rugged slopes of Three Ridges. Reach the viewpoint from which you can observe this spectacle by retracing your steps to the AT and making a right. At 0.4 mile, turn left onto a 100-foot-long side trail. From the rock outcropping you can also see what you are going to spend the day doing—dropping thousands of feet into the Tye River Valley, only to regain most of the elevation before nightfall.

Continuing the northward journey on the AT, cross the 4,060-foot summit of the Priest (no views) at 0.6 mile and begin the long descent under the thick leaf canopy of a mixed hardwood forest. Your knees and ankles will probably demand a break when you come to the only view—into the river valley—at 2.2 miles. The cheeping calls of chipmunks, and their scampering antics, may accompany you as the trail spirals down on long switchbacks. Omnivorous, the chipmunks will eat snails, insects, small birds, and even mice and snakes. In the summer, their faces are often stained by raspberry and blackberry juice, while the fall sees them running toward burrows to cache the nuts they're transporting inside bulging cheeks.

After crossing Cripple Creek at 3.5 miles, the trail makes a more direct descent of the mountain by paralleling the creek and arriving at paved VA 56 at 4.8 miles. To the left it is almost twelve miles to milepost 27.2 on the Blue Ridge Parkway. At the AT crossing, a hiker parking lot is located on the near side of VA 56 for those who want to use this spot as a trailhead. (Be aware, though, that numerous cars have been vandalized here.)

The AT continues by crossing VA 56. In 1992, members of the Tidewater Appalachian Trail Club, along with Konnarock Crew volunteers, reconstructed the suspension bridge used to get you across the Tye River. The long ascent begins with switchbacks going by numerous poplar trees, but by the time you have topped a ridgeline at 5.4 miles, oak trees have become dominant. In winter it is possible to see a farm in the valley to the right with Three Ridges standing massively above it.

Soon the route ascends steeply on an old woods road to an intersection in a small gap at 6.6 miles. You now have the option of following the AT as it bears to the right, ascending approximately 2,000

feet to traverse Three Ridges and arrive at Maupin Field Shelter, having gone nearly six miles from this intersection. Instead, so that you can enjoy the waterfalls along Campbell Creek, and to make your day a little shorter, the following description has you bearing left along the old road and taking blue-blazed Mau-Har Trail.

Following nearly level contours, your route swings in and out of large bowls and draws on the side of the mountain, passing by a couple of good springs. The roadbed fades at 7.2 miles as the trail ascends to the right on steep switchbacks. After topping the ridge and descending on a narrow, rocky pathway, you will be next to roaring Campbell Creek and its many rushing, gushing waterfalls and will begin an equally rocky and arduous ascent at 8.3 miles. Take a break at any spot that hits your fancy. A side creek, coming from a rock cleft in the hillside, is crossed at 8.8 miles as the creek drops by way of some exceptionally pretty cascades down a rock facing.

Rhododendron tunnels lead the trail to a crossing of a side creek, and cancer root grows below birch trees where the trail thrice crosses Campbell Creek, now just a small water run. Switchbacks at 9.5 miles bring you to your home for the night, the Maupin Field Shelter.

Fourth Day:

Total distance: 1.7 miles

Hiking time: 1 hour

This last jaunt is short and easy, so, depending on what you want to do with the rest of the day, you can begin at whatever hour you wish. Take the trail in front of the shelter, turning left onto the AT at 0.1 mile. Star moss lines the ascending trail and grapevines entwine on the ridgeline at 0.6 mile. Wintertime views include Three Ridges to the east and Shenandoah Valley behind the mountains to the west. The switchbacking descent begins at 0.9 mile, passing through rhododendron before coming into an open field and the end of your journey at 1.7 miles.

Now that you have enjoyed 26 miles of the AT, it may be time to contemplate hiking the rest of the trail's more than 2,100 miles. My advice? Do it! Be forewarned, though: A thru-hike of the AT may change you and your outlook on life—forever. I had been on only one overnight backpack trip before I went to Georgia to hike the AT in 1980. During the ensuing years, I've been driven to walk more than 16,000 miles in the backcountry areas of the United States, Canada, the Caribbean, and Europe. There are thousands of AT thru-hiker stories, and mine is only one. Why not make one of them yours?

36

Mount Pleasant

Total distance (circuit): 5.5 miles

Hiking time: 3¾ hours

Vertical rise: 1,400 feet

Maps: USGS 7½′ Montebello; USGS 7½′ Forks of Buffalo; Henry Lanum Trail map

The 7,500-acre Mount Pleasant National Scenic Area was designated by Congress in 1994, protecting the region from commercial use. This makes it a place you will want to come back to time and again as the years go by. Freed from the changes humanity makes on the environment by farming, road building, and logging, nature will gradually make its own changes. Rocky roadways will become covered with leaves, moss, and new growth. Open fields will overgrow, eventually turning to forest. The trees you see today will die and decay, giving way to other trees that may not even be present now. These changes are already happening; be looking for them on this fairly easy circuit, which traverses the environs of two 4,000-foot mountains. As this is on national forest lands, camping is permitted.

Drive US 60 east from Buena Vista, crossing the Blue Ridge Parkway. In 9 miles (near the Long Mountain Wayside) turn left onto VA 634. Make a right onto VA 755, which becomes dirt FDR 48. Along the way is Wiggins Spring, a true joy as it churns forth gallons of cool, clear water every hour. Past the spring, at 0.5 mile, cross the Appalachian Trail and come to a parking area. You may need to park here; in some seasons, the road beyond may be gated or become too rough for most automobiles. Whether you are able to drive or walk, continue about another 0.4 mile and turn right onto an older dirt road (FDR 51) for a few hundred feet to a small parking area and the trailhead.

Two old woods roads meet at the trailhead bulletin board. As you will be returning via the ascending road to the left, take the right one, pass through the fence stile, and gradually descend along the Henry Lanum Trail {FS #702}. (Some maps may identify this as the Pompey Mountain Trail. Its name was changed to honor the memory of a member of the Natural Bridge Appalachian Trail Club who was an ardent trail maintainer and instrumental in the protection of several areas throughout the U.S. Trailhead signs reflect this name change.)

A matting of moss makes the walking soft and easy on the feet. From June to September you should search out and stop to study the unique Indian pipe, which appears in heavily shaded areas. A saprophytic plant, it gains nourishment from decaying matter through osmosis. This herb rises from the soil on translucent, waxy looking stems. The pinkish white flower nods back toward the ground, giving the whole plant the appearance of a fancily carved soapstone pipe.

Begin a short rise at 0.8 mile and pass an overgrown clearing with black locust trees. The black locust is actually a member of the legume family and is related to peas, beans, and peanuts. Once a black locust becomes established, it propagates itself by root sprouts. This could mean that

---

Checking a map on the summit of Mount Pleasant

many of the black locust trees you see in this clearing are not individuals, but clones of one another and connected by a giant root system.

The black locust is also a succession plant that will transform this clearing into a full-fledged forest. A bacterium in its roots allows it to "capture" nitrogen from the air and use it for its own purposes. Once the tree decays, it releases this nitrogen into the ground, adding a nutrient to the soil that was previously absent or in lower concentrations. Other trees needing a more nitrogen-rich soil can then establish themselves and, probably, crowd out most of the black locusts.

Resume the descent, steeper in places, as ferns line the trail and carpet the forest floor. Cross a small stream at 1.1 miles and pass by two small springs; these flow well in the rainy season, but they should not necessarily be counted on as water sources later in the summer or fall. Cross and begin

to parallel a second water run in another 0.1 mile. A small camp could be made about 200 feet beyond the crossing. Take note of the exceptionally good job the Forest Service and volunteers of the Natural Bridge Appalachian Trail Club have done in designing and maintaining this trail. Water bars and drainage systems are strategically placed and well-built and should perform their function for a long time to come.

Be alert for double blazes at 1.5 miles as the trail turns to the left and begins to ascend. The route crosses a small stream at 1.6 miles, where the pathway becomes rougher and rockier. In 200 feet you must pay attention as the route leaves the old road, turns left onto a foot trail for 50 feet, and then right onto another roadbed.

Another turn, this one to the right, happens at 1.8 miles as the route leaves the road and passes by a well-flowing spring. Fringed phacelia put on a grand display

Blue Ridge and Massanutten Mountains

during the spring. The flowers are so numerous they make the ground look like someone has come along and cast bits of confetti throughout the forest. Close inspection of the plant reveals tiny, but deep, fringes (in botanical terms known as fimbriations) around the flowers' outer edges. The trail soon becomes steeper and rockier.

Come to a trail sign and intersection at 2.3 miles and bear to the right to take the Mount Pleasant Trail {FS #701}. In less than 0.1 mile you will pass by a shortcut trail that comes in from the left and, a little farther on, another trail to the left (often overgrown) leading to a spring. Ascend quite steeply.

Bear right at the intersection at 2.7 miles (the pathway to the left goes a few hundred yards to a viewpoint somewhat similar to that of Mount Pleasant, but with a more easterly exposure) and in 250 feet arrive at the rock outcropping on Mount Pleasant. Enjoy the nearly 360-degree view from your 4,070-foot vantage point. Behind you and to the north is Pompey Mountain, whose summit you will just miss crossing as you later continue the hike. To the northwest and west is the route of the Appalachian Trail, snaking its way across the open ridgelines of Tar Jacket Ridge and Cold Mountain (see Hike 37) and the wooded summit of Bald Knob. Chestnut Ridge is to the south. At your feet, Mount Pleasant drops quickly and steeply to the hollow created by the north fork of the Buffalo River.

Go back to the first intersection and turn left to continue retracing your steps. (Remember, right would lead to the other view.) Begin the descent of Mount Pleasant, and at 3 miles pass by the trail to your right leading to the spring. Again pass up the blue-blazed shortcut trail.

Return to the intersection with the trail sign at 3.15 miles and turn right toward Pompey Mountain. The blue-blazed shortcut trail comes in from the right at 3.3 miles. Bear left uphill toward the ridgeline. Begin descending, somewhat steeply at times, after reaching the high point of the ascent at 3.85 miles. The wooded, 4,032-foot summit of Pompey Mountain can be seen through the vegetation on your left.

After passing through a small patch of rhododendron, bear right onto an old road at 4.35 miles and gradually ascend via a switchback. You will soon begin a long, easy descent on a wide, grassy woods road. Cross through the fence stile and return to the bulletin board and parking area at 5.5 miles. An additional hiking opportunity, Cold Mountain (see Hike 37), can be reached by crossing the dirt road and following a blue-blazed trail 200 feet to a sign marking the beginning of that trail.

37

Cold Mountain

Total distance (circuit): 5.75 miles

Hiking time: 3¾ hours

Vertical rise: 1,320 feet

Maps: USGS 7½′ Montebello; USGS 7½′ Forks of Buffalo

As total public protection and domain over the entire Appalachian Trail draws ever closer to being a reality, a small, but significant, controversy has arisen among users and maintainers of the trail. Open mountaintop vistas are somewhat of a rarity in the central and southern Appalachian Mountains. In bygone days, most of these fields and meadows were kept clear by grazing cattle or other stock. Sometimes the fields were mowed for hay or kept open by controlled burnings. Should these methods, or other human manipulations, be employed or should nature be allowed to have its way, eventually turning the meadows into forests and blocking the sweeping vistas? When I first hiked the Appalachian Trail in 1980, the summit and ridgeline of Cold Mountain (identified as Cole Mountain on USGS maps) was a totally open, grassy meadow full of a variety of wildflowers. By 1991, many of the flowers were gone, having been replaced by knee-high scrub brush and young trees. A series of discussions among the Forest Service, local hiking clubs, and the Appalachian Trail Conference led to the conclusion that the rare scenic value of cleared ridgelines outweighed the desire to permit nature to take its course. Controlled burning and mechanical brush cutting is now being employed and Cold Mountain has regained the open, grassy, flowered look it had when I first encountered it.

Gaining insight into this issue is only a small reason to take this hike. In addition to the views from the summit, you will hike through mountainside meadows, into a small stand of virgin timber, and along cascading

Little Cove Creek. This hike is on national forest property, so camping is permitted. Cow Camp Gap Shelter, next to the creek, also provides a place to spend the night.

See Mount Pleasant (Hike 36) for automobile access to the beginning of the Cold Mountain hike. (These two hikes could easily be combined for a long day trip or a leisurely weekend outing.)

Begin by following the blue-blazed trail on the right side of the road from the parking area. In 200 feet come to the Hotel Trail sign, turn left, cross a fence stile, and begin following the trail, which at this point is an old roadbed. Abundant and sweet blackberries (in season) add to the enjoyment of the hike. In

0.2 mile a road comes in from the left as your route enters a wooded area where copious ferns cover the ground with rich, deep shades of green. Several springs on the left flow together to form the beginning of the north fork of the Buffalo River. The route swings away from the stream, entering an open area at 0.5 mile. Virginia and white pine, thistle, and ironweed thrive in the bright sunshine of the meadow. Look to your left for a view of Mount Pleasant.

Pay attention at 0.8 mile as the trail makes a turn to the right. It was near this spot that a former landowner, a Dr. Richeson, had a dwelling to which he would frequently invite guests. It eventually came to be known as

"The Hotel" (and thus the name for the trail). Foundations of the building are still there, but are hard to find. There is a spring on your left a few hundred feet beyond the turn. The views continue to get better as you ascend through the open field. You must be alert once again at 1 mile. The trail turns off the road to the right, crosses a small water run, enters a wooded area, and reemerges back out into the field. The pathway may be indistinct, but follow the blazed posts and you'll be on the right track. Be sure to turn around every once in a while to appreciate the scenery. Spreading below are the meadows, pines, and flowers you have just ascended through. These drop down to the north fork of the Buffalo, where your eyes will be drawn upward to the wooded slope and craggy ridge on Mount Pleasant.

A grand camp could be made on the large, flat area underneath stately old oaks at 1.2 miles. Look for the trail to veer to the right immediately after entering the woods.

Descend on a pathway softened by Virginia pine needles dropped onto the trail over the course of many years. The route becomes a little faint at 1.5 miles; watch for blazes as you slab the side of the hill with slight ups and downs. Top the ridgeline at 2 miles in a slight open area that could be used to set up a couple of small tents.

Descend to the right on a very old road lined by jewelweed (touch-me-not) and stinging nettle. If you look closely at both of these plants you will note that their tops have been nipped off at almost a uniform height. Deer feed on these plants, and they will stop chewing at the point it becomes uncomfortable for them to bend any farther. This point is known as the "browse line." In years of scarce food the browse line may be lower than normal, as the deer continue to eat downward to obtain any nourishment they can.

Begin to rise and cross Little Cove Creek, which is lined with birch trees, at 2.5 miles. There is a small spring on the left, and soon a trail to the right, at 2.75 miles, crosses the creek to Cow Camp Gap Shelter. Turn uphill to the left and, in summer, make sure to have color film in the camera for this spot. Large patches of 4- to 5-foot-high touch-me-nots grow on both sides of the trail, peppering an otherwise green understory with a multitude of red-spotted orange flowers.

Switchback to the right, ascending the old road on an almost perfect grade made for easy walking.

Intersect and turn right onto the white-blazed Appalachian Trail at 3.3 miles, where a trail relocation ascends steeper terrain. Level out at 3.7 miles and cross over rock formations on the spine of the ridge.

Break out into the open at 4 miles and continue to the open summit of 4,022-foot Cold Mountain. To give you an idea of how spectacular this spot is, my notes from scouting this hike read, "Views! Strawberries, old apple trees, butter-and-eggs. Views! Views! Views!"

To the south is wooded Bald Knob (once as open as Cold Mountain), eastward are Pompey Mountain and Mount Pleasant, and northeastward is the Religious Range—the Priest, the Friar, Little Friar, and the Cardinal. In the far distance, Three Ridges is behind the Priest, while close at hand and almost due north you can see the Appalachian Trail winding its way across the bald expanse of Tar Jacket Ridge.

Descend the ridge to enter woods at 4.8 miles. Follow the white blazes as you cross a dirt road a couple of times.

Arrive in Hog Camp Gap and turn right, tracking blue blazes along unpaved FDR 48. Watch for the blazes to turn off the road to the right, go past the Hotel Trail sign, and return to the parking area at 5.75 miles.

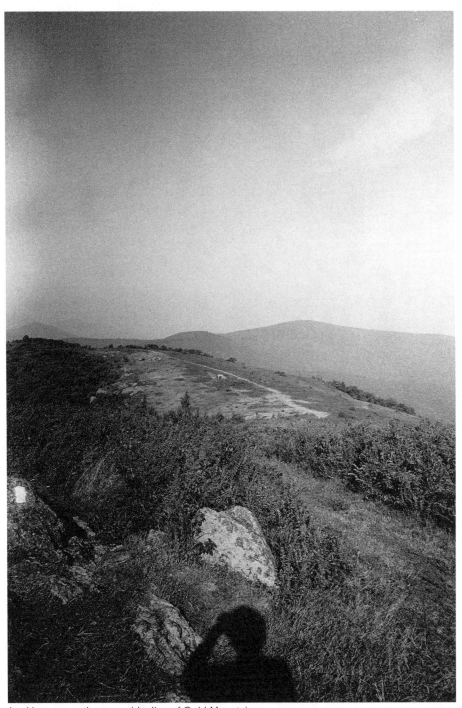

Looking across the open ridgeline of Cold Mountain

IV

Western Virginia

38

North River Gorge

Total distance (one way): 4.5 miles

Hiking time: 3½ hours

Vertical rise: 40 feet

Maps: USGS 7½´ Stokesville; North River Gorge Trail map

A thousand feet below the 2,800-foot summits of Lookout and Trimble Mountains, the serpentine North River Gorge Trail {FS 538} twists and turns on a nearly level route of exuberantly full, vibrant, and green foliage. This is a hike for those who don't need far-off vistas to feel that they are having a worthwhile woodlands experience. The lack of views is more than offset by the freedom to saunter down the gorge with almost no rise in elevation and to wander around its broad floor, searching out hidden burrows of beavers on the riverbanks or standing in far-reaching gardens of wispy ferns.

The best time to visit the gorge is in late spring and early summer, when literally hundreds of opulent pink lady's slippers will accompany you on almost every mile of the hike. This time of year also permits you to negotiate the nine fords of the river when there is still enough water flowing in the stream to make the crossings exciting and challenging. It's best to avoid the hike during the spring runoff season, and don't ever attempt to cross North River (or any stream) after heavy rains. The fords will slow your progress and you will certainly be walking in wet boots, but think of the crossings as a chance to rest for a few moments and refresh tired feet. Consider bringing along fishing gear; North River is stocked with trout by the Virginia Commission of Game and Inland Fisheries.

You will need a car shuttle, so follow the directions for reaching the Segment A trailhead of the Wild Oak National Recreation Trail (see Hike 40). From that trailhead, continue driving on FDR 95 for about 1 mile to a

paved parking area on the left side of the road. You can leave one car here, or a few hundred feet beyond, next to the gated dirt road on the left (which is where you will finish the hike). Continue with the second car, passing by Todd Lake in another 1.6 miles, where FDR 95 becomes dirt. At 1.3 miles from the lake, turn left onto FDR 95B, following it for 1 mile to the North River Campground. The campground was once a base of operations for the Civilian Conservation Corps. It is now open year-round and has vault toilets, fireplace grills, picnic tables, and water provided by a hand pump.

If you are not staying in the campground, leave your car in the parking area at the North River Gorge Trailhead, 0.2 mile beyond the campground entrance. Begin hiking by passing through the gate, and in less than 200 feet keep left on the yellow-blazed dirt roadbed. Tiny, pale bluets hugging the ground next to the roadway are hovered over by the light purple of wild geranium petals. Because all parts of the wild geranium contain tannin, it was once used as an astringent, and its leaves were brewed into a tea to treat diarrhea and bleeding ulcers.

Ford North River for the first time at 0.4 mile, passing by a wildlife clearing and crossing a side stream. The second ford is trickier, with large, slippery boulders causing your feet and ankles to twist and turn. You will make good use of your walking stick as a brace for the third ford at 0.7 mile. Because the riverbed is made of large, flat, smooth, slippery slabs of rock, there are very few cracks in which to wedge your feet to keep them, and you, from being pushed downstream by the current. Probably the best place to cross is a few feet upstream from where the trail actually comes in contact with the river. Use caution and common sense!

After the ford, the roadway becomes soft and grassy, passing a wildlife clearing at 1 mile. From May to July, the forest floor erupts in a riot of 6- to 14-inch-tall pink lady's slippers. They are next to the road, spread throughout the woods, and on the other side of the river. Like other orchids, the pink lady's slipper's exotic structure is designed to attract certain pollinators. After insects work their way through the slit in the red-veined pouch, they deposit pollen from other plants by brushing against the stigma—the tip of the pistil, or female organ. Exiting the flower by way of the two openings at the rear of the slipper, the insects then pick up that plant's pollen by grazing the anthers—the pollen-producing part of the stamen, or male organ. It appears that at one time or another almost every plant has been used for medicinal purposes, and the lady's slipper is no exception. Native Americans made a tea from its dried leaves as a cure for insomnia, and physicians, up until the 1930s, used its roots as a nerve medication. Don't, however, be tempted to touch the lady's slipper. Some people report having experienced a mild to severe skin inflammation after doing so.

At about the same time of year that the pink lady's slippers are in bloom, the vanilla-sweet smell of autumn olive, planted in the wildlife clearing at 2.2 miles, can be almost overpowering just before you ford the river for the fourth time. You will ford it again at 2.5 miles, and a sixth time at 2.8 miles.

The seventh crossing, at 2.9 miles, is a little more interesting because the trail crosses a small island that formed after the great flood of 1985. There are also a number of side streams you'll cross in order to continue to the eighth ford at 3.1 miles.

Scores of additional pink lady's slippers may keep you from being alert when

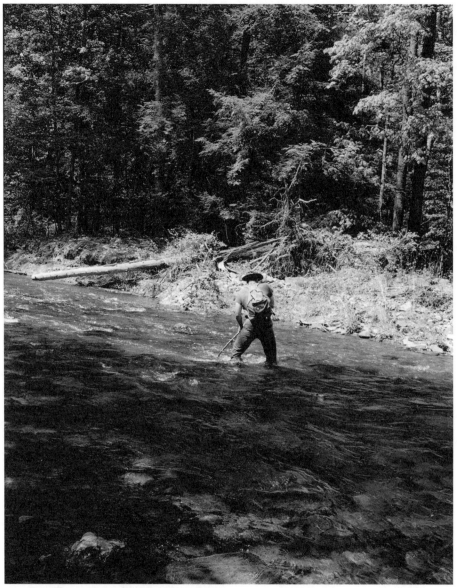

Crossing the third ford of the North River

coming to the far end of the Adirondack shelter camping area (used by Girl Scouts from Camp May Flather). The roadway continues straight, but your route makes an abrupt turn to the left to ford the river for the final time at 4 miles. It may be a little confusing after crossing the river. Do not make a turn to the right, nor follow the pathway going uphill. Instead, turn left, crossing two small streams in quick succession, and emerge onto FDR 95 at 4.5 miles.

Todd Lake Recreation Area

Total distance (circuit): 3.8 miles

Hiking time: 2¾ hours

Vertical rise: 1,120 feet

Maps: USGS 7½´ Stokesville; Trimble Mountain Trail map

Located almost at the geographical center of George Washington National Forest, Todd Lake Recreation Area can be a comfortable base from which to explore the Allegheny Mountains west of the Shenandoah Valley. Facilities in the 20-acre area include a campground with running water, hot showers, flush toilets, and huge picnic grounds. A sandy beach borders the 7.5-acre lake, and canoeists, and anyone else willing to power their boat with muscles and not motors, are permitted in the nonswimming areas of the water. Among the many trailheads within an hour's drive of Todd Lake are the Wild Oak National Recreation Trail (Hike 40), North River Gorge (Hike 38), Ramsey's Draft (Hike 41), and Shenandoah Mountain (Hike 42). See the Wild Oak National Recreation Trail (Hike 40) for directions to the Todd Lake Recreation Area.

Passing by several good views of Todd Lake, Shenandoah Mountain, and soaring Reddish Knob, and following deer trails through thickets of mountain laurel, the Trimble Mountain Trail makes it possible to take a hike right from the campground and not have to drive anywhere. Fossils found at some of the rock outcroppings show the outlines of plants that grew on the mountain as it was formed about 300 million years ago during the Paleozoic era. To reach the trailhead from the campground entrance, you can either walk the roadway back to FDR 95, turn left, and continue for a few hundred feet or simply cut downhill past the dam. If you are not staying in the campground, you can leave an automobile at the RV dump station on FDR 95, directly across from the trailhead. (Make sure you do not block access to the dumping facilities.)

From the dump station, walk across FDR 95 and follow the yellow-blazed trail into the woods, coming to an open area in 300 feet. This clearing, beginning to overgrow, was created when soil was removed to build the dam for Todd Lake. Turn right at the loop-trail intersection and ascend along an old road. Be paying attention 0.2 mile from FDR 95; the route leaves the old roadway you've been following and bears right to ascend on a narrow pathway. In the fall, you are likely to see squirrels busily harvesting the hundreds of acorns dropped by oak trees as the trail switchbacks to the right for a limited view of Todd Lake at 0.5 mile. Incredibly, all those nuts they gather are buried and concealed in individual shallow holes. The gray squirrels live in nests of leaves and twigs located in tree forks high above the ground, or in tree cavities, which they line with soft vegetation.

The trail swings around the ridge for a view to the northwest of 4,397-foot Reddish Knob, a high point on Shenandoah Mountain. Stretching for more than 50 miles, the prominent ridgeline of Shenandoah Mountain—in its southern region—marks the border of Highland and Augusta Counties, while its

A rock outcropping on the Trimble Mountain Trail

attention to the trail markers so as to stay on the correct route.

The focus of the vistas changes when the trail curves to the southern side of the mountain. The rocks at 1.2 miles overlook Elkhorn Lake (a popular fishing spot), which is surrounded by Elkhorn, Hankey, and Lookout Mountains. From 1.4 miles, the broad ridgeline the trail follows could provide nice tent sites as you descend to mountain laurel thickets in a saddle and ascend next to trees killed by an ice storm in the late 1970s. Attaining the 2,740-foot wooded summit of Trimble Mountain at 2.2 miles, the trail crosses the ridge, swinging around to another view of Reddish Knob at 2.5 miles.

Water has been nonexistent on the trail so far, so on hot summer days you may be happy to drop steeply to a spring at 2.8 miles; then resume a more gradual descent by mountain laurel to a wintertime view of Todd Lake. Mountain laurel can develop into such heavy thickets because, besides the usual cross-pollination of flowers to produce seeds, the laurel reproduces by sending up new shoots from its spreading root system. In addition, branches that touch the ground grow new roots, radiating outward and sending up shoots of their own.

northern section delineates Virginia from West Virginia. Notice that the land directly below you at this viewpoint was also used to obtain fill dirt for the dam.

Because of the large number of trees brought down by Hurricane Fran in 1996, certain sections of the Trimble Mountain Trail have been relocated in this area. The relocations are really just minor and do not significantly alter the overall length of the hike. Nonetheless, you should pay close

You will pass water sources three more times before arriving back at the loop-trail intersection and making a right to return to FDR 95 at 3.8 miles.

40

Wild Oak National Recreation Trail

Total distance (circuit): 26.1 miles

Hiking time: 3 days, 2 nights

Vertical rise: approximately 7,550 feet

Maps: USGS 7½′ Stokesville; USGS 7½′ Reddish Knob; USGS 7½′ Palo Alto (VA and WV); USGS 7½′ West Augusta; Wild Oak Trail map

Exceptionally steep ascents, miles of trail at high elevation, good water sources few and far between, two major river fords, and a rough and rocky treadway in many places—descriptions such as this may scare off timid hikers. But if you are in good shape and view these challenges as reasons to hike, the Wild Oak National Recreation Trail (WONRT) {FS 716} can be a great escape from the crowds. Just a few words of advice: An abundance of wildlife makes the entire route a favorite of hunters, so take the proper precautions if hiking during the season. In addition, the WONRT has become popular with mountain bikers; be prepared to have one whiz by you at any moment. Last bit of advice: Water is scarce, especially on the second half of the hike. Fill up with water whenever you can, and carry lots of it!

Since this is a circuit hike, you won't need a shuttle, but because the trail comes in contact with drivable roadways at three points, you could use two automobiles to split the hike into day trips—designated Segments A, B, and C by the Forest Service.

Segment A, and the beginning and ending point of the circuit, is reached by following US 250 west from Staunton. Passing through Churchville in about 10 miles, make a right onto VA 42. In 1.3 miles, turn left onto VA 760 for 3.4 miles to a left onto VA 747. Another 1.1 miles brings you to a right onto VA 730. Don't follow VA 730 when it makes an abrupt turn in 1.3 miles; keep straight, following VA 718 and making a left onto FDR 95 in an additional 1.3

CHESTNUT

Little
Bald Knob

Skidmore Fork

Skidmore Fork

Camp Todd

B Ⓟ

Springhouse Ridge

springs

Segment B

North River

Stark Pond

N

Tearjacket
Trail

Hollow

Stillhouse

0   0.25   0.5 mile

Big Bald
Knob

Dividing Ridge

Mitchell Branch

White Oak Run

Gordons
Peak

c Ⓟ

River

Bald
Ridge
Trail

R
I
D
G
E

Rattlesnake Run

Shingle

The
Pinnacle

McM

Run

Grooms
Ridge Trail

"spur" trail

Little
Skidmore
Trail

Bear Draft
Trail

Segment C

White Oak
Draft
Trail

Dowells
Draft Trail

miles. You will find the Segment A parking area in 0.1 mile, on the right.

For access to the other segments' trailheads, continue following FDR 95, passing by parking for the North River Gorge Trail (see Hike 38) in 1.1 miles, the Trimble Mountain Trail in 2.8 miles, and the Todd Lake Recreation Area (see Hike 39) in 3 miles. Continue on (now) dirt FDR 95, keeping right when you come to a T-intersection 1.3 miles from Todd Lake. (The North River Gorge trailhead and campground are about one mile to the left on FDR 95B.) Keep right in another 1.6 miles, passing by FDR 533 to Elkhorn Lake. In an additional 0.4 mile, you'll come to the next intersection, where the trailhead for Segment B is about 3 miles to the right on FDR 95, and Segment C's trailhead is approximately 2 miles to the left on FDR 96.

First Day:

Total distance: 11.5 miles

Hiking time: 8 hours

From the Segment A parking area, take the "spur" trail into the woods. This pathway was just recently constructed so hikers could avoid having to use an old woods road that had some of the largest tank traps I've ever seen. Built to discourage off-road vehicle use, one of the pits was so deep that it had developed into a permanent little pond. In about 0.2 mile, arrive and turn right onto the gray-white blazes of the WONRT. The ridgeline narrows at about 0.7 mile as the route steepens, coming to a view of Lookout Mountain. You will be traversing its ridgeline on the last day of this hike. The trail begins an immediate descent after crossing the 2,702-foot summit of Grindstone Mountain at 1.4 miles.

Passing through a wildlife clearing, resume the ascent, coming to an intersection at 2.2 miles. The Little Skidmore Trail, actually a logging access road, descends for more than two miles to Little Skidmore Fork, eventually emerging onto FDR 95. Your route continues to follow gray-white blazes uphill, going through a wildlife clearing surrounded by oak, maple, hickory, black locust, and dogwood at 2.3 miles. Despite its name, dogwood was not named for man's best friend. The tree was originally called dagwood, as its timber is so strong it was once carved into daggers. Studies of ancient civilizations show that the dogwood was as highly prized as horns for making such weapons; hence the tree's Latin generic name, *Cornus*.

The trail makes a couple of small ups and downs, ascending by patches of star moss to the main crest of Chestnut Ridge. A broad, flat knob at 4.1 miles would provide a good tenting site. From here, Groom's Ridge Trail {FS 424} descends four miles to FDR 101. Your route bears left, where thickets of mountain laurel close in on the trail and mosses cover the pathway like padded carpeting. Switchback to the left at 6.2 miles, and keep to the left when an old road comes in from the right at 6.6 miles. Soon after this, when you come to dirt Bald Knob Road {FDR 427}, be sure to turn right for a hundred yards to the most spectacular view you are going to have on the hike. Far off to the northeast is Massanutten Mountain and, on very clear days, behind it are the Blue Ridge Mountains of Shenandoah National Park. Closest to you, in the west and northwest, is the knobby ridgeline of Shenandoah Mountain, while beyond are wave after wave of Allegheny Mountain summits in West Virginia. This is such a lofty site from which to watch the sun set and rise that you may want to search out a sheltered spot along the edge of the meadow to pitch your tent and spend the evening.

Return and continue on the WONRT, crossing the very summit of 4,351-foot

Little Bald Knob. Immediately begin the long descent, passing by a limited view of Elkhorn Lake at 7.2 miles. Switchbacking off the ridgeline, follow a sidehill trail through fields of rock, entering a mountain laurel and pine tunnel at 8 miles and soon emerging into a mixed hardwood forest.

There might be a fallen tree over North River to help you get across, but use caution if you must ford it before arriving at FDR 95, the Camp Todd site, and the end of Segment A at 10 miles. There are a few campsites along the road, but for quieter and more pleasant surroundings for the night, you are going to continue into Segment B, following the gray-white blazes as they leave Camp Todd and ascend steeply along a hemlock-lined stream.

At 10.4 miles, the trail switchbacks right to gain the ridge, passing an area of recent fire activity at 10.7 miles. If hiking when the leaves are off the trees, you will see Elkhorn Lake to the southeast at 11 miles. In addition, almost in front of you is Big Bald, which you'll be crossing early tomorrow morning. You have hit your evening's destination when the trail comes to two springs at 11.5 miles (the second one is usually flowing best). Please practice no-trace camping and use your stove to cook. There are few signs of camping (and even fewer fire rings) on the entire WONRT; it would be nice to keep it this way.

Second Day:

Total distance: 9.9 miles
Hiking time: 6½ hours

In wandering around last night, you might have found, about 0.1 mile from your campsite, that the Tearjacket Trail {FS 426} goes right to descend into Ramsey's Draft Wilderness. This morning you should keep to the left at the intersection, following the gray-white blazes along the border of the wilderness area. Ascending through mountain laurel and evergreens, the treadway is softened by the accumulation of pine needles. Big Bald Knob, at 0.9 mile, was evidently an open wildlife clearing at one time, but it is gradually becoming overgrown. Near the summit, there is a short path to the left leading to a good view of Elkhorn Lake with the Shenandoah Valley and Blue Ridge Mountains visible beyond Lookout and Crawford Mountains.

Descending, the WONRT passes a couple of open areas of maples and ferns, which would make good campsites. The trail continues with quick ups and downs, passing by several other possible camps, and arrives at an overgrown wildlife clearing and pond (many deer prints in the soft mud) at 1.8 miles. Swing left of the pond and bear left, descending steeply away from Ramsey's Draft Wilderness on the gray-white-blazed pathway. (The trail ascending from the far end of the pond is the Bald Ridge Trail {FS 496}, which runs along the eastern border of the wilderness area.)

Make a short side excursion off your wintergreen-lined pathway at 2.4 miles. Mitchell Branch to the left is the last sure water you will come across for the rest of the hike. After taking proper precautions in treating the water, drink your fill and be sure to carry enough to get you through the rest of today, tonight's dinner, and the long, dry walk along Hankey and Lookout Mountains tomorrow.

The WONRT now descends gradually on an old road along Dividing Ridge, arriving at FDR 96 and the end of Segment B at 4.2 miles. Continue on into Segment C, climbing steeply by blueberries and wintergreen. Wintergreen's evergreen leaves and bright red berries add a welcome splash of color to an otherwise brown and gray forest in the colder months. Its fruit is an important food source for many animals in the winter. Mice

Crossing the North River

and chipmunks nibble away at the fleshy berry; deer, grouse, and bear swallow the fruit whole, and after their bodies absorb the digestible part, they drop the seeds somewhere else—a classic example of how animals help disperse seeds.

Unfortunately, the climb becomes even steeper at 4.6 miles before you attain the ridgeline. This hard labor continues with several ups and downs to a knob at 5.9 miles, where Dowell's Draft Trail {FS 650} drops for about three-and-a-half miles to US 250 near West Augusta. Your route swings left into a gap before climbing to attain a grassy area surrounded by oak and hickory at 6.2 miles—the first peak of Hankey Mountain, 3,407 feet above sea level. When you come into the wildlife clearing at 6.6 miles, the trail begins to follow a woods road. You could camp just about anywhere you wish along the broad crest of the mountain, but as the walking is now fairly effortless, it is easy to put in a couple more miles before stopping for the night.

At 7 miles, White Oak Draft Trail {FS 486} drops to the right for about two-and-a-half miles to US 250 near Whites Store. Continue on the roadway, topping the second peak of Hankey Mountain (3,450 feet) at 7.2 miles. There is a dazzling display of wild azalea next to the road as it descends along the mountain crest. Dogwood adds bits of white when the route enters a clearing and the roadway becomes well surfaced. The trail makes use of this road, open to motorized traffic during the hunting season (usually mid-October to the end of December), for the next few miles.

You will pass by five more clearings. If you can keep count, make it to the fifth and largest clearing at 9.9 miles before setting up camp, although any one of these open areas would provide fairly good tent sites.

Third Day:
Total distance: 4.7 miles
Hiking time: 3½ hours

After shouldering your pack and heading out for the day, pay attention when the main road descends to the left. You want to keep right on a less-traveled roadway, following the gray-white blazes. The road splits again at 0.2 mile; keep right, passing through a field and descending on a steep, grassy woods road. Join up with another road at 0.5 mile, staying right and going by Bear Draft Trail {FS 535}. (Bear Draft descends for approximately three miles to arrive at VA 728 near Stribling Springs.) Keep left at 1 mile when another roadway joins up with your route.

The roadbed ends at 1.7 miles and the trail becomes a pathway, soon making a steep descent in a deep woods with thick undergrowth. It is obvious that few people use this portion of the WONRT, and after so much road walking, you will welcome the feeling of isolation as you negotiate minor ups and downs. Begin the final descent at 3.1 miles, using a couple of switchbacks along the way.

Be alert at 3.7 miles. At one time the trail made an abrupt downhill turn to the right. Now, however, you want to switchback to your left (avoiding what looks like a well-used pathway straight ahead) and continue downhill to a footbridge that enables you to get across the North River with dry feet. Until recently hikers faced a somewhat dangerous and tricky ford of the river, having to choose their own route through the rippling waters.

Soon after crossing the river, step over FDR 95 and quickly come to the "spur" trail where a right turn will bring your 3-day excursion away from the world of motor vehicle travel to an end as you return to the Segment A parking area at 4.7 miles.

41

Ramsey's Draft

Total distance (circuit): 8.3 miles

Hiking time: 6 hours

Vertical rise: 1,080 feet

Maps: USGS 7½′ West Augusta;
U.S. Forest Service Ramsey's Draft
Wilderness map

In 1912, a team of U.S. Forest Service employees headquartered at an inn named the Mountain House walked, drove, and otherwise surveyed the mountains, hills, and valleys of Highland, Bath, and Augusta Counties. The recommendations contained in their reports led to the 1913 purchase of more than 38,000 acres on and around Shenandoah Mountain—some of the first property to be acquired for the Shenandoah National Forest, which eventually grew to be the present-day, 1.1-million-acre George Washington National Forest. Recognizing that much of the land still existed in its pristine state—never having been logged—the area has been managed essentially as a wilderness by the Forest Service since 1935. The Virginia Wilderness Act of 1984 ensured that lands around Ramsey's Draft will remain this way for generations to come.

Framed by Shenandoah Mountain, Tearjacket Knob, and Bald Ridge, Ramsey's Draft flows freely through these high Allegheny Mountains. From its headwaters of spewing springs at nearly 4,000 feet in elevation, the stream drains the wilderness's 6,500 acres. Up until the 1960s, it was possible to drive more than 3 miles upstream from US 250 on a road made passable by the construction of 11 fords by the Civilian Conservation Corps in the 1930s. Automobile traffic came to an abrupt halt in 1969, when rainwater from Hurricane Camille—the same storm that did so much damage to the Tye River Valley (see Hike 34)—wiped out most of the man-made enhancements at the stream crossings. While

not downplaying the need to negotiate the numerous fords, posthurricane Forest Service literature spoke of the joys of using the flat surface of the old road to hike along the draft. That information had to be updated when the great flood of November 1985 not only caused the roadbed to deteriorate and, at some spots, completely disappear, but even changed the course of the stream in several places. In February 1996 Hurricane Fran caused more changes in the stream channel and blew over scores of trees, making travel along the drainage system even more difficult. Today's visitors definitely have to be more determined than those of the past.

Don't let flood-damaged terrain deter you from taking this hike to explore the wilderness. The quiet, isolated hillsides of Road Hollow, a mile of gentle, nearly level walking in the deciduous forest on Shenandoah Mountain, and an easy descent amid the vintage hemlocks next to Jerry's Run are all things that will help you forget the stresses and strains of modern life. And besides, you will have a chance to see first-hand the effects of hurricanes and floods on a mountain river valley.

Take US 250 west from Staunton, passing through Churchville. About 14 miles from the small hamlet, turn right onto FDR 68 and into the Forest Service's Mountain House Picnic Area. The area was named for a tollhouse on the Staunton-to-Parkersburg turnpike constructed before the Civil War. Being approximately 20 miles from Staunton, Mountain House was about as far as a team of horses could comfortably pull a wagon in a day, and the station became a popular overnight destination. It was a place to let the horses rest prior to making the long haul over Shenandoah Mountain and for travelers to enjoy indoor lodging and an evening meal

for all of 35 cents. A local legend maintains that, during the War Between the States, an inebriated Confederate soldier, patronizing the house while on break from his duties at the breastworks on top of the mountain, made advances toward Mrs. Rogers, the proprietor. More than annoyed by his attentions, she dispatched the soldier to an early grave by using a rolling pin to deliver a number of blows to his head.

From the picnic area, which has toilet facilities and a water pump, continue on FDR 68 for a few hundred feet to the trailhead parking area. Begin the hike on Ramsey's Draft Trail {FS 440}, walking by the Bridge Hollow Trail {FS 442} as it goes to the right and ascends about two miles to connect with the Bald Ridge Trail {FS 496}, which runs along the eastern border of the wilderness. At 0.1 mile, make a left onto the Road Hollow Trail {FS 448}. Bridge Hollow and Road Hollow Trails were constructed during the summers of 1988 through 1992 by members of the Student Conservation Association. The nonprofit, educational organization provides high-school and college students the opportunity to volunteer their services and work for public lands throughout the country. You should thank these young folks for their hard labor, because prior to 1992 this circuit hike would have been longer, and you would have had to walk several miles along heavily-traveled US 250 to complete it.

Road Hollow Trail leaves the hemlock trees along Ramsey's Draft and ascends in a forest of mountain laurel, blueberries, and pines. At 0.5 mile, cross over a small water run after having swung into the first of eight draws that you walk into during the ascent. The highway sounds of US 250 finally begin to fade at about 1 mile, when the trail makes a wide arc to the north and the road makes a horseshoe bend to the southwest. With the

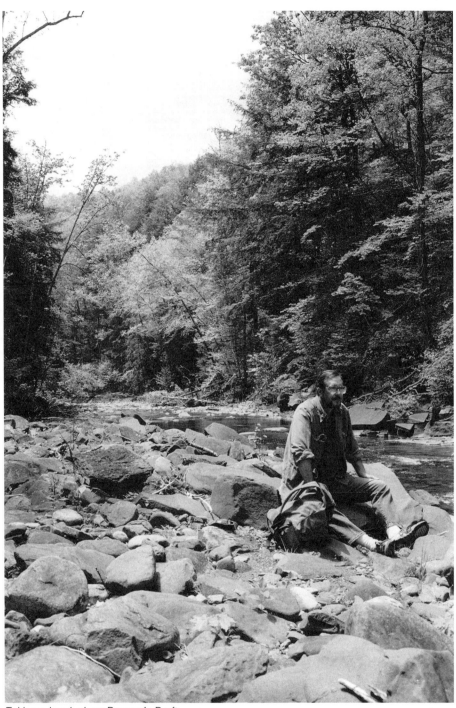

Taking a break along Ramsey's Draft

gain in elevation, the evergreens become less common, replaced more and more by deciduous trees; in the spring, the draw at 1.75 miles is adorned by dozens of dogwood trees in bloom. Commonly mistaken for the flower, the pink and white that you see on the trees are actually leaf bracts encircling the petals of the dogwood's small blossom. Look inside the bracts to see the true beauty of the state flower of Virginia. The tree's green berries appear around the first of September, about the same time its leaves are changing to a deep, dark crimson. As the leaves drop off, the fruit turns a shiny red, providing the forest with some color for the cooler months ahead.

Road Hollow Trail ends when it tops the ridge and meets the Shenandoah Mountain Trail {FS 447} at 2.6 miles. To the left, it is one and four-tenths miles to the Confederate Breastworks Overlook on US 250. You, however, want to make a right to walk along this wonderfully built and nearly level pathway as it swings around a hollow at 3 miles, where there are some limited views to the west. Although the mountainside drops off steeply, the trail continues at a level contour and is almost wide enough for two people to walk abreast. The broadly flat ridgeline at 3.5 miles may make you wish you had brought a tent so that you could camp amid the hemlocks, hardwoods, and pines.

A short distance from the wilderness boundary, leave the Shenandoah Mountain Trail (see Hike 42 if you would want to keep following that route) to make a right and descend on Jerry's Run Trail {FS 441}. Cross the run a couple of times before coming to a large grassy lawn at 4 miles and an old chimney marking the site of the Potomac Appalachian Trail Club's Sexton Cabin, which was dismantled in keeping

with the spirit of returning Ramsey's Draft to wilderness status. Beyond this good campsite, the trail swings left, continuing downhill to cross the stream again as the valley becomes narrower and hundreds of hemlocks keep the forest looking green throughout the year. Be careful on an eroded section of trail at 4.9 miles—in times of high water you may have to follow a scrambling trail around fallen trees, taking care not to tumble into the creek. The route crosses Jerry's Run twice more and enters a wide valley of hemlocks where jack-in-the-pulpits are unusually abundant. Be watching for the trail to make a faint, abrupt turn at 5.6 miles to recross the run and end as it meets the Ramsey's Draft Trail at 5.8 miles.

Turn downstream to follow the old roadbed and cross Jerry's Run for the final time before fording Ramsey's Draft for the first of many times. In fact, allow plenty of time from here to the end of the hike, because for the next 2 miles you are more or less on your own. The roadbed disappears in many places, and you will have to make your own decisions as to what route to take around hundreds of blowdowns and giant boulders and logs carried down the mountainsides by raging waters. The draft is a native-trout stream, but since the flood of 1985 changed their habitat, the fish are reported to be not as abundant nor reaching the size of their ancestors. The beaver population must also have diminished, because the only signs of activity look years old.

Passing by a large Forest Service structure and the Road Hollow and Bridge Hollow Trails, arrive back at the parking area at 8.3 miles, possibly exhausted, but certainly richer in spirit from the experience.

42

Shenandoah Mountain

Total distance (one way): 10.6 miles

Hiking time: 6 hours

Vertical Rise: 1,400 feet

Maps: USGS 7½′ McDowell; USGS 7½′ West Augusta; USGS 7½′ Palo Alto (VA and WV); U.S. Forest Service Ramsey's Draft Wilderness map

The Shenandoah Mountain Trail may well be the easiest long-distance excursion you can take in the mountains of western Virginia. Following a route first dug by the Civilian Conservation Corps during the Great Depression, the route, sometimes wide enough to invoke visions of a carriage road, traverses the spine of Shenandoah Mountain for more than 10 miles. Along its entire distance there are no places where your calf muscles will begin to ache from having to work hard to get you up steep inclines, nor will there be any pressure on your knees or jolts to your ankles from making long, rapid descents. Unlike other ridgeline trails, which seem to go up and over every knob and knoll, this pathway skirts these natural fluctuations, negotiating what little bits of elevation changes it does have by means of gradual grades or gentle switchbacks. Because of this ease of travel and the fact that good, level campsites can be found every few miles, the Shenandoah Mountain Trail is the perfect place to bring the kids for an overnight hike or to break friends into the pleasures of backpacking in some extremely isolated backcountry (Highland County is one of the least populated in the state) without introducing them to the rigors of a more rugged terrain. Be sure to carry enough water; it is not readily available right on the route.

The trail has so many good things going for it that it's a worthwhile hike anytime of the year. In spring there are thousands of azaleas and other wildflowers in bloom, the green leaves of maple, birch, oak, beech, poplar, and other deciduous trees provide deep shade to keep hikers cool on hot summer days, and, because the forest has such a variety of vegetation, walks during the fall leaf season are more colorful than in many other parts of the state. The wide pathway, gentle grade, and quite frequent heavy snowfalls of winter make the trail a good proving grounds for novice snowshoers.

Since this is a one-way hike, a car shuttle will be necessary. The shuttle involves many miles of dirt road travel, so allow ample time. Drive US 250 west from Staunton, and in about 20 miles—immediately after crossing the Calfpasture River—make a right onto VA 715. Stay on this route (which eventually becomes dirt FDR 96) for 6.4 miles to make a left turn onto FDR 95. In 3.2 miles you will pass a sign identifying Camp Todd, and 4.1 miles beyond that, stay left on FDR 95 at the junction with FDR 85. In 0.4 mile more you must be paying close attention, as the trailhead for the Shenandoah Trail may be marked only by a faint blaze on the left side of the road. If you find yourself in West Virginia,

turn around and look again for the trailhead—eventually you will find it located about halfway between the West Virginia border and the FDR 85 and FDR 95 junction. Leave one car here (there's not much room, so make sure it is well off the road) and retrace your route all the way back to US 250. Make a right onto US 250, pass by the Mountain House Picnic Area and Ramsey's Draft trailhead (see Hike 41), and in 7.3 miles park at the overlook on top of Shenandoah Mountain.

Before you "officially" begin your hike of the Shenandoah Mountain Trail, take the 20-minute interpretive trail looping through trenches remaining from the days of the Civil War. To prevent Union forces from using the Staunton-to-Parkersburg turnpike (now US 250) to gain access to the Shenandoah Valley from the west, Confederate soldiers under the command of General Edward Johnson constructed a network of breastworks on the western side of Shenandoah Mountain in March 1862. On April 18, despite the strategically placed fortifications, Union general Robert Milroy's superior forces caused the Southern men to abandon what had become known as Fort Edward Johnson. The occupying army subsequently built additional breastworks on the eastern side of the ridge to check the flow of Confederates to the west. Yet on May 5, the combined armies of Stonewall Jackson and General Johnson were enough of a threat to make Milroy retreat and give the mountain back to the Confederacy.

Once back at the parking lot, start your longer hike by taking the right branch of the breastworks loop trail, staying more or less level to swing around the knob; do not follow the unauthorized trail going uphill. At 0.2 mile, turn right off the interpretive trail to begin following the Shenandoah Mountain Trail {FS 447}. Hikers are surprised to see wild turkeys this close to the road, but they are often spotted here because the oak and hickory trees provide plenty of mast for the healthy flocks inhabiting the Allegheny highlands. The golden yellow flame azalea can be seen throughout much of George Washington National Forest, but notice that it is the pink azalea thriving here on Shenandoah Mountain.

At 1.4 miles, the Road Hollow Trail {FS 448} (see Hike 41) heads off to the right, descending to the Ramsey's Draft trailhead off US 250. Stay left, slabbing the western side of the ridgeline. The green fields along Shaws Fork can be seen through breaks in the vegetation at 1.8 miles. The hillside drops off steeply, but the trail remains level and almost wide enough for two hiking partners to walk side by side. At 2.3 miles, come onto a broad flat area of hemlocks, hardwoods, and pines, where you may be tempted to set up camp. Here you will pass a sign letting you know you've entered the Ramsey's Draft Wilderness, and a few hundred feet beyond the sign you'll see Jerry's Run Trail {FS 441}, which descends right 0.2 mile to a water source and continues about two more miles to reach the lower elevations of the wilderness area.

Staying left, it becomes evident that most

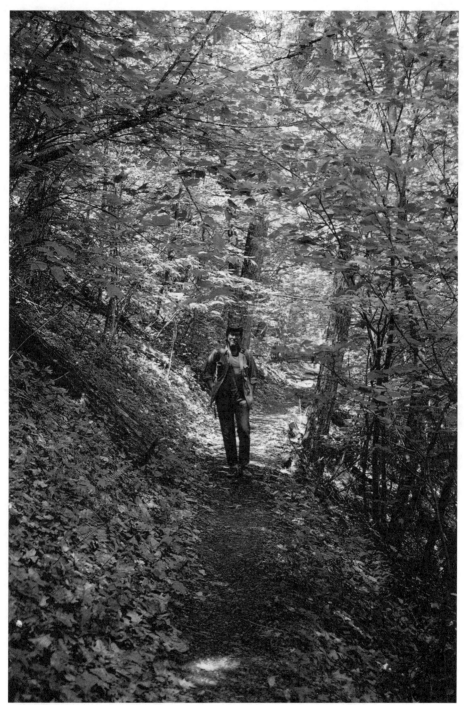

Hiking on Shenandoah Mountain Trail

people use the Shenandoah Mountain Trail for access to the wilderness area, because the pathway is now very obviously less used. The temperature may drop as much as 10 degrees (anytime of year) when the route enters a stand of hemlocks; as you have now walked 3.3 miles from your car, use this as an opportunity to get off your feet and listen to the restful sounds of the winds passing through the evergreen boughs.

Continuing along the ridge with minor ups and downs, the decline in human foot travel is accompanied by a corresponding increase in the signs of wildlife—deer tracks, bear scat, and turkey scratchings. In the spring and early summer, as you pass through a small gap at 4.7 miles you may hear the water of Al's Run, a tributary of Jerry's Run, dropping down the mountain to the right. If you are hard up for water you could bushwhack down to it; just remember it'll be a steep climb back to the trail. Of course, you could enjoy the jack-in-the-pulpits on the way down and back up.

A grassy area at 5.2 miles is another inviting campsite, and those who wander around this small mountain lawn may have their hearts skip a beat when a grouse or two suddenly come flying out of the underbrush, flapping noisily just a few feet in front of startled faces. Diminutive bluets, whose pale color replicates that of an early morning sky, line the trail at 6.4 miles, where the left prong of Ramsey's Draft becomes audible below the ridgeline. Shortly beyond this, another broad, grassy, flat area would provide additional, nicely situated tenting spots. From here, the Sinclair Hollow Trail {FS 4470} drops to the left about two miles to reach FDR 64 next to Shaws Fork. Keeping to the right, the Shenandoah Mountain Trail makes one of its rare climbs by switchback to gain a few hundred feet and arrives at the intersection with Ramsey's Draft Trail {FS 440}, which comes in from the right at 7.2 miles. Once again it may be tempting to set up camp in the flat grassy gap, especially when the wet-weather spring is flowing well. It is located about a hundred feet down the west side of the mountain, directly opposite the trail junction.

Continue on the Shenandoah Mountain Trail, leaving the wilderness area at 7.5 miles, where the route is high above the Brushy Fork Valley to the northwest. If you are using the Forest Service's 1988 Ramsey's Draft Wilderness map, you may be looking for the Tearjacket Trail {FS 426} to intersect your trail at this point. It won't. The map contains a major error, and the Tearjacket Trail actually meets up with the Ramsey's Draft Trail near Hiner Spring, well within the boundary of the wilderness area. (USGS maps show the correct route of the Tearjacket Trail.)

Soon the Shenandoah Mountain Trail, now sometimes a little overgrown, makes a short ascent through azaleas, whose delightful fragrance is so strong that it eclipses any other smells that may be present. Swinging around the ridge at 8.4 miles, there is a limited view of Little Bald Knob (see Hike 40) to the east. When the trail begins its long, gradual descent at 9.1 miles, your eyes will be drawn beyond ridge after ridge to some of the loftiest mountains of West Virginia rising along the northwestern horizon. The large leaves of the striped maple give the woods a lush green, almost rain forest look just before the trail makes its final drop to cross the Little River and come to an end at 10.6 miles on FDR 95.

FDR 95 is a gateway to a multitude of hikes in this part of George Washington National Forest. Looking at the descriptions for North River (Hike 38), Trimble Mountain (Hike 39), and the Wild Oak

National Recreation Trail (Hike 40) may make you wish you had brought enough supplies to stay out here for at least another week. And, if you want more hiking on Shenandoah Mountain, the Shenandoah Mountain Trail has another section of about 20 miles that heads southward from the Confederate Breastworks on US 250.

43

Elliott Knob/Falls Hollow

Total distance (one way): 9.0 miles

Hiking time: 6 hours

Vertical rise: 2,060 feet

Map: USGS 7½' Elliott Knob

Elliott Knob, the summit of Great North Mountain, is not only the highest point in Augusta County but also the loftiest height obtained in all of George Washington National Forest. Although this hike involves a vertical rise of more than 2,000 feet to reach the summit, the elevation is gained gradually over the course of almost 5 miles. Enjoyment and inspections of assorted spring and summer wildflowers can make the ascent seem even easier, and the downhill portion of the journey has charms of its own, providing a forest and environment quite different from that found on the mountain's ridgeline. A stream drops through the narrow canyon of Falls Hollow in an extensive series of cascades, best appreciated in the spring and early summer when the flow is at its highest volume.

To do the complete hike as a one-way trip will require a car shuttle. Take VA 254 west from Staunton, and in about 8 miles, in Buffalo Gap, continue straight onto VA 42. In just a short distance VA 688 comes in from the right. Stay on VA 42, but be paying close attention to the odometer because 2.4 miles from this intersection you need to pull into the unmarked Falls Hollow trailhead parking area on the right side of the road. Leave one car in the large turn-around next to the gated road. Take the second car and backtrack to make a left onto VA 688, ascending almost 4 miles to the top of the ridge. Be looking for a small, possibly unmarked parking area on the left side of the road in Dry Branch Gap.

Walk through the gate and follow yellow-blazed North Mountain Trail {FS 443},

gradually rising on an old road along the ridge. At 0.2 mile, the route becomes a pathway on the west side of the mountain. When you swing around a spur ridge, Elliott Knob looms high on the horizon to the south. Because Forest Service history shows that North Mountain never had any great number of inhabitants living on it, the old fruit trees you pass by once the trail gains the top of the ridge hold an air of mystery. Did the trees sprout from some hiker's discarded lunch half a century ago? Were the seeds secreted away by a squirrel and then forgotten? Or did some valley dweller use the mountaintop as an orchard?

Next to the trail and growing 1 to 2 feet tall is wild geranium, with its pink and purplish flowers of five petals. After the petals drop off, an elongated ovary becomes part of the seedpod, which resembles a bird's head with a long beak rising up from the stem. Europeans hundreds of years ago named the plant cranesbill, and even the word *geranium* comes from the Greek *geranos,* which means "crane."

Learning to "read" a forest as you walk through it can tell you of past events. When you level out a bit at 1 mile, note how the trees on the left side of the trail are thinner and younger looking and stand amid old stumps and logs that are almost completely rotted, while to the right the trees have broader trunks and there are few, if any, stumps. This pretty much leads to the conclusion that this high up on the mountain, loggers only timbered the eastern slope. (If, however, you were to drop down to the west, where the mountainside is not so steep, you would find ample evidence of logging.)

Rounding the side of a knob, look to the west for views into the Calfpasture Valley and out to Shenandoah Mountain (see Hike 42) on the Highland-Augusta County line.

Along the trail, wild azalea grows just about at eye level, and crow's foot, a club moss resembling running cedar, is at your feet. Jack-in-the-pulpit pops up between the boulders, which are covered in a soft, 3-inch layer of moss. Many people think that the green, white, or purple sheath with a hood—the pulpit—which surrounds and covers "Jack" is the plant's flower. Actually, the sheath is just a leaf bract, and in order to see the diminutive flowers you need to lift up the hood and look inside to find them clustered around Jack's base. When you come back here in the fall, the pulpit will have fallen away and red berries will have replaced the flowers. After putting the plant's roots through an elaborate cooking process, early Native Americans pounded them into powder to be used as a type of flour. Hence, jack-in-the-pulpit's other name, Indian turnip. Don't try eating a raw root, though—it's quite poisonous.

If you have worked up a thirst by the time you've gone 1.8 miles, you are in luck, because an unmarked side trail to the right leads to the somewhat-dependable Buffalo Spring in less than 500 yards.

Birch trees are a part of the forest now, and gooseberries are abundant in the understory in late summer. It is possible to eat this ½-inch, rounhd, translucent green relative of the currant right off the shrub, but they will taste better when cooked into a jam or jelly with sweeteners added. Traversing the east side of the mountain, the fire tower on Elliott Knob comes into view. By midspring, pink lady's slippers will have popped up trailside here. At 4.4 miles, turn right and ascend on graveled Elliott Knob Road, but be paying attention when what appears to be the main dirt road swings right to a communications installation. The North Mountain Trail turns left to descend off the knob, but you want to keep straight,

Jack-in-the-pulpit

subsequent nap, the sunshine beaming down on Elliott Knob becomes too warm, it is possible to retreat to cool shade in the stands of spruce planted by the Civilian Conservation Corps in the 1930s.

When ready for the next phase of this excursion, retrace your steps back down the road, walking past the two segments of the North Mountain Trail and coming to multiple springs (a couple of which are boxed and piped) gushing out of the mountain on the left side of the road, 5.1 miles after beginning the hike. There are some nice campsites beneath larch and spruce around the wildlife pond and across the road. After descending on the steep roadway, your knees and ankles are going to be thankful when you can turn left onto the gently sloping Falls Hollow Trail {FS 657} at 6.2 miles. Pay attention because most likely there will not be a sign identifying the trail, only blaze marking.

For a small burst of refreshing flavor, chew on a leaf of wintergreen. Also known as teaberry, it is the groundcover next to the trail growing on creeping stems and erect branches of 2 to 6 inches with shiny, oval, evergreen leaves. Native Americans used extracts from the plant to lessen the pain of a headache or discomforts of a fever, and they obviously knew what they were doing, because wintergreen contains a concentration of methyl salicylate—or, as most of us call it, aspirin.

At 7 miles, come to an old road in a forest of hemlocks and plush green moss. Go upstream a couple of hundred feet to see the first of many falls you're going to enjoy while in Falls Hollow. After a snack break, follow the roadbed downstream, passing numerous falls and, in some places where the gorge becomes steep and narrow, rising high above the stream. The cascades of these narrow stretches are

walking amid bleeding heart and climbing on a grassy roadbed.

At 4.7 miles, spread out the picnic blanket and enjoy lunch in the clearing on top of 4,463-foot Elliott Knob. Luckily, you don't have to climb the fenced-off fire tower—built in 1958 but abandoned when aircraft took over the job of fire detection in the 1960s—to enjoy the fine panorama. The ridgeline of Great North Mountain courses northeast and southwest. Shenandoah Mountain is to the west, and to the east, across Little Calfpasture Valley, is the Virginia Department of Game and Inland Fisheries' Wildlife Management Area on Little North Mountain. (Consider visiting the area someday to wander around its 17,500 nearly trailless and roadless acres. Except during hunting season, you could most likely be the only person on all of that acreage.) If, during lunch and maybe a some of the most impressive in Falls Hollow, but be extremely cautious if you decide to drop off the trail to get a closer look—Forest Service records show that more people are injured from slips and falls at waterfalls than at any other type of site. If hiking during spring runoff season, be prepared for high water when fording the stream at 7.4 miles and then again a few feet beyond that.

At 7.7 miles, the route begins to swing away from the creek and soon becomes a major dirt road in an area of new growth after recent logging activity. It could be easy to become confused in the maze of roads passed within the next mile, but the roadway to stay on is the one that is the best maintained and is obviously the main route through the series of clear-cut areas. At a turn in the road in one of the clear-cuts, at 8.5 miles, Elliott Knob can be seen to the west, soaring high above and dramatically illustrating the more than 2,000 feet you have dropped since being on its summit. In a few feet, faint blazes show the trail going off to the left, but it is just as easy to stay on the road because the trail returns to it in several hundred yards. Passing through a gate, find your shuttled automobile awaiting your return from hiking 9 miles in the more than 1 million acres that make up the George Washington National Forest.

44

Laurel Fork

Total distance (circuit): 14.0 miles

Hiking time: 8½ hours, or an overnight backpack trip

Vertical rise: 2,300 feet

Maps: USGS 7½′ Thornwood (VA and WV); USGS 7½′ Snowy Mountain

Laurel Fork, a tributary in the headwaters of the Potomac River, flows through a high-altitude region on the Virginia–West Virginia border that more closely resembles the forest lands of New England and Canada than the central or southern Appalachians. Red spruce, red pine, and birch thrive here, interspersed between tall sugar maples and oaks. Dozens of beaver ponds flood the mountain valleys, creating the tannin-darkened bogs that are so well associated with natural areas in Maine, New Hampshire, and Vermont. In addition to the usual assortment of Appalachian Mountain wildlife—turkeys, black bears, deer, mink, and raccoons—the area is home to snowshoe hares and is one of the few places in Virginia to have a known population of northern flying squirrels.

Old railroad grades, abandoned since logging operations ceased around the turn of the 20th century, provide ready-made and gently sloping access routes to the region's inner reaches. Although the Forest Service reports a somewhat heavy hiker use, the area's nearly 11,000 acres provide plenty of elbow room. I have never run into more than a handful of people each time I've hiked here, and in fact, on a Fourth of July weekend I saw only two other hikers the entire time I was on this 14-mile excursion.

From the US 220–US 250 junction in Monterey, travel on US 250 west for about 20 miles to reach the junction of US 250 and WV 28 near Thornwood, West Virginia. Make a right, following WV 28 for 6.7 miles to turn right onto FDR 106 (a sign will identify the Locust Springs Picnic Area). In 0.5 mile, bear left onto FDR 60, making a

right onto FDR 142 in another 0.3 mile. Continue on FDR 142 for 0.4 mile to the picnic area. If you are arriving late in the day you will be happy to know that camping is permitted here.

Facing the picnic area, walk to the right and take the Locust Springs Run Trail {FS 633}, descending gradually past the spring on a wide, old railroad grade in a forest of hemlock, birch, and mountain laurel. The trail is grassy and soft from years of dropped evergreen needles, and the songbirds and sound of the brook make for relaxing walking. In order to avoid a couple of stream crossings and some muddy spots, a high-water trail goes off to the left at 0.6 mile. The main pathway crosses the stream twice before the two routes meet up again at 1 mile. Enjoying the peace, beauty, and solitude of this high altitude through which you are walking, continue downstream, crossing the run a few more times before stepping over a side stream and making a right to ascend steeply on a different portion of the Locust Spring Trail—identified on Forest Service maps as FS 633A.

When the pathway begins following an old railroad grade at 1.5 miles, the gain in elevation is so gradual that you'll put forth little effort to achieve it. It is often worthwhile to leave the route, searching for shreds of evidence from the days when steam engines ran up and down these narrow valleys. At 2 miles, beaver dams and their resulting ponds have flooded the valley below. From where you are standing, it is possible to make out the individual sticks in the dams, but if you don't mind climbing back up, it's more interesting to drop to the valley floor for an even closer look at the beavers' handiwork. After felling a tree, a beaver trims off its branches in convenient sizes and carries them with its teeth to the dam or lodge site. Dam construction is adapted to local conditions—to lessen the pressure from a fast-moving creek, the dam will be bowed upstream, and in times of high water, the beaver will fashion temporary spillways. Although beaver ponds can be a nuisance to humans by flooding agricultural fields or blocking the route of a pathway, they also provide a place for insects to lay eggs, supporting a fish population that feeds on the insect larvae. In turn, the fish provide nourishment for osprey, mink, bears, and other birds and mammals.

At 2.4 miles, you must be alert for, and take, the blue-blazed pathway ascending steeply to the left. (If you miss the turn, you will eventually come to FDR 106, where you need to make a left for several hundred yards to rejoin this route description.) At the top of the narrow ridgeline is a small parking area just off FDR 106; you, however, want to continue straight across the ridge, dropping on Slabcamp Run Trail {FS 600} and keeping to the left when passing through an old gate. The beaver ponds on your right and the open fields of wildflowers the trail passes through will leave no doubt in your mind that you are walking in a transplanted section of the Great North Woods. Cross the stream at 3.1 miles and enter an evergreen forest, where the pathway shows so little evidence of use that you could swear you are walking on an animal track. In summer, the display of wood sorrel is simply outrageous—its small, pink-veined petals and green leaves cover literally every inch of boulders and ground close to the creek.

You may have to adjust your stride a bit to adapt to the spacing of the "ripples" on the pathway when you begin following the railroad grade at 3.8 miles. This stretch of uneven ground is the result of the railroad track and its ties being removed when logging operations ceased. However, at one

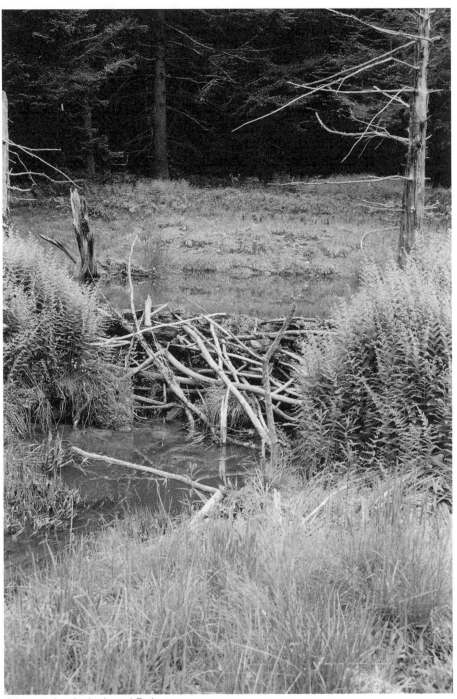

A beaver dam in the Laurel Fork area

time so many trees were being felled in this hollow that it required two tracks to haul them out. Look to the opposite side of the valley and you can see the contour of the other railroad grade.

Eventually the grade you are following will deteriorate to the point that you might as well give up trying to stay dry; just continue downstream, rock hopping from one spot to the next. It really doesn't matter if you get your feet damp because they are going to get soaked when you ford Laurel Run, a native-brook trout stream, at 5.5 miles.

After wading through the run, turn right onto the Laurel Fork Trail {FS 450} and walk through tunnels of rhododendron. (If you wish to shorten this hike by four miles, you could make a left on Laurel Fork Trail and continue for about half a mile to rejoin this hike description at the 10.4 milepoint.) At 5.8 miles, bear left to ascend the Christian Run Trail {FS 599}.

There is a heavy growth of almost neon green moss on the rocks and boulders as you ascend the railroad grade next to Christian Run. By the time you cross the run at 6.8 miles, the stream has become nothing more than a trickle and the landscape flattens out, with ferns lining the less steep and rocky pathway. While the trail is faintly obvious in the meadow at 7.2 miles, there are arrowed markers guiding you to the depression slightly to your left. Upon reaching the gap, turn left onto the dirt roadbed of Cold Springs Run Trail {FS 634} and continue to ascend for a distance. At 7.9 miles, be sure to take the right fork and descend. Also, be paying attention at 8.6 miles, where you do not continue straight but instead make a left to keep on the well-blazed Cold Springs Run Trail. This narrow valley is an exceptionally beautiful repeat of the other small hollows you've traveled—a multitude of wood sorrel, moss, rhododendron, and railroad tie "ripples."

Reaching Laurel Run at 9.9 miles, turn left to follow it upstream past widespread beaver activity and, in June, pink lady's slippers. The valley gradually widens as you come to an obviously large campsite on your right at 10.4 miles. You can either spend the night here or, if you don't want to face a river crossing first thing in the morning, ford the stream now to find a tent site on the opposite side.

Once you are across Laurel Run, the Locust Springs Trail is a short distance upstream from the large campsite; the Buck Run Trail {FS 598} is the old railroad grade that begins to ascend the mountain just a short distance downstream. Follow the Buck Run Trail as it goes by tens of thousands of richly green wood-sorrel leaves. So many little shamrock shapes spread across the forest floor that you probably wouldn't be surprised if you happened upon a leprechaun propped up against a moss-covered rock. After crossing the stream at 12 miles, swing to the left to continue the ascent, soon crossing it again and bearing left. You will be headed downstream for a short distance before climbing via switchbacks. Upon coming into an open area at 13.2 miles, make an abrupt left onto a pathway through a planted evergreen forest, working your way around numerous beaver ponds. Turn right onto a grassy roadbed, pass through a gate to bear left onto a dirt road, and return to the picnic area at 14 miles.

Visiting and exploring places such as Laurel Fork can help to refresh and revitalize our spirits, enabling us to truly understand what Emerson meant when he wrote, "In the woods is perpetual youth."

45

Hidden Valley

Total distance (circuit): 5.6 miles

Hiking time: 3 hours

Vertical rise: 120 feet

Maps: USGS 7½′ Warm Springs;
U.S. Forest Service Hidden Valley Trail
System map

Hidden Valley has changed so little since the Warwick Mansion was built here in the mid-1800s that the area was used to film the 1993 post–Civil War movie *Sommersby.* According to publicity releases, after a search in 15 states, Hidden Valley was chosen because "its rugged and remote hill overlooking the pristine Jackson River presented an unspoiled, stark but picturesque setting . . . You could shoot 360 degrees and not know you were in the 20th century."

Happily, this is not just Hollywood hype. In any direction you gaze, there are no high-power utility lines cutting across the hillsides or communication towers and radio dishes rising above the ridges. In fact, other than the Warwick Mansion and its few outbuildings, a couple of Forest Service structures, an old, overgrown fence line, and a dirt road that part of the hike follows, there is scant evidence of humans ever having been in the valley.

Archaeological digs indicate the presence of Native Americans in the valley more than 8,000 years ago. The first settlement by European immigrants wasn't established until 1740, but only the most skilled researcher could find any trace of this small community that was abandoned after being burned in 1754 during the French and Indian War. In 1788, Jacob Warwick obtained the property in Hidden Valley that was to be passed onto his grandson, Judge James Warwick. The judge, using the labor of slaves, had his mansion built out of bricks formed from mud along the Jackson River, and his plantation, known as Warwickton, endured until he and his wife passed away

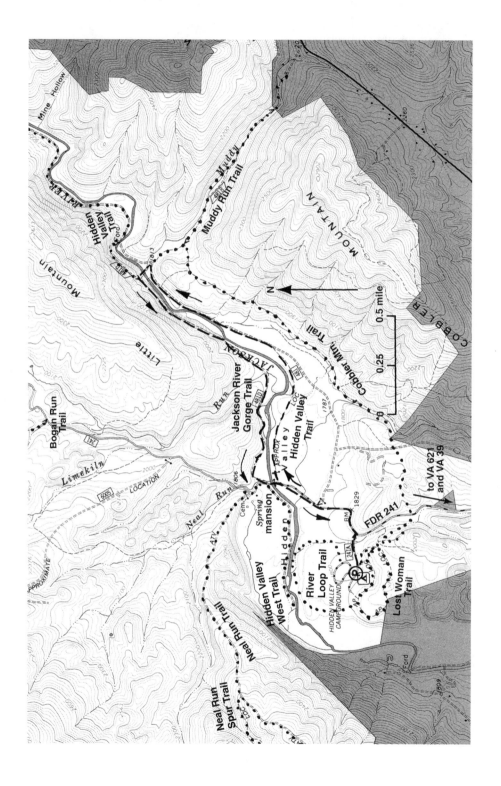

in the late 1890s. The land and mansion went through a number of owners, eventually falling into disrepair by the 1960s. However, a renovated Warwickton is now once again a working farm (on a smaller scale) and was opened to the public as a bed and breakfast in 1993.

You can reach Hidden Valley by following VA 39 west from Warm Springs for 1.5 miles before making a right onto VA 621. In 1 mile, bear left onto FDR 241, arriving at the Hidden Valley Campground on the left side of the road in 1.8 miles. Drive the campground road and park in the trailhead lot for the Lost Woman Trail, an enjoyable pathway of two short, interconnecting loops in the forest above the campground.

Walk the campground entrance road back to FDR 241 at 0.3 mile, turning left onto it as it becomes dirt. The reason the area was named Hidden Valley soon becomes obvious. The open meadows and fields along the Jackson River are more or less encircled by Back Creek Mountain and the long, heavily forested ridgelines of Cobbler, Warwick, and Little Mountains. The river provides the only naturally occurring access route. Coming to the junction at 0.9 mile, make a right close to the river and begin following the route of the Hidden Valley Trail {FS 481}.

Enjoy the walk through this quiet valley surrounded by luxuriant greenery that covers the encompassing hillsides. The open views of the meadows fade when the roadway enters the woods at 2.2 miles, soon coming close to, but well above, the Jackson River. Look along ground-hugging rhododendron limbs and on rocks in the moist draws of the hillside and you just might spy a lizardlike red-spotted newt. Spending a great portion of their lives in the water, newts, like salamanders, may wander miles from their home stream but al-most always return to breed. Researchers say that the nervous systems in some newts are able to develop a "map" of the terrain they cross and that the information can be recalled when it is time to return. The red-spotted newts have an additional mechanism at their disposal—they can detect Earth's magnetic field and are able to use it as a directional reference!

After crossing Muddy Run at 3 miles, many fishermen make use of the route bearing to the right, the one-mile Muddy Run Trail {FS 481B}. Many of these sportsmen come back with reports of a healthy population of wild rainbow trout in this side stream. Unless you are going to do some exploring up Muddy Run, keep to the left on the roadway, crossing the Jackson River on a superbly designed and constructed suspension bridge at 3.2 miles. On the far side of the bridge, the Hidden Valley Trail bears right; you'll turn left onto Jackson River Gorge Trail {FS 481D} on a cliffside above the river.

By the very nature of the terrain and vegetation this riverside pathway travels, it may often be a frustrating pathway to negotiate. You can be almost assured of getting wet feet when crossing moist bottomlands, and if the trail has not been brushed out for awhile, quick-growing briars, brambles, and other entangling plants may make the route hard to follow and certainly will leave evidence on your skin of your walk through them. If you find the trail in such condition you may want to retrace your steps back to the campground, but if you are feeling adventurous and don't mind a little bit of adversity, continue onward, passing by an old fence line at 3.8 miles.

The trail soon drops into the damp bottomland, and you may have to decide on the best way to get through. Take solace in the abundance of wild strawberries, whose

The bridge across the Jackson River

juicy concentration of flavor puts their cultivated relatives to shame. Deer tracks are
often seen around the swampy area at 5
miles before you make a left onto what is
the main throughway through the valley,
FDR 241. Passing by the Greek revival–
style Warwick Mansion (placed on the National Register of Historic Places), cross
the Jackson River and come into the area
that served as Vine Hill, Tennessee, while
Sommersby was in production. In a matter
of just a few months, the film company built
a small community of about a dozen structures, filmed the movie, and then dismantled the set, leaving (at Forest Service
request) several outbuildings next to the
mansion as the only evidence of their activities. You will soon meet up at an intersection with the Hidden Valley Trail, where you
should bear right and retrace the steps with
which you originally began this hike, returning to the campground at 5.6 miles.

46

Lake Moomaw

Total distance (round trip): 6.6 miles

Hiking time: 4½ hours

Vertical rise: 1,700 feet

Map: USGS 7½′ Falling Springs

There are few places in Virginia where you can legally camp on public land next to a large lake and not be situated in an often crowded and noisy developed campground. The primitive campsites at Greenwood Point on Lake Moomaw can be reached only by boat or by hiking the moderately strenuous 3.3-mile Greenwood Point Trail—thereby limiting the number of people who will put forth the effort needed in order to be camped close to you. You will be rewarded with a quieter camp of much less human activity, where you can enjoy golden sunrises and pink sunsets reflected in the lake and secluded coves in which to take a leisurely swim (no lifeguards, so take care) or idly read a book. This isolation does bring some responsibilities your way, though. There are portable sanitary facilities at the site but no potable source of water, so you will have to carry in all that you're going to need. Also, be aware that there are only five authorized campsites at Greenwood Point, and during the summer vacation months these are often filled quickly by boaters. Start your hike early enough in the day so that if you find all the sites filled, you have enough time to walk back to one of the developed campgrounds.

The building of Lake Moomaw and its dam was originally authorized by Congress in 1947, but construction by the U.S. Army Corps of Engineers didn't begin until 1965. With completion of the work in 1981, the lake reached its present length of 12 miles and width (at its widest) of 2½ miles, with a surface area of 2,530 acres enclosed by more than 43 miles of shoreline. The Army Corps retains the responsibility of managing flood

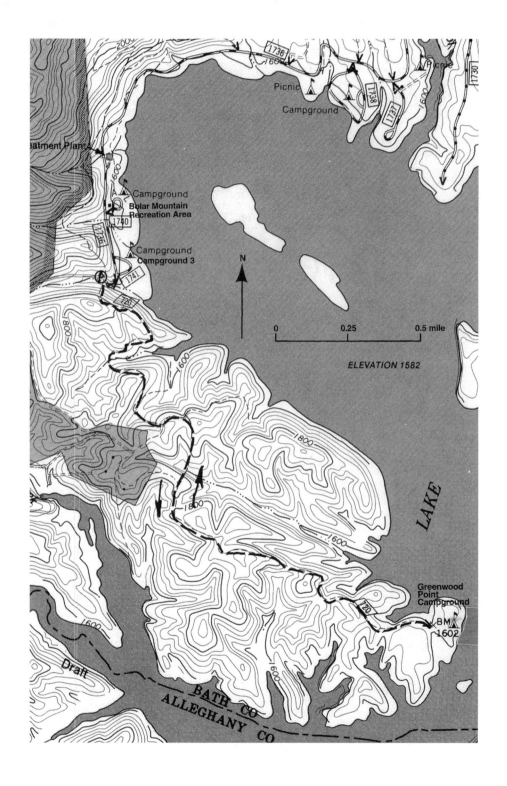

Picnic

Picnic

Campground

Treatment Plant

Campground

Bolar Mountain
Recreation Area

Campground
Campground 3

N

0   0.25   0.5 mile

ELEVATION 1582

LAKE

Greenwood
Point
Campground

BM
1602

Draft

BATH CO

ALLEGHANY CO

control and water quality and maintains a visitor center at the dam, but the Forest Service administers the surrounding lands.

Spread around the lake are numerous developed campgrounds, picnic areas, swimming beaches, boat-launching ramps, marinas, and fishing access sites. Among other fish, the lake contains bass, trout, northern pike, catfish, and crappie. The Bolar Mountain Recreation Area on the northern side of the lake is one of the most developed spots, and in addition to the Greenwood Point Trail {FS 720}, the area has the approximately 2-mile Grouse Point Overlook Loop Trail {FS 721}, providing a couple of good views of the lake.

To reach the Bolar Mountain Recreation Area, follow VA 39 west from Warm Springs, passing by VA 621 (access to Hidden Valley, see Hike 45) in 1.5 miles. Continue up and over Back Creek Mountain to make a left onto VA 600, which you follow to its intersection with VA 603. Make a right onto the Forest Service road to arrive at the recreation area, a U.S. Fee Area. The Greenwood Point Trail begins from a trailhead parking lot next to the entrance of campground 3.

Walk across the footbridge and start an immediate ascent on steep switchbacks, attaining the ridgeline in less than 300 yards. With views of the lake through the vegetation, you will be on a downward trend on the grassy ridge when the trail makes an abrupt switchback to the right. The route soon follows an old road for less than 300 feet before switchbacking left off the roadway to gain elevation on a steep grade, only to cross the ridgeline at 0.9 mile and descend by dogwood, maple, hickory, oak, and abundant cancer root. A parasite upon the roots of trees, especially oak, cancer root has amazingly small yellow flowers. But the flower is probably not what will catch your eye at first—it will be the stem. It produces no chlorophyll—the substance that gives plants their green color—so its entire stalk is a sort of yellowish brown. Because the scalelike leaves resemble a pinecone, its Latin name (Conopholis) is derived from the Greek words conos, meaning "cone," and pholis, meaning "scale." Cancer root is also called squawroot, having been used by Native Americans to treat menstrual disorders.

Climb steeply out of a narrow draw to cross another ridgeline at 1.3 miles, only to drop down and repeat this process again. Having attained the final ridge, which will deliver you to Greenwood Point, there will be an old trail coming in from the right at 2 miles, where you will bear left onto a wide and well-built pathway in a mixed hardwood forest. As it does in cancer root during the summer months, the absence of chlorophyll plays a part in the look of the woods in the fall. Not only does chlorophyll give the leaves their green color, but it also produces simple sugars to nourish the trees. The leaves also contain yellow pigments—carotenoids—that are masked by the chlorophyll. Cooler temperatures and less daylight signal the leaves to quit making the sugars, and as the chlorophyll breaks down, the green fades and the yellows, browns, and oranges emerge. Autumn's reds and purples come from other pigments called anthocyanins, which develop in the sap of leaves as a result of a complex interaction between sugars, phosphates, and other chemicals. An early fall of bright, sunny days and cool nights (but not below freezing) will produce the most brilliant colors.

Continuing along the ridge, descend gradually to arrive at the Greenwood Point Campground at 3.3 miles. Pitch the tent, have a little lunch break, and then go exploring—there are many miles of shoreline

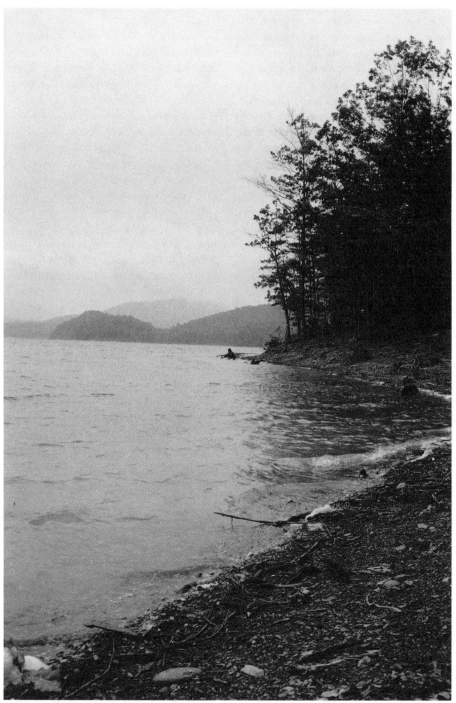

The shoreline at Greenwood Point

from which to fish and acres of trailless woodlands waiting to be discovered. And, if you strike up a friendly conversation with some of your neighbors who arrived by boat, you may get a free ride around the lake or a chance to try your luck at a bit of waterskiing. In a day, or two, or three, or whenever you finally decide to go home, simply retrace your route back to campground 3.

47

Rich Hole Wilderness

Total distance (one way): 5.8 miles

Hiking time: 3½ hours

Vertical rise: 980 feet

*Maps: USGS 7½' Longdale Furnace;
USGS 7½' Nimrod Hall*

In May 1988, more than 6,000 acres on and around Mill and Brushy Mountains were designated as the Rich Hole Wilderness. Like Saint Mary's Wilderness (see Hike 33), Rich Hole is a beneficiary of the 1975 national law that permits places where the evidence of human activity is gradually being reclaimed by natural processes to fit within the definition of a wilderness.

In 1827, Colonel John Jordon built an iron-producing furnace in Longdale, about a mile from the present-day boundary of the wilderness. Due to America's voracious appetite for materials with which to build its expanding cities and transportation systems, the colonel's business thrived. Roads soon ribboned the hillsides so that iron ore could be mined and hardwood trees could be harvested for timber and charcoal to fuel the furnaces. By the time the factory closed in the early 1900s, only the steeper and most inaccessible areas of what are now Rich Hole had escaped this activity.

Recognizing these nearly pristine spots as rather unique and rare in the eastern United States, the U.S. Forest Service has managed them as a primitive area since it acquired the property in 1935; the logged and mined areas that are included in the wilderness have now had well over half a century to return to a somewhat more natural state.

In one of nature's interesting twists of fate, even the unlogged areas are not as they once were. Many of the tall trees you see today were a part of the understory until the chestnut blight of the 1930s. The death of the American chestnuts liberated

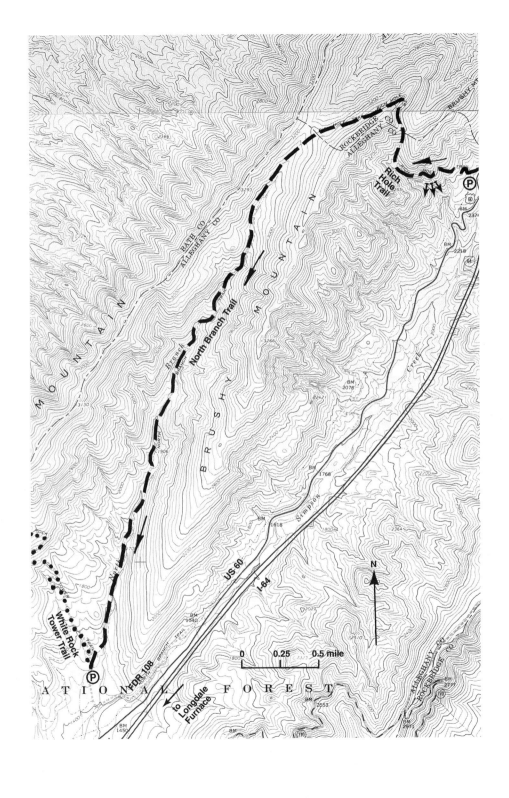

the oaks and hickories to become the dominant species. In turn, some of these trees were damaged or killed in the massive Easter ice storm of 1978, changing the look of the forest again.

Despite a gain of nearly 1,000 feet in a little more than 1 mile, the walk is a moderate one. Although the trail is relatively short, there is so much to see, enjoy, and experience in Rich Hole that you should consider making this an overnight hike and not just a day trip. Either way, don't pass up this chance to hike into a lush and green part of Virginia where, more than likely, you will not see another person or even signs of other people the entire time you are on the trail.

You are, however, almost guaranteed to see evidence of black bear. In 1958, an inspection team from the Wilderness Society recommended the suitability of Rich Hole as a wild area based almost exclusively on its large bear population. Of course, that was several decades ago, and bears move about from year to year, but each time I've been to Rich Hole I've seen more piles of scat per mile than any place I've hiked. Other signs that will help you identify whether there are any bears around are tree trunks marked by long, scraping claw marks and rocks and boulders that have been overturned as the bears searched for grubs, termites, and other insects.

Unless you want to walk several miles on US 60 after completing this hike, it will be necessary to have two cars for a shuttle. Exit I-64 at Longdale Furnace, going east on US 60 for about 1.5 miles to a left turn onto FDR 108. Come to the trailhead on the right in 1.5 miles and leave one car in the small parking area. Return to and continue east on US 60 for 3.6 miles to a small graveled parking lot on the left with a sign identifying the Rich Hole Wilderness.

Begin the Rich Hole Trail {FS 464} by leaving the parking area to walk on a blazed old Forest Service road. In 0.1 mile your route begins a series of switchbacks, ascending the mountain at a more than 10 percent grade. The forest is a mixture of chestnut oak, red oak, white oak, white maple, and sugar maple. Evergreens become more numerous for a short distance as the trail grade moderates a bit at 0.3 mile.

In the rhododendron and mountain laurel shrubs found at 0.5 mile and 0.6 mile from leaving the trailhead, rock outcroppings to the left provide lofty views to the south of 3,000-foot North Mountain and motor vehicles speeding along I-64, paralleling Simpson Creek in the valley below.

Avoid the old trail coming in from the left at 0.7 mile, where the trail steepens once more; you may find it worthwhile to leave the trail at 0.9 mile to explore the natural bowl to your left. Rich Hole receives its name from the deep, nutritious, organic soils found in heads of drainage systems such as this. Amid the mature black locust it is possible to find remnants of a former homestead. Old apple trees are the most obvious signs, but you might also locate a cabin's crumbling foundation, a decaying farm implement, or a rusting metal pail.

After a short, steep climb at an almost 50 percent grade, Brushy Mountain's ridgeline, separating North Branch from Alum Creek, is reached at 1.1 miles. There are no official pathways dropping down into the Alum Creek drainage to the right, yet this area contains one-third to one-half of Rich Hole's acreage and promises an excellent wilderness experience for those equipped with backcountry skills and appropriate maps.

Your trail begins its descent from the ridge into large stands of rhododendron on a well-built treadway. A good, but waterless, camp

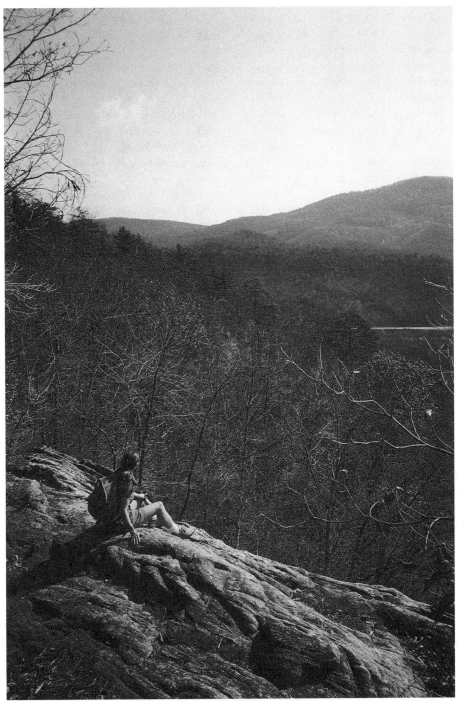
The view of North Mountain and I-64 from Rich Hole Wilderness

could be made where the trail crosses a level spur ridge at 1.6 miles. Other campsites can be found on the moist land the trail passes through at 1.9 miles. A spring, the source of North Branch, will provide water in all but the driest of seasons.

A rare club moss, sometimes known as crow's foot, grows prolifically in the middle of the pathway at 2.2 miles. You will recognize this point because the ground will be covered by what appear to be miniature evergreen trees.

Cross North Branch for the first time at 2.3 miles, soon entering a grove of towering hemlocks. Cross the creek again in 200 feet and then again in 500 more feet.

The next 2 miles of scenery the rough and rocky trail passes through make any walking or hardships you have had to endure all worth it. Tall, straight poplar trees vie for dominance with red maples and several different kinds of oaks, and elegant fern fronds dance in the breeze over neon green moss-covered rocks in the creek. Although there is a plethora of spots suitable for great tent sites, there are almost no traces of anyone ever having camped here. This apparent lack of use is even more amazing in light of the fact that the Forest Service classifies North Branch as a native-trout stream.

Be alert at 3 miles; the trail makes a sudden switchback to the right to cross the creek. The route crosses the stream 12 more times before the hike comes to an end. Abundant spring runoff may make these crossings a little tricky, and an interesting situation develops in the fall when the flow of the creek diminishes: The hardwood trees drop so many leaves onto standing pools of water that it becomes next to impossible to distinguish solid ground from liquid creek bed. Pick your steps carefully or you will end up with wet feet.

Wintergreen, with its evergreen leaves (and rich red berries in the fall), is a major part of the groundcover; a small cave can be found in the rock facing to the right at 3.7 miles. Rocky treadway is replaced by a wide, grassy woods road at 4.4 miles, and pines become numerous once again as the road brings you to your shuttled car, FDR 108, and the end of the hike in 5.8 miles.

Lightly utilized and rarely maintained White Rock Tower Trail {FS 466} starts about one mile to the right up FDR 108. This trail could be used to extend your trip for another seven to eight miles, but it is best to contact the Forest Service about its present condition and accesses before setting out to walk it. Excellent nearby hikes are in Douthat State Park (see Hikes 48 and 49) and Dry Run (see Hike 50) near Clifton Forge and Covington, each just several miles to the west via I-64.

48

Beards Mountain

Total distance (circuit): 7.1 miles

Hiking time: 4½ hours

Vertical rise: 1,360 feet

Maps: USGS 7½ Healing Springs; Douthat State Park map

Rising north of Clifton Forge and attaining heights of more than 2,600 feet above sea level, blueberry bush–covered Beards Mountain separates the Cowpasture River Valley from the Wilson Creek Valley. Situated on Beards Mountain's western slopes and the eastern edge of Middle Mountain and nestled along Wilson Creek is 4,493-acre Douthat State Park. Six hundred men of the Civilian Conservation Corps–stationed at three separate campsites–worked on developing the park, fabricating cabins and other buildings along with roads, bridges, trails, and a 50-acre lake contained by a rock spillway dam. One of the six original state parks in Virginia, Douthat was opened to the public on June 15, 1936. Its blend of recreational opportunities makes use of many of the still-standing CCC constructions, and the park therefore was designated a National Registered Historic Landmark in 1986. The park offers interpretive programs during the usual heavy-use months, rental cabins (plus a large lodge with six bedrooms), three campgrounds, hot showers, a camp store, a restaurant, a dumping station, swimming, boat rentals, and picnic areas and shelters. Douthat Lake and Wilson Creek are stocked with trout and licenses are available in the park, so bring the rod and reel. (Fishing the stocked area requires a special daily permit.) The park is reached by exiting I-64 and following VA 629 north from Clifton Forge for about 5 miles.

With a system of interconnecting trails totaling more than 36 miles (more than any other state park in Virginia), almost countless circuit hikes can be taken. This

hike along Beards Mountain provides an opportunity to get away from the crowds at the lake and campgrounds, study a mountaintop environment, and explore numerous, seldom-visited hollows.

Begin by walking behind the visitor center, picking up blue-blazed Beards Gap Trail, and passing by the park's maintenance building, which originally was the blacksmith shop for the CCC camp. Enter the woods and cross the stream the first of nine times as you ascend the narrow valley. The narrower side hollows you pass invite off-trail explorations. It's hard to get lost if you stay close to these minivalleys' small streams, in which you might find a frog or a salamander. Salamanders, like frogs, are amphibians, not lizards, and must keep their skin damp, so you will never find them far from some source of moisture. And, although they spend very little time in water, you may see a box turtle poking along one of the streams. There is no mistaking this reptile because, of all the turtles in the United States, this is the only one able to "box" itself in completely by closing its shell. Continuing on the main pathway, there is a good wintertime view of Middle Mountain on the western border of the park from a switchback at 1.1 miles.

Upon reaching Beards Gap at 1.2 miles, orange-blazed Brushy Hollow Trail goes right for three and a half miles to VA 629 near the park entrance. You want to bear left and rise on yellow-blazed Mountain Top Trail. Now on the crest of Beards Mountain, you will soon take the 0.1 mile side trail on the left to a viewpoint overlooking the interior of the park. Unless this overlook has been recently maintained, you may not have much of a view, but you only expended a little bit of energy and have walked through a part of the park you would have otherwise missed.

Return to the main trail, turn left, and come to the junction at 1.7 miles with blue-blazed Buck Hollow Trail. Since you are going to make use of this pathway later in the hike, keep right on yellow-blazed Mountain Top Trail. In just a few feet, keep right again when passing by white-blazed Mountain Side Trail. After encountering a grand vista of Middle Mountain and the 1,000-foot-higher Warm Springs Mountain rising behind it, attain a knob at 2.4 miles with a wintertime view of pastoral Cowpasture River Valley to the east. With its headwaters far to the north near the Highland-Bath county line, the Cowpasture River has created one of the most visually pleasing valleys in western Virginia. The river joins the Jackson River (which is dammed near the West Virginia–Virginia border, creating Lake Moomaw—see Hike 46) southeast of Clifton Forge to form the James River.

The reason this trail was named Mountain Top is obvious as you continue along the crest of the ridgeline to another knob at 2.8 miles. Yet here on the park's border with the George Washington National Forest, you will leave the heights and follow your route when it drops steeply to the left for a short distance before descending at a more gradual rate. At 3.8 miles, keep to the left and begin following white-blazed Mountain Side Trail. (Orange-blazed Ross Camp Trail descends right for seven-tenths mile to VA 629.) The Mountain Side Trail winds in and out of small draws, keeping on an almost even contour of about 2,000 feet and reaching its termination at the junction with Mountain Top and Buck Hollow Trails at 5.1 miles.

Make a hard right, descending the switchbacked, blue-blazed Buck Hollow Trail to take the side trail to the left at 5.6 miles. Once again, this viewpoint overlooking the interior of the park may be overgrown, but it

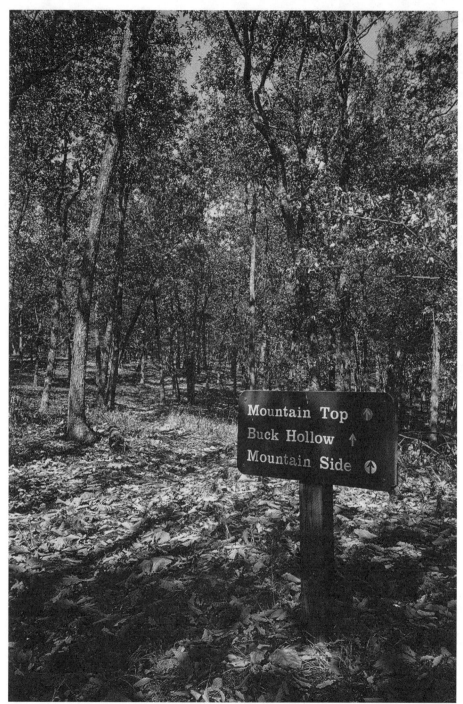

On the ridgeline of Beards Mountain

is still an enjoyable walk through a mixed hardwood forest and an additional chance to see one of the park's many white-tailed deer. Returning to the main trail, continue the descent as the hollow becomes wider and you cross a couple of small (possibly dry) water runs.

Buck Hollow Trail comes to an end when it runs into white-blazed Wilson Creek Trail at 6.6 miles. VA 629 is just a few feet in front of you, but make a left onto Wilson Creek Trail, following it across a wooden footbridge and past the Buck Lick Interpretive Trail on the right (a worthwhile three-tenths mile walk). Ascend on a woods road, passing by cabins and leaving the utility line right-of-way to enter the woods on the left. Crossing under another set of utility lines, keep to the right; don't follow the right-of-way to the left. Soon, Wilson Creek Trail terminates at VA 629, but to avoid walking the paved roadway, keep to the left on a gravel road, returning to your car at 7.1 miles.

Don't leave the park just because you've finished the hike. If it is a hot day, your best bet is to head to the lake for a refreshing dip. If you have been walking in a cold rain, sipping a cup of coffee in the restaurant will warm your insides. And, if you've used a little foresight, your tent is already set up in the campground and waiting for you to crawl in to get a good night's sleep before taking off on tomorrow's hike.

49

Tuscarora Overlook

Total distance (circuit): 9.6 miles

Hiking time: 6 hours

Vertical rise: 2,180 feet

Maps: USGS 7½' Healing Springs; Douthat State Park map

This excursion into the western and southern regions of Douthat State Park (see Hike 48 for directions) is probably best done in the early spring. Not only will the trees still be leafless so that the views will be more extensive, but the two waterfalls you encounter will be running at their highest and most impressive volume.

Leave your car at the entrance parking area of campground C and walk across Wilson Creek on the low-water bridge into the campground and past Beards Gap Hollow Trail (on which you will be returning). Across from the bathhouse and next to campsite 33, make a left into a woods of pine and oak on yellow-blazed Tobacco House Ridge Trail. Some of the trees and shrubs you pass may have galls on them. Galls form on almost every plant in the world and are not a cancer or some other disease but the plant's reaction to an attack by a parasite (which could be a bacteria, fungus, eelworm, mite, or insect). Rarely will a plant be affected by the formation of a gall. Rather, this abnormal increase in the number or size of cells isolates the parasite and helps to localize any poisons it may produce.

A break in the vegetation at 0.5 mile provides a pleasant spot, especially early in the morning when songbirds are most active, to overlook Douthat Lake. The Tobacco House Ridge Trail comes to an end upon meeting blue-blazed Blue Suck Falls Trail at 0.9 mile. This trail descends right to VA 629, but it also ascends to the left and that is the direction in which you need to turn. Early settlers noticed that wildlife was attracted to the salt from high-sulfur-content springs in the area of

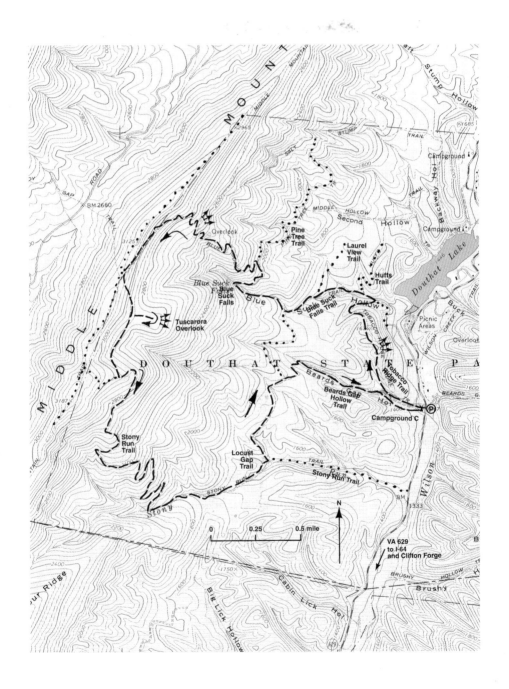

Douthat State Park and that the animals would stand above the springs to inhale the vapors—thus the name "suck."

At 1 mile, gold-blazed Huff's Trail bears right toward the northern portion of the park; keep left on Blue Suck Falls Trail. Keep left again when white-blazed Laurel View Trail comes in from the right at 1.2 miles. Conversely, bear right upon reaching the junction with yellow-blazed Locust Gap Trail at 1.5 miles. (You could follow Locust Gap Trail left for about a mile and rejoin this hike description at the 8.6 mile-point. This would shorten your hike by about 6 miles, but you'd miss the waterfalls and views.)

Continuing to ascend on Blue Suck Falls Trail, which is now steep and rocky, come to the falls, which drop about 50 feet down a rock facing lined by mountain laurel and rhododendron. Your route crosses the stream just below the falls and swings around the side of the mountain on a pathway still supported by rock cribbing constructed in the 1930s by the Civilian Conservation Corps. Keep left at 2 miles when yellow-blazed Pine Tree Trail comes in from the right; pass by two excellent views of Wilson Creek valley bordered by Beards Mountain. The stone bench at 2.5 miles provides a place to rest and enjoy the view, but take the short side trail to the right to Lookout Rock at 2.7 miles for an even better vantage point on this vista of wave after wave of undulating Virginia ridgelines.

Returning to the main trail, continue to the end of Blue Suck Falls Trail at 3.6 miles. A short pathway to the right provides access to George Washington National Forest's Middle Mountain Trail {FS 458}. You want to bear left, descending on yellow-blazed Tuscarora Overlook Trail, taking the side pathway left to Tuscarora Overlook at 4 miles for a view unsurpassed anywhere else in the park. Douthat Lake sparkles more than 1,000 feet below you, and now that you are high above the elevation to which Beards Mountain to the east attains, you can see far beyond it—into Cowpasture River Valley and all the way out to Rough and Mill Mountains, well over 10 miles from where you're standing. To the southeast it is even possible to see a bit of four-lane I-64 snaking toward Lexington. The rustic cabin at the overlook was originally built by the CCC and later used as a fire warden's station; it was restored in the late 1980s. It is not available for overnight stays and should only be used in case of an emergency. Because the Tuscarora Indians inhabited North Carolina (and later New York and Ontario) and not Virginia, it must be assumed that this overlook is named for the Tuscarora sandstone that forms the upper layer of the mountains in the region.

Returning to the main trail, make a left and contour along the mountain in an upland environment of hardwoods and mountain laurel to where the Tuscarora Trail ends at 4.6 miles. A portion of orange-blazed Stony Run Trail ascends right to connect with the Middle Mountain Trail. However, you will follow its orange blazes as they descend to the left. Be alert at 5 miles! Do not take the old trail straight ahead, but bear left to swing around the ridgeline and begin a series of long, well-graded switchbacks down the steep slope of the mountain. After entering a rhododendron tunnel at 6.9 miles, cross scenic Stony Run and bear right onto a 100-foot-long side trail to Stony Run Falls. This is a great place to stop and relax on a warm, dry day. Tiny bits of mist from the falls add moisture to the air, and thick growths of rhododendron block the sunlight to provide dark patches of shade. It's interesting to see how the

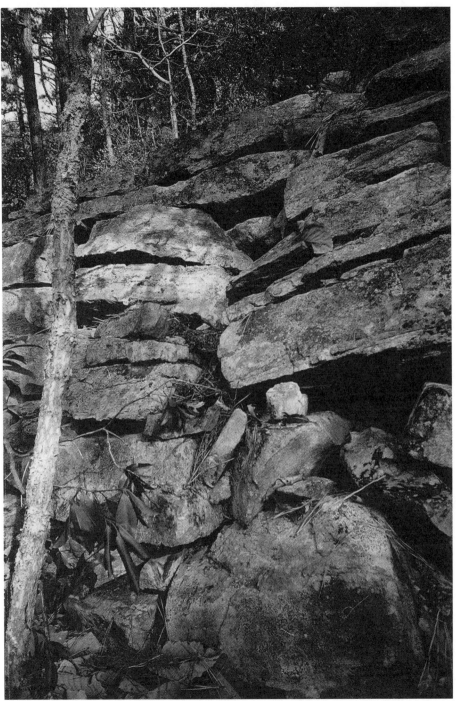

Rock cribbing built by the CCC to support the trail

rhododendron is affected by its environment; in some places it grows tall and straight while in others it is twisted and gnarled.

Return to the main trail to continue downstream as the valley becomes wider and more open. At 7.7 miles, Stony Run Trail continues right for one and a half miles to VA 629. You'll bear left onto yellow-blazed Locust Gap Trail, swinging around several spur ridges with little change in elevation to the next intersection at 8.6 miles. Locust Gap Trail continues left for about a mile to intersect Blue Suck Falls Trail; you should bear right to drop quickly along white-blazed Beards Gap Hollow Trail, crossing the water run several times. Keep a sharp eye out at 9.2 miles and you might notice an old telegraph wire connector in an evergreen tree. In the days before wireless radios and phones, the only contact with isolated outposts—such as the cabin at Tuscarora Overlook—was by way of telegraph lines. If you watch closely when hiking in Virginia on a pathway going to the site of an old lookout station, you will likely find some kind of evidence of this form of communication.

Turn right onto a dirt service road at 9.3 miles, keeping left when another road joins it in a few hundred feet. After crossing a wooden footbridge, turn right onto the paved campground road. If you are near the campground in early morning or evening, there's a good chance of seeing a raccoon or an opossum. The opossum is the only marsupial (meaning it carries its young in a pouch) in the United States. When the young are born they weigh less than a tenth of an ounce each, measure about one-half to two-thirds the size of a honeybee, and an entire litter of 13 could easily fit into a tablespoon. Opossums live in abandoned burrows or hollow trees and are often seen walking along a tree's lower limbs; clawed feet and a strong prehensile tail make them excellent, if somewhat clumsy, climbers.

Follow the campground road across Wilson Creek and to your car, ending the hike at 9.6 miles. If you have also done the Beards Mountain hike (see Hike 48), you've now completed an exploration of some of the eastern, western, and southern portions of Douthat State Park. Take a look at the park handout map and you will see that by combining the Salt Stump, Pine Tree, Middle Hollow, Heron Run, and Backway Hollow Trails you can accomplish an approximately 4-mile discovery trip into a segment of the park's northern district.

50

Dry Run

Total distance (one way): 9.7 miles

Hiking time: 6¼ hours

Vertical rise: 1,640 feet

Maps: USGS 7½′ Covington; U.S. Forest Service Fore Mountain Trail/Dry Run Trail map

A moderately easy ascent of Warm Springs Mountain, passage close to Big Knob and Bald Knob—two of the highest points in the Allegheny Mountains of Virginia—and a pleasurable descent along tumbling Dry Run make this excursion a good choice for a long day trip or an overnight hike.

A number of years ago, the US Forest Service officially combined what were known as the Skyline and Dry Run Trails into the Dry Run Trail, and portions of these two pathways are used for this hike. Many maps, however, and even signs along the route may still designate the two as different and distinct trails.

Because this is a one-way walk, a car shuttle will be necessary. Exit I-64 at Covington and follow US 60 and US 220 east and north toward downtown. In 1.4 miles, US 60 forks left; take US 220 to the right. Be watching for East Cypress Street in another 1.4 miles, where you turn right to follow it 0.3 mile to its dead end with gated FDR 339. Park one car (there is very little room, so be sure you are off the pavement) and retrace your route back toward the interstate. Be watching for the left turn you need to make onto East Dolly Ann Drive (VA 625), 0.9 mile before you would return to the interstate exit. Paved VA 625 becomes dirt FDR 125 in 1 mile. Continue on FDR 125 for 4.6 miles to a trailhead sign for the Skyline Trail {FS 417} directly across the road from gated FDR 448. Be sure to watch your odometer; the trailhead sign may be obscured, removed, or possibly, by the time you take your walk, replaced with a sign designating this as the Dry Run Trail.

Two roads diverge from the large parking area. Do not take the level, gated road to the right. Your route begins by following the ungated, rough, four-wheel-drive road that ascends to the left. The first few feet are a little steep, but soon the road takes on a gradual and gentle grade.

If you are hiking when leaves are off the trees, be sure to turn around every so often to peruse emerging growth on the hillside across the valley, which is the result of fairly recent logging operations on Fore Mountain. If you are hiking during warmer months, walk in cool shade, courtesy of a mixed hardwood forest spreading its canopy over the road.

At 1.1 miles, and again in a few hundred feet, roads come in from the right. Keep to the left on the main road at both spots.

Come to a T-intersection at 1.3 miles. Bald Knob is visible to the right (no views from its summit, though). Bear left and continue to ascend, staying on the main roadway when old roads come in from the right and then the left. The road makes its first major switchback to the right at 1.8 miles.

Reach the top of the ridgeline at 2.3 miles, where the road becomes gated. Look toward the northwest for a view of Big Bald before crossing the gate. Now the slightly undulating road, receiving no motorized traffic, takes on a completely different feel. There are few ruts or potholes, leaves and other decaying vegetation make the walking a little softer, and bushes and other underbrush lining the roadway appear healthier and more abundant.

Begin to descend at 2.5 miles. To the right of the trail is a large outcropping that invites exploration. Enjoy this natural "jungle gym," but there are cracks, crevices, and drop-offs, so keep an eye on the children.

Before the two trails were combined, the Skyline Trail officially ended as you come into a wildlife clearing. Posted signs about 300 feet to the right let you know that the land is private property. Look for red diamond blazes to your left, which mark the former beginning of the Dry Run Trail {FS 471A}. Follow the blazes along a short pathway for 200 feet, turn left, and ascend along an old woods road. The route takes on a different feel again. The terrain is more rugged; rock outcroppings and jumbles of boulders are on both sides of the roadway. Stop for a few moments to enjoy the isolation you have obtained. With the possible exception of a passing airplane, you will probably hear no other signs of human life. Listen for the wind coming across the ridgeline from the west, rustling leaves and creaking tree branches. In an area this quiet, the sounds made by tiny squirrels hopping through dry leaves on the ground may become exaggerated and be perceived as the movements of larger animals, such as foxes, bobcats, or deer, which also make their home in this forest.

In 3.2 miles the route levels out somewhat as you slab the mountainside just below the ridgeline. Where the road makes a swing to the left at 3.4 miles, several small, flat spots could provide a campsite for an overnight stay.

A side trail to the right at 4 miles leads, in one mile, to an overlook to the west. This trail is not well marked nor maintained and should probably be followed only by the adventurous. I suggest checking on its current condition at the ranger station in Covington before deciding whether or not you want to take this side trip.

A well-flowing spring is located on the right at 4.2 miles.

Cross the ridgeline at 4.8 miles and begin the descent to Dry Run. The route narrows; laurel has begun to reclaim the edges of the roadway. Pass through a draw in the

Dry Run

mountainside at 5.3 miles; this is actually the headwater area of Dry Run.

Trees that have fallen at 5.6 miles show the great expanse of root systems that are required to sustain the life of a tree. The route becomes a well-built, narrow, sidehill pathway supported by rock-wall cribbing. You are walking high above Dry Run, which you can hear working its way down the hollow.

Swing right at 5.9 miles to begin descending along a spur ridge to come to a grove of hemlocks lining Dry Run. Groves such as this often become favorite places for those who walk through forests on hot, humid days. Hemlocks are very tolerant of the shade of taller trees or of those growing higher up on the mountainside. As a result, the sun is blocked by both the overstory trees and the spreading branches of the hemlocks, making temperatures sometimes 10 or more degrees cooler than the surrounding woods. This area is also a good place to look for opportunities to cool yourself in the many inviting wading pools of the run.

Cross Dry Run at 6.1 miles and continue downhill, paralleling the stream. Evidently, in times of high water the trail becomes part of the stream; the pathway is rough, rocky, and a little faint at 6.5 miles. Just continue descending along the same side of the stream and you will eventually find orange blazing to mark your route. Small campsites can be found along this stretch.

Be paying very close attention to the blazing at 7.6 miles, where you should not continue to go straight on an obviously well-used trail. This may be all right for hunters and fishermen who wish to continue to follow Dry Run, but the trail you need to take makes an abrupt turn to the left and recrosses Dry Run.

Switchback uphill, eventually working your way high above the stream. The route again takes on another kind of feeling. The pathway is soft from a cushiony layer of moss. Hardwoods and pines have replaced the hemlocks around the creek (which can no longer be heard) and galax and trailing arbutus help stabilize the soil that had been disturbed by construction of the trail.

Come onto wide, graveled FDR 339 for the final descent. Although walking along a road littered with the rusting remains of every kind of modern appliance you can think of—stoves, refrigerators, washers, dryers, microwave ovens, televisions, and more—may not be the best way to end a hike, it is still possible to appreciate the natural surroundings. Sumac grows well and is one of the first trees to leaf out in early spring. About this same time coltsfoot adds its bit of yellow along the roadway. Later, in early fall, the sumac's leaves turn a crimson red several weeks before other leaves begin to change color. Honeysuckle and greenbriar seem to be doing their best to overtake the edge of the forest.

A bend in the road at 8.6 miles permits views of the Westvaco pulp mill in Covington and of the mountains to the west and south. The hike ends at 9.7 miles as you come to the gate. Your shuttled automobile sits on Cypress Road ready to whisk you away to your next exploration of Virginia's natural wonders. Happy trails.

Index

Index

Let Backcountry Guides Take You There

Our experienced backcountry authors will lead you to the finest trails, parks, and back roads in the following areas:

50 Hikes Series
50 Hikes in the Adirondacks
50 Hikes in Connecticut
50 Hikes in the Maine Mountains
50 Hikes in Coastal and Southern Maine
50 Hikes in Maryland
50 Hikes in Massachusetts
50 Hikes in Michigan
50 Hikes in the White Mountains
50 More Hikes in New Hampshire
50 Hikes in New Jersey
50 Hikes in Central New York
50 Hikes in Western New York
50 Hikes in the Mountains of North Carolina
50 Hikes in Ohio
50 Hikes in Eastern Pennsylvania
50 Hikes in Central Pennsylvania
50 Hikes in Western Pennsylvania
50 Hikes in the Tennessee Mountains
50 Hikes in Vermont
50 Hikes in Northern Virginia

Walks and Rambles Series
Walks and Rambles on Cape Cod and the Islands
Walks and Rambles on the Delmarva Peninsula
Walks and Rambles in Dutchess and Putnam Counties
Walks and Rambles in Westchester and Fairfield Counties
Walks and Rambles in the Western Hudson Valley
Walks and Rambles on Long Island
Walks and Rambles in Ohio's Western Reserve
Walks and Rambles in Rhode Island
Walks and Rambles in and around St. Louis

25 Bicycle Tours Series
25 Bicycle Tours in the Adirondacks
25 Bicycle Tours on Delmarva
25 Bicycle Tours in Savannah and the Carolina Low Country
25 Bicycle Tours in Maine
25 Bicycle Tours in Maryland
25 Bicycle Tours in the Twin Cities and Southeastern Minnesota
30 Bicycle Tours in New Jersey
30 Bicycle Tours in the Finger Lakes Region
25 Bicycle Tours in the Hudson Valley
25 Bicycle Tours in Ohio's Western Reserve
25 Bicycle Tours in the Texas Hill Country and West Texas
25 Bicycle Tours in Vermont
25 Bicycle Tours in and around Washington, D.C.
30 Bicycle Tours in Wisconsin
25 Mountain Bike Tours in the Adirondacks
25 Mountain Bike Tours in the Hudson Valley
25 Mountain Bike Tours in Massachusetts
25 Mountain Bike Tours in New Jersey
Backroad Bicycling on Cape Cod, Martha's Vineyard, and Nantucket
Backroad Bicycling in Eastern Pennsylvania
Backroad Bicycling in Connecticut

Bicycling America's National Parks Series
Bicycling America's National Parks: Arizona & New Mexico
Bicycling America's National Parks: California
Bicycling America's National Parks: Oregon & Washington
Bicycling America's National Parks: Utah & Colorado

We offer many more books on hiking, fly-fishing, travel, nature, and other subjects. Our books are available at bookstores and outdoor stores everywhere. For more information or a free catalog, please call 1-800-245-4151 or write to us at The Countryman Press, P.O. Box 748, Woodstock, Vermont 05091. You can find us on the Internet at www.countrymanpress.com.